SECOND EDITION

COLOR OF JUSTICE

Culturally Sensitive Treatment of Minority Crime Victims

Brian K. Ogawa

Director, Crime Victims' Institute
Office of the Attorney General
State of Texas

Allyn and Bacon

Boston • London • Toronto • Sydney • Tokyo • Singapore

This book is dedicated to my children,
Brent Kalani Masanobu and Brooke Noelani Akemi,
and to
Masanobu Frank, Bessie Emiko, and Tsutako Alice Ogawa,
who endured much in America for the sake of their children

Editor in Chief, Social Sciences: Karen Hanson
Series Editorial Assistant: Heather Ahlstrom
Marketing Manager: Susan E. Brown
Production Editor: Christopher H. Rawlings
Editorial-Production Service: Omegatype Typography, Inc.
Composition and Prepress Buyer: Linda Cox
Manufacturing Buyer: Megan Cochran
Cover Administrator: Jenny Hart

Copyright © 1999 by Allyn & Bacon
A Viacom Company
160 Gould Street
Needham Heights, MA 02194

Internet: www.abacon.com
America Online: Keyword: College Online

Previous edition, copyright © 1990 by Dr. Brian Ogawa, Office of the Governor, State of California, Office of Criminal Justice Planning

Library of Congress Cataloging-in-Publication Data

Ogawa, Brian K.
    Color of justice : culturally sensitive treatment of minority
crime victims / Brian Kenji Ogawa.
        p.   cm.
    Includes bibliographical references (p.   ) and index.
    ISBN 0-205-28061-7
    1. Minorities—Crimes against—California.   2. Victims of crimes—
Services for—California.   3. Pluralism (Social sciences)—
California.   I. Title.
HV6250.4.E75O34   1999
362.88'089'009794—dc21

                                                        98-5359
                                                        CIP

Printed in the United States of America
10 9 8 7 6 5 4 3 2 1   03 02 01 00 99 98

Published in cooperation with and by permission of: Office of the Governor, State of California, Office of Criminal Justice Planning, 1130 K Street, Suite 300, Sacramento, California, 95814.

CONTENTS

Preface   vii

1   Introduction   1
La Famosa Jessica   2
Multicolor Hologram   4

2   Increasing Cultural Sensitivity   6
Racial and Ethnic Demographics   8
    Color Lines   8
    Minorities and the Census   11
    The United States' Cultural Identity   13
    Diversity within Diversity   19
Cultural Keys   21
    The Blues   22
    Chants   23
    Dichos   24
Historical Perspectives   25
    Legacy of April 30   25
    Subjugated but Not Defeated   29
Minority Family Patterns   33
    Native American Children   34
    Hawaiian *Ohana*   37
    Strengths of African American Families   38
    La Familia   40
"False Culture"   42
    Asian American Patriarchies   42
    Machismo   44

3   Impact of Crime on Minorities   48
Minority Crime Statistics   49
Vulnerability to Crime   51
    Murder on Twin Peaks   51
    Asian Children   53
    Children of Migrant Farmworkers   55
    Home Invasions   56
    La Migra   58
Misconceptions   63
    Black Girls Are Not Good Girls   63
    More Than Shame   66
    Just Another Day   70
Cultural Response Patterns   72
    Brick in the Purse   72
    Verbalization and Demonstration   74
    Who Suffers?   76
    A Better Life   77
    Oklahoma City Bombing   78

4   Racism and Hate Violence   82
Rising Conflict of Differences   83
    Bias-Motivated Crimes   83
    Racial Uniforms   88
    Offensive or Funny?   90
Us against Them   93
    The Homeless   93
    Korean Merchants and Black Customers   95
    White Straight Males   97
    Homophobic Panic   101
    Right to Go Anywhere   104
    Yellow Peril Revisited   106
Racism and Crime   113
    Charles Stuart Is Not a Black Male   113
    Killing Fields   115
    Hooty Croy   119

5   Improving the Criminal Justice System   124
Communication and Outreach   126
    Why Not English Only?   126
    Self-Translation   129
    First Contact   133
    Community Oriented Policing   135
    Partnerships with Refugee and Immigrant Groups   138

Prerequisites for Service   *141*
    We Are One Color—Blue   141
    Prejudicial Attitudes and Behavior   144
    Shoes at the Door   145
Minority Perceptions of the Criminal Justice System   *147*
    Experiences from Native Countries   147
    Whites Enslaved the Blacks   148
    Dying to Be Heard   151
Restorative Justice   *154*
    Victim Impact Panels   155
    Native American Justice Systems   157
    Ho'oponopono   160

6   Redesigning Victim Services   162
Multiculturalism in Victim Services   *163*
    Color Blindness   164
    Cross-Cultural Counseling   165
Minority Mental Health Systems   *172*
    Latino Cultural Values   172
    Black Churches   175
    Asian American Orientation   179
    Indian Shamans   180
Culturally Competent Approaches   *182*
    Exodus from Hostility   182
    Fort Mojave   186
    Compton Storefront   189
    Sense of Belonging   190
    Pais Libre   192
    Reaching for the Sky   193

Epilogue   197

References   199

Index   211

PREFACE

The criminal justice system in the United States is designed for the fair administration of legal protections and the equal provision of public safety. There is little doubt that the present system embodies both prevailing strengths and lingering deficiencies. Law enforcement policies, penal codes, and prosecutorial and judicial procedures have been continuously revised, including efforts toward more timely and compassionate treatment for victims of crime. There were in 1997, for example, approximately 30,000 pieces of legislation at the federal, state, and local levels addressing crime victims' rights and services. Regrettably, the particular needs and concerns of racial and ethnic minority crime victims have hardly been represented in these reforms.

Mental health and social service delivery systems have primarily mirrored the ideas and promulgated the interests of the majority. The pluralistic character of our country, however, requires the honest reappraisal and refashioning of how *all* victims are best counseled, assisted, and supported. Bold brush strokes of colors must infuse the overall pale canvas of justice in the U.S. and its indiscernible texture of crime victim treatment.

Color of Justice is the first major book to present the significant challenges facing the criminal justice system as it seeks to serve victims of crime within the increasing racial pluralism and ethnic diversity in present-day society. Through an overview of current problems and major issues, the personal accounts of victims and survivors, and descriptions of innovative and promising programs, this book introduces the premises for and requisites of culturally sensitive treatment.

Color of Justice is intended for anyone, either student or professional, who desires a greater awareness and appreciation of the impact of violent crime on minorities and a more inclusive understanding of recovery from the traumatic effects of victimization. It is a comprehensive planning resource; a guide to program development and practice; and an indispensable handbook for criminal justice policymakers, law enforcement and legal professionals, judges and court personnel, victim advocates, sexual assault and family violence counselors, and social service and mental health providers.

The original edition of *Color of Justice* was the culmination of a major focus on the needs of racial and ethnic minority crime victims sponsored by the Office of Criminal Justice Planning (OCJP), Office of the Governor, State of California. I served as the consultant to OCJP's Minority Victims Project during a 1990 sabbatical year from my position as Director of the Victim/Witness Assistance Division at the Department of the Prosecuting Attorney, County of Maui, Hawaii. During the course of the project, graduate intern Karen McGagin was invaluable in conducting research, providing perceptive comments, and offering unfailing enthusiasm. I also benefited from working closely with the Minority Victims Advisory Committee, which met periodically to ensure that the purposes of the project were met and the contents of the book were representative and accurate. The members of this state-wide committee reflected a variety of university faculty members, criminal justice professionals, and victim service specialists, as well as diverse minority groups.

Since the original edition of *Color of Justice* was published, the crime victims' field has changed in significant ways. Crime victims' bills of rights have become a part of the constitutions in the majority of the states, and an amendment to the U.S. Constitution has recently been introduced. Certification of victim service programs and providers has been instituted in several states along with national programs to help convey and ensure professionalism. Continuing education conferences and seminars have been held to train those in criminal justice and human services who work with minority crime victims. Colleges and universities have begun to include instruction on victim issues, supplementing more traditional criminology and victimology courses. Law enforcement officials have adopted the philosophy and practice of community-oriented policing in many jurisdictions, including those serving minority communities. The Office for Victims of Crime, U.S. Department of Justice, has also included multiculturalism in its national agenda for crime victims for the next millennium. The need for an updated and revised edition of *Color of Justice* was apparent.

In preparing the second edition of *Color of Justice,* the following were most helpful: Gary Howard and Donald Currier, Office of Criminal Justice Planning, State of California; Commander Sadie Darnell, Gainesville, Florida Police Department; Dr. Karen Huggins Lashley, Oklahoma City; Helen M. Thueson, Victim Services, Waco, Texas Police Department; Dr. Michelle Batchelder, University of Texas; Regina Sobieski, MADD National Victim Services; Joseph Myers, Executive Director of the National Indian Justice Center; Beth Binstock, U.S. Attorney's Office, District of Montana; Dr. Katharine Lawson, Abundant Grace Fellowship, Memphis, Tennessee; Nahela Hadi, National Multicultural Institute, Washington, D.C.; Karen Parker, Department of Human Services, Austin, Texas; Drew T. Durham, Deputy Attorney General for Criminal Justice; Laurel Kelly, Director Victims' Services and Special Projects; and Sally Griffiths, Administrative Assistant of the Crime Victims' Institute, Office of the Attorney General, State of Texas.

Finally, to the crime victims and survivors whose stories are shared in this book, those who serve them well, and the many colleagues who befriend and teach me everyday, I extend my warmest gratitude.

1

INTRODUCTION

Circle of the Eagle

Circle of the Eagle

Sam English is a Chippewa Indian now living in Albuquerque, New Mexico. This painting was originally commissioned by the National Indian Justice Center. It formed the centerpiece of a conference on Promoting Child Protection In Indian Country, held in Green Bay, Wisconsin, in 1988.

For most Native Americans, the eagle is an important symbol of protection and spirituality. It forms a circle of life and harmony embracing the Indian family. To stand outside this circle means to lose one's pride and one's proper relationship with others. The family therefore stands together in the center of the circle with their feet and the father's hair ties firmly rooted in the mother earth.

Within the shoulders of the eagle are portrayed ancestors and elders who pass on language, culture, and spiritual truths. Eagle feathers have a highly spiritual significance. The feathers of the eagle are given only at significant passages of life, such as birth and coming of age. In this painting they represent emerging love, protection of children, and the journey of healing.

LA FAMOSA JESSICA

Jessica Morales was an exceptional child. She was born premature and barely two hours later, overcome by an intense high fever, lapsed into a coma. For weeks, Jessica lay without movement as doctors desperately searched for an explanation. Then one day, Jessica unexpectedly regained consciousness. The doctors were baffled by the course of events but shortly thereafter allowed her parents, Francisco and Claudia, to take their infant daughter home.

Within weeks, however, Jessica returned to the hospital. A cranial shunt had to be inserted to drain fluids that were exerting pressure on her brain. Although the procedure was successful, the doctors expected Jessica to suffer severe and permanent brain injury. Instead, she miraculously recovered without any real impairment. Among the hospital staff, she became known as *"la famosa Jessica"* (the famous Jessica) because of what she had overcome so early in life.

Jessica grew to be a happy and bright child. Her father said, "She liked music, to dance. She smiled all the time." She wanted to be *numero uno*, the best in whatever she did. By the time she reached the third grade at Victory Boulevard Elementary School, Jessica was also eager to assist her teacher by translating for the other Spanish-speaking children. Her dream was to become a nurse because she wanted to keep people from dying.

On July 25, 1989, at 2:25 P.M. Jessica was in front of her home on the way to visit a friend. Suddenly a car veered across the boulevard, leaped a curb, grazed a tree, and then struck her. The impact hurled her 60 feet through the air. Jessica died almost immediately of massive internal and head injuries. A neighbor who heard the horrible sounds of the crash came running to the scene. He saw the young girl's lifeless body on the ground and covered her with his jacket, protecting her from the hot afternoon sun. Other neighbors, most of them Hispanic, began to gather. Jessica's parents were summoned from work.

A police officer arrived. He asked if anyone had seen what had occurred. No one responded—they had not actually been witnesses. The officer, in apparent disgust and derision, then remarked, "Why don't any of you speak English?" The man who had provided his jacket for Jessica, an African American, looked up angrily from where he was kneeling beside her. He softly but firmly answered that if he, the officer, was to serve this community, *he* had the responsibility to be bilingual.

The crowd that assembled became increasingly mixed in racial composition. At one point, forming a circle around Jessica, they bowed their heads and offered prayers. The death of this child had stunned each one of them. Differences in language and ethnicity did not preclude the common experience of grief.

Before they were married, Francisco had emigrated to Los Angeles from Mexico and Claudia from Guatemala. Their most meaningful encounters with non-Hispanic people prior to their daughter's death were with the customers of the fast-food Mexican restaurant where they both worked. July 25 changed all that. Their tragedy touched many people's hearts. That even strangers showed concern was a source of strength for Jessica's parents. One couple offered one of their own cemetery plots for Jessica's burial. Others visited and donated money to offset funeral expenses. Claudia was overwhelmed that her boss shed tears at the funeral service for her daughter. Over the many years that she had worked for him, he had expressed little emotion toward his employees. Jessica's classmates also dedicated two books for their school library in her memory, and composed a gentle and thoughtful letter in Spanish for her parents. Francisco and Claudia have kept the letter in a frame, displayed in their home, as a remembrance of their special child.

Claudia cries each day for her daughter. Not being there to caress and comfort Jessica as she lay dying has brought her unbearable anguish. Francisco and Claudia have been sustained by concern for their younger daughter, April, and *la fe* (faith in God). April is seeing a child therapist at a community clinic for Latinos. For one week after her sister's death, April refused to be alone in her bedroom. She was fearful that she would fall into a "sleep" as Jessica had in her casket. But three months later, April said she wanted to die so that she could see her sister again.

Jessica's parents now feel little animosity toward the drunk driver who killed their daughter. He was convicted of vehicular manslaughter and sentenced to two years in prison. Just months before their daughter's death, the Morales family had returned to the Catholic religion. At the sentencing hearing, Francisco and Claudia gave the defendant a Bible, inscribed with the words of a *cancion* (a song) written to honor Jessica by the man who had first rushed to her aid. The Morales now feel a sense of new life, more love, and unity among them. God, they believe, had been preparing them for what was to happen.

A few friends and acquaintances have criticized Francisco and Claudia for feeling forgiveness rather than hatred toward the defendant. They have, in fact, experienced an array of emotions over time. Initially, they were puzzled and angry at the defendant, who after his arrest had been released from custody almost immediately on bail of only $2,500. Francisco's brother-in-law, on the other hand, had been arrested for riding a bicycle on a sidewalk while intoxicated and was incarcerated for one week! Francisco and Claudia also wondered why they were never kept informed of the criminal proceedings but had to depend on the newspapers. They had met the assistant district attorney handling the case only once—for a brief 15 minutes before the sentencing hearing. They were, moreover, slighted by a support group for those grieving over lost loved ones at the hands of drunk drivers. The group has yet to invite them to a meeting. Francisco and Claudia believe that they must have been largely ignored because they are Latinos, speak little English, and live modestly in an old rented house in a nondescript neighborhood.

Jessica's parents requested that I use their true names so that their story could be told without fabrication. Their child, fragile at birth, had become a little girl with effulgent energy and contagious hopes. It was as if she had undergone a rebirth. And now the Morales' believe Jessica has been reborn again, not only into heaven but also in their lives. Life in Claudia's homeland of Guatemala had been difficult, and she had fiercely mistrusted people prior to Jessica's death. But Claudia has since changed. Before, she had vowed that if anyone hurt her daughter Jessica, she would kill that person. Now she realizes that her precious child has given her a *corazon* (a heart) of compassion and understanding.

When I came to visit, Francisco and Claudia welcomed me to their home because they wanted to help others who have experienced a similar misfortune. Near the end of our visit, they smiled and asked what I would actually write on behalf of minority victims. I promised to convey, as best I could, what they and other survivors had shared. Carefully selecting a treasured photo of Jessica from her purse, Claudia presented it to me. Her eyes were brilliant with tears of sorrow and thankfulness. I kept Jessica's photo beside me as a constant companion during the first writing of this book. It was my anchor in the flood of information and storm of opinions around any discourse on minority issues. Jessica Morales is *everyone's* child, for she is a symbol of all that we hold dear in life.

MULTICOLOR HOLOGRAM

All victims of crime are susceptible to being mistreated by uncaring, misinformed, or antagonistic individuals and/or an overburdened, ponderous, and jaded criminal justice system. These are insensitivities and injustices that victims of every race and ethnicity have endured. The events that befell Jessica Morales' family in the aftermath of her death, nevertheless, form a composite of the *distinct* experience of many minority crime victims. There are psychological responses to crime, community resources, cultural practices and beliefs, and matters of social acceptance, racism, and discrimination that characterize and set apart minority populations in the United States.

This book is a compendium of general principles, practical approaches, and key points for defining culturally sensitive treatment of crime victims. The needs of all minority groups, however, were not able to be addressed within the constraints of a single volume. The focus is, therefore, on the four largest categories of racial minorities—African Americans, Asian/Pacific Island Americans, Hispanic Americans, and Native Americans. Immigrants and refugees from Latin America and Southeast Asia are included, and a discussion of the Pacific Island population is limited primarily to Hawaiians, in deference to their status as native peoples in the United States and their relative numbers here in comparison to other Pacific Islanders. Asian Indians are also not discussed because of their somewhat unique cultural and religious experience.

This book is a primer of how violent crime affects victims in our multiracial and multicultural society. All segments of the criminal justice system and the full complement of victim services are responsible for discerning and implementing approaches that acknowledge diversity. However, it takes genuine openness to cross color lines with skill and grace rather than refuse, through habitual disinterest or intense scorn, to engage others in this manner. Awareness of color lines form the vanguard of our philosophies and approaches regarding criminal behavior and victimization.

The thematic chord of *Color of Justice* is not a blanket indictment of the criminal justice system or a sweeping polemic of discrimination in U.S. society. All of us, from every race and ethnicity, must present incisive questions and remedy obvious errors. The most direct path to accomplish this is to heed what minority victims themselves tell us concerning how they have been treated. Doing so may elicit discomfort, disagreement, and controversy. But the concerns of these victims should not be expediently dismissed or continue to be unmet. Their accounts are compelling and real. *Color of Justice* is in essence a forum for their stories of pain and frustration, and of survival and recovery. Hopefully, this book can be described as a type of multicolor hologram, wherein images of culturally *insensitive* treatment recede and are replaced with a deepening respect for others different than ourselves.

2
INCREASING CULTURAL SENSITIVITY

Hawaiian Blessing
Water, Ti Leaf, Salt

From ancient to modern times ceremonial blessings have been an important part of the Hawaiian culture. Each element used has special significance and conveys the interrelationship of human beings, nature, and spirits. *Wai* (water) comes from the heavens. It is not only a reminder of the life bestowed by the gods but also the purest means to literally touch, taste, and immerse in the divine. The Hawaiian word for wealth is accordingly *waiwai*, for one is enriched by an abundance of fresh water and through reverence for its creative source.

Wai is contained in a *pola* (bowl) of koa or milo wood. As a sign of respect, *lai* (*ti* leaves), rather than one's hands, have direct contact with the water to be sprinkled on the place or object to be blessed. *Ti* leaves symbolize the generosity of the gods to provide for human needs. In ancient times they were used to make protective capes, to bundle and transport personal property and goods, to cool one's body from fevers, and to cook and store food. *Ti* leaves were also symbols of peace. Warriors would hold up *ti* plants to indicate they were approaching without hostility. *Pa'a'kai* (salt), representing "to preserve" or "to restore," may be either sprinkled upon the ground to be blessed or added to the water.

By waving *ti* leaves laden with *wai* over an area the *kahu* (priest) cleanses it of any unseen negative forces or purifies it from any misfortune already experienced. A place where death, injury, or violence has occurred, for example, is often blessed so that recovery can begin.

Chapter Overview

- Racial and Ethnic Demographics
- Cultural Keys
- Historical Perspectives
- Minority Family Patterns
- "False Culture"

The United States is in the midst of sweeping social transformation; for the first time in U.S. history, racial and ethnic minorities are reaching numerical parity with the white majority. As this multicultural society unfolds, we are discovering what has always been the gift and vibrancy of the United States. Experiencing contact with other cultures, nevertheless, is filled both with the possibility of acquiring new values and perspectives but also with the added caution of misperceiving unfamiliar traditions and practices. This chapter presents some of the central issues surrounding cultural pluralism and provides a series of topics to enhance appreciation for specific ethnic belief systems and traditions.

RACIAL AND ETHNIC DEMOGRAPHICS

Color Lines

A century ago, W. E. B. Du Bois, the distinguished black writer and teacher, wrote these words:

> Herein lie buried many things which if read with patience may show the strange meaning of being black here at the dawning of the Twentieth Century. The meaning is not without interest to you, Gentle Reader; for the problem of the Twentieth Century is the problem of the color line. (Du Bois, 1903, p. xi)

Du Bois did not state that *a* problem of this century is the problem of the color line. He intentionally emphasized that it is *the* problem. In analyzing the prophetic aspects of this statement, Ben Reist, a modern liberation theologian, agrees with Du Bois:

> He [Du Bois] was, in fact, right in far more convoluted ways than he could have known, for the problem of the Twentieth Century is the problem of the color *lines....* What is centrally involved here is a question of *perspective....* For the white liberal is profoundly persuaded that whereas ethnic oppression is terrible, painful, destructive, and thus urgently awaits solution, it is nevertheless only one of a series of problems.
>
> Precisely this condition is what Du Bois sought to unmask. For the ethnically oppressed, all of the so-called people of color, oppression is real, permanent, and unavoidable. It cannot be dislodged from the psyche by any maneuver, simple or complex. It is constant as the breath of life itself.... And in the light of this exposure one can at least get a handle on that highly emotional term "racism." A racist is one for whom ethnic oppression is one of a series of problems. (Reist, 1975, pp. 18–19)

This, of course, does not mean that the problem of the color lines is the *only* problem we face today. Environmental protection, world peace, gender discrimination, and economic stability are some of the other pressing issues we can no longer afford to ignore. But, as Du Bois and Reist argue, the problem of the color lines is the problem that informs and is interrelated with all other problems. If we fail to meet this problem, we may well set the stage for catastrophe in all others.

Color lines across the United States are indeed rapidly being redrawn and reshaded. There are now multiple lines alongside the predictable and persistent barrier between black and white. One wonders whether our uneven successes, fractured attempts, and tiresome ineptitude to mend black and white divisions in the past foretells our ability and wisdom to handle what is imminently before us. States such as California, New York, New Jersey, Illinois, Massachusetts, Texas, and Florida with large minority populations must, without hesitation, take effective measures to prepare for the inevitable.

Leobardo Estrada, one of the nation's foremost demographers, notes that the many changes people in the United States are encountering today precipitate feelings of *powerlessness* and *incompetence*. This country, he states, is in transition. There is economic restructuring in the world, the polarization of income (the decline of the middle class), a glut of complex information processing systems, bewildering pressures on family life and personal identity as well as eye-opening demographic trends. To resist these changes is unrealistic and fruitless. And so we vent our frustrations and soothe our uneasiness by targeting those whom it is convenient to blame, namely minorities, especially immigrants (Estrada, personal communication, August 22, 1990).

Psychiatrist Robert Jay Lifton also argues that the "boil of prejudice" seems to explode during periods of social and political upheaval. When prevailing systems begin to disintegrate or break down, people experience loss of meaning and a "death anxiety" (Bass 1990, p. E16). To counteract this fear and to reassert their "cultural immortality," they feel compelled to persecute those who do not share their values and beliefs. Dominant groups, according to Lifton, constantly attempt to exert their dominance by victimizing others. This disturbing pattern of human behavior, in other words, has psychological underpinnings.

Racial tensions, however, are not just between whites and non-whites. William Henry, for example, writes:

> Blacks, who feel they waited longest and endured most in the fight for equal opportunity, are uneasy about being supplanted by Hispanics or, in some areas, by Asians as the numerically largest and most influential minority—and even more, about being outstripped in wealth and status by these newer groups. Because Hispanics are so numerous and Asians such a fast-growing group, they have become the "hot" minorities, and blacks feel their needs are getting lower priority. (1990, p. 30)

It is ill advised and ultimately self-defeating to view the emerging color lines as a threat or negative occurrence. "Once America was a microcosm of European nationalities," states Molefi Asante, chairman of African American Studies at Temple University. "Today America is a microcosm of the world" (as cited in Henry, 1990, p. 29). Manuel Perry, a futurist with the Lawrence Livermore Laboratory, enthusiastically endorses this fact and argues that these differences of race, culture, and language should be looked upon as opportunities to "go global." Ethnic diversity allows a state, region, or nation to operate successfully in the world community. The front lines of international politics and economics, in other words, will be where diversity is accepted and fostered (Perry, 1990). The idea of color lines *blending* for a common purpose should obviously be more appealing than having these same color lines bitterly clash.

The problem of the color lines is certainly not something from which we can shield ourselves. U.S. society is becoming increasingly and irreversibly pluralistic in its racial and cultural composition. The white majority population is proportionately *decreasing* at the same time that there are dramatic percentage *increases* among minorities, particularly Hispanics and Asians.

- In 1960, for example, there were only 877,934 Asians in the United States, .5% of the nation's population. In 1985, however, Asians numbered over 5 million, or 2.1%. This represents an increase of 577% compared to the 34% growth rate of the general population (Takaki, 1989). By the year 2030, Asian Americans (including Pacific Islanders) are projected to number 23 million or 6.6% of the U.S. population (U.S. Bureau of the Census, 1997b).
- Projections for the U.S. population into the next millennium (the year 2000) are 71.8% white, 12.2% black, and 11.4% Hispanic. By the year 2030, however, these percentages will be 60.5% white, 18.9% Hispanic, and 13.1% black (U.S. Bureau of the Census, 1997b).

This shift is even more dramatic in several states:

- In the state of California, by the year 2010, 34% of the residents will be Hispanic (U.S. Bureau of the Census, 1997a). By the year 2020 it is estimated that there will be over 39.6 million California residents, or about 38% more than in 1990. The population will then consist of 40.1% white, 37.7% Hispanic, 7.5% black, and 14.2% Asian and other. The white population, in other words, will no longer be the majority (Department of Finance, February 1988).
- In Texas the projections are that 65% of the state will be Hispanic in 2010 (U.S. Bureau of the Census, 1997). Between 1990–2030, the state will grow at the rate of 20.4% for the Anglo population, 62.0% for black, 257.6% for Hispanic, and 648.4% for other. Of the total change in population, in other words, 87.5% will be due to growth in minority populations. Almost 75% of this growth will be due to immigrants and their first generation descendants (Murdock, Hogue, Michael, White, & Pecotte, 1997).
- Florida, New York, New Jersey, and Massachusetts will also increasingly have significant percentages of Hispanic residents. Florida, for example, in 2010 will have a population which is 18% Hispanic (U.S. Bureau of the Census, 1997a).

Much of this changing pattern will come from foreign immigration into the United States. In 1996, Asia was the leading source of new immigrants with 34% of the total, not counting refugees and the undocumented. Since 1985, the leading source of Asian immigration has been from the Philippines, with an average of 50,000 entering the U.S. annually. Immigration from China and Vietnam, for the period 1994–1996, both averaged 40,000 immigrants per year; Korea was 15,000, and Taiwan was 10,000 (U.S. Immigration and Naturalization Service, 1997b).

The U.S. Bureau of the Census (1997a) lists Latino immigration over the period 1971–1994 as follows:

Area of Origin	Percent
Mexico	61
Central America	14
South America	16
Cuba	8

The resident Hispanic population in the United States in 1990 somewhat reflected this immigration pattern with 60% of the Hispanics considered Mexican, 12% Puerto Rican, 5% Cuban, and 23% other Hispanic (U.S. Bureau of the Census, 1997a). Mexicans generally reside in the southwestern states, Puerto Ricans in the New York/New Jersey area, and Cubans in Miami. Overall, immigration from Europe is decreasing, although the rise in the immigration of particular groups such as Armenians and Eastern Europeans may continue.

Minorities and the Census

The actual number of blacks, Asians, Hispanics, and Native Americans is believed to be higher than recorded amounts. Minorities, some believe, are overlooked five times more often than whites. The 1990 Census of the United States, for example, was conducted and tabulated by a staggering number of workers—350,000. The rate of initial returns was, nonetheless, a disappointing 64%. This translated into 43 million census questionnaires that were left unanswered, about twice as many people in the United States as ever before who had either failed to or refused to mail back census forms. Even then, some of the forms received by the Census Bureau had been submitted by pranksters. There were fictitious names such as "Paula Nesians," persons who said they were born "in the state of inebriation," and occupations listed as "driving people crazy."

The recruitment, training, and mobilization of additional census takers to go door-to-door to conduct interviews had mixed results. Minority community activists referred to inappropriate assignments as a major stumbling block. In Oakland's Chinatown, for example, a Chinese American is said to have been designated to interview residents although he spoke no Chinese. Black interviewers were slated to canvass Latino neighborhoods, but stopped after calling on home after home of non-English-speaking families. Reports in San Diego County suggested that many census takers who were sent to migrant camps never left their cars. They did not want to venture into the warren of shacks and caves that Hispanic laborers ranging in numbers between 5,000 and 35,000 call home (Haddock, 1990b, p. A-10). The unique situation of the nation's homeless, a large number of whom are minority persons, also posed a dilemma for the Census Bureau and compounded the problem of a thorough outreach—knocking on doors does not reach people who live without doors.

A post-enumeration survey (PES) was conducted of 150,000 households nationwide in targeted census blocks for chronically undercounted neighborhoods in an attempt to adjust for the undercounting, which has marked decades of census taking. The survey came as the result of a lawsuit brought by civil rights groups, including the Mexican-American Legal Defense and Education Fund (MALDEF) and the National Association for the Advancement of Colored People (NAACP), by cities, including New York and Los Angeles, and by others. In a court settlement in July 1989, the U.S. Department of Justice agreed to issue guidelines to make the adjustments possible.

An accurate census count is critical for a host of purposes. The National Advisory Council on Indian Education, for example, reports that the actual 1980 Native American population was 6.7 million but that the officially recorded figure was only 1.4 million. The 1990 Census counted almost 2 million Native Americans (U.S. Bureau of the Census, 1995). National authorities on providing mental health, substance abuse and family counseling services to Native Americans rely on these population figures in their research studies and clinical recommendations (Trimble & Fleming, 1989). Measuring both the need for and adequacy of services is obviously affected. Such an undercount affects everyone because it affects millions of dollars in federal aid to states, political representation in Congress and the Legislature, and the calculation of statistics such as crime rates, all of which are based upon census figures.

There are numerous reasons why minorities have chosen not to respond to the census. These include mistrust of government inquiries, inability to read English, reluctance to reveal the number of occupants in living units, and fear of disclosing immigration status. For the Vietnamese, for example, the census was not only something to which they were unaccustomed because it had no counterpart in their native country, it also caused some of them to remember hiding their male children during the war to protect them from the draft. Requests for detailed information on their family members naturally elicited concern about how that information could be used. Census data was, after all, studied by the U.S. government to locate and assemble Japanese Americans for relocation during World War II. Although individual information was kept confidential, statistical profiles and tallies pinpointed which neighborhoods contained concentrations of Japanese American residences (Haddock, 1990a, p. A-17).

The Census Bureau in 1990 sought to overcome the difficulties of reaching and reassuring minority groups by such tactics as placing pro-census messages in Chinese fortune cookies, drafting sermon outlines for black ministers extolling the virtues and biblical antecedents of the census, hiring translators and "community awareness specialists," establishing a multilingual toll-free telephone line, making questionnaires available in Spanish, and consulting with former gang members, Catholic priests, and Native American tribal leaders (Haddock, 1990c, p. A-26).

Five minority-owned advertising companies were also chosen to reach ethnic communities. Slogans were coined. Blacks were called upon to "Stand right up for who you are." Latinos were told *Esta es la nuestra*—"This is our chance." And Native Americans were encouraged to "Listen to the drum. Answer the Census. It counts for us." Apparently, these promotional efforts were somewhat marginally received or, in the opinion of some, lacked proper execution (Mitchell, 1990, p. A-11).

University of California, Berkeley, statistics professor David Freedman likens the census and the PES to counting fish in a lake without draining it. You capture a certain number of fish, count them, and throw them back. Somehow you determine that not all the fish were counted so you catch another number and extrapolate a new number based on a margin of error. "But people aren't fish," Freedman emphasizes. "Different kinds of people will react differently to being surveyed… [Some] people don't want to be either captured or recaptured" (as cited in Haddock, 1990c, p. A-26).

Some also may not want an accurate census for political reasons. Previously uncounted minorities, for example, could change the party affiliation of dozens of congressional and state legislative seats. This "potential disruption of the process of the orderly transfer of political representation" is cited by some as one reason the Secretary of Commerce may withhold any adjustments to the census (Gleick, 1990, p. 8). As James Gleick of the *New York Times* has written:

> Many officials wish the count could be free of politics, free of subjectivity, fuzz-iness and tinkering. There are strong psychological reasons to embrace the idea that a count of every individual is a national event, galvanizing all Amer-icans to work together toward a shared goal.... [But] when the nation's great-est and most troubled exercise in counting finally comes to an end—when the last form flicks through the machines, when the last enumerator turns in the last Questionnaire Misdelivery Record Nonresponse Follow-up, when the last lawsuit is filed—the 1990 census seems certain to stand as a bleak landmark in the annals of arithmetic (p. 7).

One of the major issues in the 2000 Census may be the controversy on the inclu-sion of a new "Multiracial" category. The number of mixed marriages has grown from 150,000 in the 1960s to more than 1 million in 1990. Racially-mixed children number roughly 2 million. In 1790, there were three racial categories delineated in the census: free white male, free white female, and slave. The racial breakdown remained black and white for 70 years until American Indians, then Chinese, and later other Asian groups were added. In 1980, the census added the ethnic choice of "Hispanic or Non-Hispanic." In 1990, there were 250,000 Americans who checked the "Other" category and listed more than one race (Eddings, p. 22).

The controversy stems from the potential effects that a new multiracial choice could have on entitlements, discrimination, and political power. Most African Americans, for example, could claim to be multiracial because of the history of slaveholders impregnating slaves. There would thus be statistically fewer blacks. The National Council of La Raza and the National Association for the Advance-ment of Colored People have testified before Congress against a census change. Thirty agencies studied the issue over a three year span and unanimously recom-mended that no multiracial category be added but that individuals could mark as many racial categories as they wanted. Census and agency reporting would detail the combinations by which people described themselves. The largest effect is expected to be on other groups with higher intermarriage rates than blacks or whites (Barr & Fletcher, 1997).

The United States' Cultural Identity

The late Edward Abbey was an environmentalist who made keen, acerbic observa-tions about the condition of the earth. His best known novel, *The Monkey Wrench Gang*, inspired the formation of the controversial direct-action environmental group Earth First! Abbey's viewpoints, however, not only criticized the relentless pollution of nature but also the mismanagement of the human ecosystem. He ardently bemoaned the fact that despite 40 years of unprecedented economic growth in the United States, our nation is beset with mass unemployment; permanent poverty; an overloaded welfare system; violent crime; rotting cities; a poisoned environment; eroding farmlands; the destruction of forests, lakes, rivers and seashores; and the extermination of whole species of plants and animals.

Much of what ails the United States, according to Abbey, is a "simple gross quantitative increase" of population and industry. His solution was essentially to halt "the mass influx of even more millions of hungry, ignorant, unskilled and culturally–morally–genetically impoverished people" into our country.

> Let's be honest about this. These uninvited millions bring with them an alien mode of life that is not appealing to the majority of Americans. For one thing, we prefer democratic government. We still hope for an open, spacious, uncrowded and beautiful society…. The United States has been fully settled, and more than full, for at least a century. We have nothing to gain, and everything to lose, by allowing the old boat to be swamped. (Gilliam, 1990, p. 18)

Abbey may have been motivated by his prescriptions for the protection of the earth's resources. We, as residents of the United States, are undoubtedly wasteful and arrogant consumers and are generally unheedful of warnings regarding the depletion of our world. He was, however, at the same time a crass proponent of xenophobia. The United States may very well need a careful reevaluation of immigration patterns, but a doomsday prediction and nativist hysteria about hordes of foreigners befouling the cultural and social landscape by their inferiority belongs on the compost pile of errant thinking (see also Perea, 1996).

Others have also deplored the expanding multicultural makeup of the United States. They insist that a uniform culture and set of values are necessary to keep us prosperous as a nation. Allan Bloom, a social commentator, has said:

> Obviously, the future of America can't be sustained if people keep only to their own ways and remain perpetual outsiders. The society has got to turn them into Americans. There are natural fears that today's immigrants may be too much of a cultural stretch for a nation based on Western values. (As cited in Henry, 1990, p. 31)

Is the United States in jeopardy? Yes, if we limit our perspective of this country to what is at present the dominant culture. No, if we allow for the continuing development of that culture into a new and less oppressive form. The country will not disintegrate because of a feared "riot of cultures." A greater threat exists from any one culture obstinately attempting to maintain or gain preeminence over what it considers to be its lesser adversaries. As Thomas Bender, a historian at New York University, argues, if the cultural center of the United States cannot hold, then that center must be redefined. The process for this, he says, is a "continuing contest among social groups and ideas for the power to define public culture" (as cited in Henry, 1990, p. 31).

In the United States today, the outcome of this process will be ever changing. There will likely be more than a single popular culture. As Paul Fussell of the University of Pennsylvania remarks, the concept of a country having only one culture is as bereft of merit as the boredom of a "global village." This does not mean, however, that the United States will become chaotic. Immigrants are attracted to this country at least in part because of its institutions and values. Society changes its newcomers more than its newcomers change society. At the Sesame Restaurant in Houston, for example, as described in a *Time* magazine article entitled "Beyond the Melting Pot," a Korean immigrant owner has trained Hispanic immigrant workers to prepare Chinese-style food for a largely black clientele (as cited in Henry, 1990, p. 29).

Where there is a commonly acknowledged purpose to cooperate, in other words, persons from different cultures can benefit from one another. That purpose may be the simple practicality of free enterprise, steady employment, or good food. It may also be the evolution of more grandiose endeavors such as international relations, global economics, or human rights. How competent we will be in investigating the opportunities afforded by a multicultural society rests on our willingness to forfeit our past notions of what "real Americans" look like, how they act, and even how they speak. The faces depicted in a Norman Rockwell painting personify the United States of yesterday, not tomorrow.

Years ago, I visited the Oakland Museum in California to hear a lecture by a renowned glass artist. An exhibit of his works included a magnificent bowl radiant with hues of blue, magenta, and emerald. In describing the procedures he employed to achieve the colors and design of the bowl, the artist stressed the preference for starting with colorless glass which is as free from impurities as possible. Firing this glass to an intense level of heat, he carefully added colors and decanted the mixture into a graphite crucible. The graphite, a black lustrous carbon, was able to withstand the heat changes and remain stable without transferring its properties onto the cooling glass beyond its form. The result was a unique piece of sculpture.

This is a metaphor for forging a new cultural identity for the United States. The colors and design of this identity are traced already in the irrepressible movement toward a truly multiracial nation. Impurities of any type that foster injustice or subservience are cast out. The crucible becomes a composite of the principles that govern our democratic institutions. These principles must not be compromised in the mistaken belief that they cannot withstand the transforming of this country now in progress.

A reflection of how willing and astute we are in achieving this identity is how we are educating the youngest generation of students. By the year 2000, nearly one-third of all children in the United States will be from minority groups (Wheeler & Baron, 1994). All children should, therefore, hear positive messages about their own racial and ethnic heritages and those of other children. One program with this end is A World of Difference, which was originally developed in Boston in 1985 by the Anti-Defamation League of B'nai B'rith but is now available in major cities across the country. It is a prejudice awareness and reduction campaign in which the centerpiece is teacher training. The program was introduced in central California after a high school student in Sacramento told her class and her teacher that all

Chinese should be exterminated! A parent of one of the students, who was of Jewish heritage, was horrified at this unexpected reminder of the Holocaust. Through her initiative A World of Difference was introduced into the area and received the enthusiastic support of government, business, and community organizations.

Efforts to educate young students about minority cultures, however, have not always been as wholeheartedly received. Proponents of multicultural education claim that textbooks and curricula perpetuate a truncated view of life and history in this country. Although degrading caricatures and racist depictions have been removed from most educational materials, there remains scant attention given to the contributions and achievements of minorities. Students are instead given heavy doses of our European roots.

Many texts, for example, describe Christopher Columbus' "discovery" of the New World but make no mention of the vast migration and settlement patterns of Native Americans who preceded him. Many texts briefly note the Chinese work on the transcontinental railroad, whose labor was used to facilitate Manifest Destiny, but do not credit the Chinese for developing California's fishing and shrimping industries and reclaiming the tule swamps of the Sacramento–San Joaquin Delta for rich farmland. Many texts describe the conditions of slavery and the Civil War, but they do not teach respect for the full humanity of those who were forced to become slaves, nor do they highlight the substantial role of black soldiers in the Union victory. The list goes on.

K. W. Lee, editor of *Korea Times* magazine in Los Angeles, is one of many critics of school textbooks that are Eurocentric:

> They defy and destroy the sum total of experiences of people with different civilizations in history. That to me is the most unpardonable crime of all. Not to kill people physically but to kill people's memory. That's what publishing companies are doing to our children. (As cited in Kang & Waugh, 1990, p. A-14)

By omitting a multicultural approach to education, it is said, textbook manufacturers deprive minority students of a link to their heritage and an important source of self-esteem. Young children need role models and heroes. Not all of these have to be of the child's same race. But by being exposed to a variety of persons and deeds a greater number of children would be more likely to emulate them. Even though self-esteem itself is not a prerequisite for scholastic attainment—a child with self-pride can still receive poor math grades—the content of education must still be accurate and inclusive. An incomplete education leaves all of us less proud of our heritage. Children need to be aware of their own culture *and* those of other groups.

In 1960, when Yolanda Woo began her career as a teacher, her colleagues strongly disapproved when she taught her sixth-grade class about the Day of the Dead, a Mexican tribute to ancestors. The other teachers felt that the students were learning witchcraft! Woo is amused to find that such ethnic festivals are now popular subject matter in many classrooms. Other teachers seize the opportunities provided by the arrival of Cinco de Mayo, Black History Month, or the Lunar New

Year to instruct their students about different cultures. Carla Anders of Lazear Elementary School in Oakland, California, goes even further. Her school is 85% Hispanic, but Anders weaves together lessons about African American, Asian American, Native American, and other cultures into virtually every aspect of her teaching. One class project, for example, was to make papier-mâché renderings of famous black women.

In Hawaii, all public elementary schools have a formalized Kupuna Program whereby the children learn Hawaiian culture through the weekly visits of *kupunas* (elders) or *kumus* (teachers). There is a saying, *Oi ka 'aka 'a na maka* ("while the eyes are still open"), which admonishes young people to learn from the old people while they are still alive. The oldest kupuna on Maui is "Auntie" Alice Kuloloio, an octogenerian dynamo, who shows the children how to prepare Hawaiian foods, sing Hawaiian songs, appreciate Hawaiian values, and make simple conversation in the Hawaiian language. "Show me your *manamana limas*," she encourages a lively class of first-graders, and they wiggle their fingers in the air (Spalding, 1990, p. A-1).

Responding to the reality that the majority of the public school students in California are non-white, state educators have established guidelines for history and social science textbooks and educational materials. California guidelines, as outlined in the document "History–Social Science Framework," promise basic cultural literacy for these students:

> Whether treating past or present, textbooks…must portray the experiences of men, women, children and youth as well as different racial, religious, and ethnic groups…. Materials that ignore the importance of cultural diversity in United States history or world history are unacceptable (Kang & Waugh, 1990, p. A-14).

The school districts in California, which number over 1,000, buy more textbooks than any other state, comprising roughly 10% of the national textbook market. In 1990, nine publishing companies submitted textbooks for review and potential purchase by the state. This decision was a far-reaching one, for these books were to be California students' main introduction to history and social science into the next century. Seven of these publishers' programs were rejected by an evaluation panel of 60 classroom teachers and university professors, leaving only two that were recommended for approval. On July 20, 1990, by a vote of 10 to 3 (with three members absent and one abstaining) the state's 17-member Curriculum Commission voted to approve an elementary through junior high series and one eighth-grade text. Joyce King, an African American professor of teacher education at Santa Clara University on the commission, however, publicly disagreed with the views of her colleagues. She voted against approval because some of the recommended books contain "justifications and trivialization of unethical and inhumane social practices, namely racial slavery." King had previously argued unsuccessfully for the section in the state guidelines called "National Identity" to be changed to "Multicultural Identity" (Waugh, 1990, p. B-3).

The other black and Asian members of the commission also raised concerns over the lack of cultural diversity in the textbooks. Roger Tom, curriculum director of the San Francisco Unified School District, believed that they did not meet the needs of his area's student population—at that time, 85% minority with Asian Americans alone comprising 45% of the total student body. Nevertheless, on October 12, 1990, the State Board of Education voted to accept these textbooks.

The proponents of multicultural education in other states have likewise met opposition. Political science professor Andrew Hacker, of New York's Queen's College, for example, warns that actual historical events are sometimes replaced by elaborate myths created for the purpose of bolstering the self-esteem of minority children. The rhetoric of certain racial platforms and passionate advocacy of them, he insists, interfere with imparting essential and truthful knowledge (as cited in Henry, 1990, p. 30). Others state that minorities are being misdirected and misled by the concerns for a diverse education. Miller states bluntly that "self-esteem won't solve a kid's math problem" (1990, p. A-21). One resident of Palo Alto wrote the following to the editor of the *San Francisco Examiner:*

> The great figures in American history, whether in politics, science, industry, education or literature are almost all of European ancestry. The American civilization has European roots. It will do our country no good to distort history just to soothe the pride of the many groups who come from other cultures. That most of the ethnic groups want to preserve some of their cultural traditions is commendable and nothing keeps them from doing that. But they are Americans now and it isn't necessary to rewrite history to make them feel at home here. (Ross, 1990, p. A-16)

It is clear that this letter unintentionally reiterates the arguments *for* and not against multicultural education. Its writer exemplifies the limited knowledge of the history of minorities in the United States. He also raises the important issue of who belongs in this country. Minorities have too often been shunned as outsiders. At a gas station near the city limits of Monterey Park, California, for example, where the majority of residents are now Chinese, a sign was erected displaying two slanted eyes with the query: "Will the last American to leave Monterey Park please bring the flag?"

Cultural literacy helps to form the basis for inclusion by highlighting both past and potential contributions by diverse peoples. It argues for retaining rather than relinquishing cultural identity as a means for them to move into and be an integral part of the larger society. The right of minorities to belong in the United States stems from more than their mere presence here or the benevolence of European Americans. Their range of identities has yet to be fully recognized. The San José telephone directory lists columns of Nguyens, outnumbering the columns of Joneses. A white Southerner now living in New York may discover that the only other people in the phone book with her last name are black families, descendants of slaves owned by her ancestors. The identity of this country, in other words, is finding both new and neglected sources of cultural identification.

Diversity within Diversity

Generalizing persons into large groups is part logic and part insult. The logic derives from the desire to highlight similarities, to promote cohesion, and to convey a larger political or cultural identity. We therefore speak of this country's people from African, Asian, Latin, European, Pacific Island, and Native descent. Their collective geography and history suitably and persuasively bind these persons together. The variety *within* populations, however, is often as great as between them. These "finer distinctions" (Hecht, Andersen, & Ribeau, 1989, p. 178) exist within groups because there are different ways of being one particular ethnicity. This fact is sometimes obscured by our categorizations.

The term Indian, for example, was a misnomer applied to the Arawak tribe of the southeastern United States by an errant Italian navigator who had set sail for India. It is now (mistakenly) used to describe all the native populations of the Western Hemisphere. Those who fall into the category of American Indians, however, are federally recognized to belong to approximately 550 separate nations and tribes with 187 different languages (U.S. Department of Justice, 1994). The largest of these is the Navajo Nation. Its reservation covers an area that spans New Mexico and Arizona, almost the size of West Virginia. The second largest is the Cherokee Nation in Oklahoma. California has the greatest total number of Native Americans of any state, who are dispersed among 100 tribal organizations, reservations, and rancherias. Some of the tribes have only a few members living on several acres, whereas others number in the thousands and live throughout the state. Ortiz, moreover, summarizes the diversity within diversity of Native Americans through this query about Pueblos:

> In confronting any question having to do with the Pueblos of New Mexico and Arizona, considered as a group, we must first ask whether it makes any sense at all to lump them together for any purpose. After all, the term Pueblos today encompasses some forty thousand people speaking six mutually unintelligible languages and occupying thirty-odd villages stretched along a crescent of more than four hundred miles. In other words, we must consider whether the term *Pueblos*, like the term *Indian*, only denotes an artificial category invented by Spanish invaders of the sixteenth century for their own purposes and perpetuated in our time by anthropologists and other non-Indians for their own, presumably more exalted, purposes. (1994, p. 296)

If we delve into the category called Asian American, we discover a commingling of Chinese (23% of Asians in the United States), Filipinos (19%), Japanese (12%), Koreans (11%), Asian Indian (11%), Vietnamese (8%), Laotian (2%), Cambodian (2%), and others (12%) (U.S. Bureau of the Census 1997). Upon further inquiry, we find that Okinawans, although frequently regarded as Japanese, have their own distinct dialect and sub-culture. Likewise, Filipinos, whose roots extend back to days of Spanish colonization, are often more Spanish than Asian in their traditions (e.g., their adherence to Catholicism is of Spanish origin).

We would be presumptuous indeed to consider an Irish Bostonian, an Anglo-Saxon California yuppie, a Jewish Greenwich Village artist, and a New Age Polish vegetarian as all the same blend of European Americans because they are white. We would also be foolish to homogenize the experiences of Puerto Ricans, Cubans, Guatemalans, Mexicans, Argentinians, and Panamanians by classifying them all as Latinos. To give an example, not everyone who lives in Mexico speaks Spanish; there are native populations, those of Mayan and Aztec descent, living in remote areas who are not Hispanic. No one is, in fact, *just* what we label or classify them. *All* races and ethnicities are more variegated than we usually imagine.

Infused throughout our racial and ethnic identities are, furthermore, the distinctions of gender, age, generation (first, second, etc.), degree of acculturation, place of residence (regional and local), and socioeconomic status. People must be recognized for their individual traits within a larger cultural grouping. Individuals, for example, have varying levels of ethnic identification related to length of residence or parents' residence in the United States, language spoken in the home, and whether or not their marriage is interracial (Young, 1993, p. 109–110). An "ecological fallacy" (Robinson, 1950, p. 351) occurs when we fail to consider cultural variables *between* individuals. Among the Vietnamese, for example, I have met both young, Paris-educated, computer literate professionals and elderly, refugee farm workers from mountainous villages, who had never before held a writing instrument of any kind.

Of African American homogenizing, Julia Boyd, an African American psychotherapist, has written:

> Categorizing women of color as neatly packaged groups defined by customs and traditions might be an easy task, if the groups were not made up of individuals.... There are many models of black womanhood. Black women are distinct individuals who make choices as to the many ways in which they gain their strength. There are black women who may not always look to their ethnic and cultural traditions for subsistence, but it is very likely that on some level such a woman will periodically seek comfort that only her community or family of origin can provide. This attention to both group and individual needs may sound complex...[but] being of one body yet sharing many voices is the daily life and strength of black women. (1990, pp. 230–231)

There is also enormous diversity among African American males. In 1945, after our release from an internment camp for Japanese Americans, my parents, brother and I returned to the Los Angeles area—homeless. For much of the first year, we shared the small, rented home of a generous and welcoming black postal worker and his wife. My parents had known him before they were interned and respected him as a hardworking and quiet-spoken man. Later, we moved to a predominantly black and Mexican section of the city. I can recall the fear that I felt as I walked to Garfield Elementary School each morning around the derelicts who had strewn themselves across the sidewalk outside liquor stores. They never harmed me, but I did a lot of sidestepping and running.

After nine years we moved again. In our new neighborhood, there was an elderly, black man who lived near us. He stood in the middle of the street daily, waving his arms, and shouting obscenities at "the white devils." Our next-door neighbors were a black dentist, a prominent citizen of the area, and his wife, who was related to government officials in the Virgin Islands. The dentist was also a talented water colorist who portrayed African Americans in tropical and festive settings wearing bright and billowing outfits. Occasionally, the neighbor would come out of his house and attempt to calm the old man.

During my undergraduate studies at UCLA, I had several classes with the basketball legend Lew Alcindor, who later changed his name to Kareem Abdul Jabar to play professionally for the Los Angeles Lakers. I would marvel at Lew ducking to walk through doorways and dominating his opponents in basketball when he played in Pauley Pavilion. But on April 4, 1968, during my graduate work in East Asian Studies, my life took an unexpected turn. On the date of my 23rd birthday, Martin Luther King, Jr. was assassinated in Memphis. His life had always commanded my attention, but now his death caused an abrupt change. My career goals subsequently centered on theology, counseling, and race relations.

Forty years after my family had lived with the postal worker, I was reminded of his kindness in a startling way. I was the director of a prosecutor-based victim assistance program in Hawaii and was assisting a family whose young daughter had been raped. The defendant eventually decided to enter a plea of *nolo contendere*. As I reviewed the presentence report on the defendant, I was stunned to see the name of the defendant's father. His father had moved to Los Angeles without his family around 1940, and the defendant, though born in the Midwest, had been raised by his single mother in Hawaii. The defendant therefore never really knew his father—who was the very same person who had befriended my family!

In other words, in every race there are those imbued with hospitality and warmth, those who have lapsed into drunken stupor, those who vainly rail against their plight, those who exhibit a refinement and artistry beyond their common origins, those who excel at physical and athletic prowess, those who are extraordinary in courage and sacrifice, and those who stumble because of their upbringing and circumstances. All of these images must be woven into our understanding of persons of any color.

The labels that we employ, including those in this book, are no more than conveniences for describing and understanding one another. All crime victims deserve to be treated as *individuals* and not just according to victim types and categories. Minority victims also are deserving of individual respect and not just as members of a particular race. We must assume diversity within diversity even as we generalize between groups. The more variety that we uncover, in fact, the more likely that we will recognize our overlapping and common qualities.

CULTURAL KEYS

Social cognition refers to the ways in which knowledge about people is acquired and processed (Gudykunst & Gumbs, 1989, p. 204). One of the most accessible but misappropriated ways to understand people of different cultures is to appreciate their literary folklore, traditional ceremonies, and creative expressions. Triandis (1972) referred to such tangible and visible aspects as "objective" and "surface" culture because they could easily be examined, observed, felt, heard, and tasted. Too often, forms of expression which are important elements of minority cultures are viewed apart from their historical or spiritual roots. They are superficially perceived as quaint or primitive, or commercialized for entertainment and amusement. As Leigh and Green state, "As Black traditions, artistic and musical efforts fulfill more than simply entertainment functions as they are also collective representations of the concerns of the Black community. Like Black ministers, entertainment figures often embody and articulate values and sentiments widely shared among Blacks" (1979, p. 137). These forms of communication and preservation, however, are key to learning about the cultures they represent. They are paths to appropriating the "subjective" and "deep" culture representing values, norms of behavior, world view, and attitudes. As Cushner states,

> Like the iceberg, whose 90 percent remains hidden from view, there are subjective elements of culture that are also hidden. These aspects of deep or subjective culture…are more potent and more substantial in that they are critical in providing support and structure for what is seen, as well as more dangerous in people's interactions and understanding. It is the deep aspects of culture… that must be examined and understood if interactions across cultural boundaries are to be effective. (1996, p. 215)

The Blues

Blues music is a uniquely African American musical style. Its history can be traced from its probable birthplace on the Dockery Plantation in the Mississippi Delta to the clubs of Chicago, which is now arguably the blues capital of the world. In the 1920s down-home blues was called "race music" and mistakenly considered a low art form. In the thirties there was New Orleans stride style of piano music, and in the forties and fifties blues-based be-bop jazz. Although dismissed by some younger blacks as the outdated music of their parents and grandparents, blues enthusiasts argue that contemporary funk and rap music are in the same tradition as blues. They speak from the soul and experience of black people—their laments and hardships, their aspirations and longings. Alice Walker, in *The Temple of My Familiar*, provides this fascinating description of a blues musician:

> Arveyda lived in the clothes she made for him, earning himself finally the nickname "Bird," or, as he loved to translate it, "Charlie Parker the Third." Wrapped in his feathered cape, his winged boots, he sent his soul flying to Zede while holding his body, his thought, his attentions on Carlotta, whom he did not cease to love…. Arveyda thought and thought about the problem; his music, so mellow and rocking, became tortured and shrill. Sometimes in

rehearsal and even in performance he played his guitar in a trance. Arveyda's music was so beautiful no one minded how long he played.... Arveyda and his music were medicine, and seeing or hearing him, people knew it. They flocked to him as once they might have to priests. He did not disappoint them. Each time he played, he did so with his heart and soul. Always, though he might be very tired, he played earnestly and prayerfully.... He played for his dead mother and for the father he'd hardly known; the longing for both came out of the guitar as wails and sobs. There was a blue range in his music that he played when he was missing them. (1989, pp. 23–24)

The blues traveled with African Americans as they moved from the South to the North and from Louisiana and Texas to California. The story lyrics and the emotional intensity of the blues, therefore, mirror black history. Hugh Merrill, author of *The Blues Route,* however, tells of being dismayed after a blues performance at a club in the Atlanta suburb of Buckhead, which he describes as "a glittering corn-pone Beverly Hills on the northside of town" (Ross, 1990, p. 5). The patrons are apathetic to the blues and treat it as live background music. Merrill thereafter embarks on an odyssey to rediscover the blues in the cities where it still vibrates with purity and fire. He visits Watts, "the Harlem of Los Angeles," San Francisco, and Oakland, among others, on his quest. Merrill passionately defends the blues as the most indigenous of American music and therefore something to be preserved and appreciated. As Ross states, "Despite its deepest roots in black life in the American South, its themes are universal, its truths shared by anyone" (p. 5).

Chants

There are millions of people from the United States mainland who visit the Pacific Islands of Polynesia and Micronesia each year. Ancient dances and chants are performed by island natives for the entertainment of tourists and visitors. These dances and chants, however, represent much more than a social pastime or merriment for these native people. They carry religious and spiritual meaning by transmitting the values and beliefs of the past.

The cadence, pitch, and intonation of particular chants in the Hawaiian culture, for example, have their own significance. All words within a chant must be precise. In ancient times any omission or alteration of even a single word could mean death for the chanter. The chant had to be absolutely reliable for all those who listened to it and for each succeeding generation. In ancient times, Hawaiians had developed no written language fully, not because of inability to construct written forms, but due to their preference for oral history in order to safeguard and authenticate what was being passed on.

In other words, they believed anyone could alter written documents, but the chanters were strictly instructed to adhere to what was entrusted solely to them. Chants are therefore rich with wisdom and purpose, tradition and obligation. They are not just the odd, rhythmic sounds of "primitives."

The Three Counsels

There was once a boy who ran away from home. This boy had three bad habits: he would not stick to a purpose, he meddled in other people's business, and he would always lose his temper. He had traveled only a short distance when he left the highway for a trail and came across an old man. He questioned who he was, and then became upset when the old man did not reply.

Finally, the *viejito* (little old man) spoke, saying he was a peddler of advice and for a peso he would instruct the boy. The boy had only three pesos, but he gave one to the old man and was told, "Don't leave a highway for a trail." The boy was angry at such meager advice, so the viejo offered to say more for another peso. The second advice was, "Don't ask about things that don't concern you." Again, the boy became angry, but eventually parted with his last peso, only to hear, "Don't lose your temper." And the old man vanished.

The boy, continuing his journey with his pockets empty, soon met a stranger who galloped up to him on a black horse and urged him to take a "shortcut" into the city. The boy, however, refused and stayed on the main road. He came upon a ranch house and was invited to dinner by a bandit seated on the porch there. At dinner, when a man's head was served to the boy for his meal, he decided he'd better not ask any questions. The bandit therefore showed the boy the skeletons of those who had been too inquisitive about the head. Because the boy had not been nosy, he was given three mules and a horse, each mule having two bags of gold tied on its back.

On the road again, the boy met another bandit who demanded to know what was in the bags. Instead of losing his temper, the boy said simply that he preferred not to tell. "Speak or I shall kill you!" warned the bandit. "Do as you must," the boy answered. Pleased with the boy's calm wisdom, the bandit allowed him to pass.

Later, the boy prospered in the city and married. Best of all, his wife also did not leave the main road for a path, asked no questions about matters that did not pertain to her, and always kept her temper. (West, 1988, p. 99, paraphrased)

Dichos

A closer consideration of Mexican American *dichos* (sayings) and prose narratives helps to further our cultural awareness and enables us to benefit from their message. Almost every cultural group has peculiar proverbs and sayings which summarize advice on a wide range of topics such as romance, social etiquette, and overcoming hardships. These allow both the common folk and the educated elite to share simple truths and observations about life. Proverbs and sayings, moreover, have a cross-cultural aspect in that the proverbs and sayings of many cultures share common insights.

John West, in his book *Mexican-American Folklore*, demonstrates this point by mentioning how the Mexican proverb to be *entre la espada y la pared* (between the sword and the wall) is very similar to the English "between the devil and the deep blue sea" and "between a rock and a hard place." There are also certain dichos that non-Hispanics can readily adopt as their own:

> *El que adelante no mira, atras se queda.* (He who doesn't look ahead, stays behind.)
> *Los adagios de los viejos son evangelios chiquitos.* (The adages of old people are little gospels.)
> *No hay consejos como los que el tiempo da.* (There are no counsels like those that time gives.) (1988, pp. 40, 44)

The guidance conveyed through Mexican American prose narratives, as demonstrated in "The Three Counsels," speaks to all peoples. This folktale follows a familiar and easily remembered pattern of describing persons and situations in groups of threes. There are the three primary characters of the boy, the old man, and the wife. There are three bandits, three mules with bags of gold, and three guiding principles. These principles have universal applicability and not just relevance for Mexican Americans. The literary folklore of other peoples, in other words, not only offers a glimpse into their cultural values but also provides practical instruction for us. Such stories are generally appealing and can be easily recalled. They capture our attention through their exaggeration and fable-like quality. The search, in other words, for the meaning of various oral and written traditions and cultural expressions is well rewarded.

HISTORICAL PERSPECTIVES

Crime victims have racial and ethnic identities preceding and greater than their victimization. Their self-concepts and response to trauma occur within the context of not only prior personal experiences but also the social history of their primary affiliate group. Minority victims have histories that, in fact, include injustice, oppression, dislocation, and hardship. These events permeate minority life in the United States. The histories of Southeast Asians and Native Americans are two examples of the significant role that histories play in understanding and serving victims from minority cultures.

Legacy of April 30

Vietnam had been a colony of France since the late nineteenth century. In 1954, under the leadership of Ho Chi Minh, the Vietminh were able to defeat the French forces at Dien Bien Phu to regain their country's independence. Vietnam, however, was soon torn apart with the northern portion aligned with China and the Soviet Union and the southern portion allied with the United States. A civil war had begun. The bordering countries of Laos and Cambodia became staging grounds and supply routes, and their peoples became inevitable allies and covert forces in the struggle. The longer the war continued, the more it escalated to become a torturous conflict of military atrocities, decimation of the civilian population, collateral "hidden wars," and political entanglements by the super powers.

But on April 30, 1975, the government of South Vietnam collapsed. Saigon had been under siege, and there was constant bombardment by advancing North Vietnamese troops. The city's population was in panic and chaos. As the city burned, fires too numerous to count engulfed it "like dragon's teeth," smearing the horizon with "the color of death." U.S. citizens were evacuated first but thousands of Vietnamese, many of whom were military personnel and their families, managed to escape by the only possible route: a massive and dramatic airlift (Takaki, 1989, pp. 449–450).

In the aftermath, 130,000 Vietnamese found refuge in the United States in 1975. Many of these were educated, spoke some English, and had arrived with their families intact. Among these refugees was Thien Cao, a community relations officer with the Garden Grove Police Department. His father, who had received his early military training in the United States, had been the commander of a South Vietnamese Army communications unit of 3,000 soldiers. Thien recalls how the family initially settled in Akron, Ohio. Despite his level of formal training, Thien's father, unable to find other employment, worked as a building custodian. He was eventually fired, however, because he did not know how to operate a floor waxing machine properly! Determined to make a better life for himself, he studied to be an engineer and in 1982 moved his family from Akron to "Little Saigon" in Southern California.

Hundreds of thousands of Vietnamese escaped the communist regime in the years following 1975. Socially and educationally, they were quite different from those who had earlier fled Saigon. Most did not speak English, and 40% were ethnically Chinese. This "second wave" of refugees from rural areas and coastal villages left on overcrowded boats and endured the pillaging of Thai pirates and the rape and death they cruelly meted out. Those who survived were forced to wait in camps in Thailand for months or even years before they could go to Australia, Canada, France, or the United States. By 1985, there were 643,200 Vietnamese in the United States. Forty percent had settled in California, particularly in the counties of Orange and Santa Clara. At present, besides the first airlift refugees and the following wave of boat people, 20,000 Vietnamese enter the United States each year, classified as family reunification immigrants under the Orderly Departure Program that was signed between Vietnam and the United States in 1979.

Many of the Vietnamese have successfully pursued professional careers or established businesses. In 1990, for example, Bolsa Avenue between Garden Grove and Westminster in Orange County housed 800 Vietnamese shops and restaurants alone. The rapidity of Vietnamese achievement in the United States has been linked to their ability to establish a community infrastructure and familiarity with American life. Vu-Duc Vuong, the director of the Center for Southeast Asian Refugee Resettlement in San Francisco, has become the first Vietnamese American to run for political office. Though unsuccessful, Vuong, 42, sought election to his city's Board of Supervisors. The son of a Saigon tailor, he had come to the United States in 1968 on a college scholarship. He obtained master's degrees in international relations and social work, and then earned a law degree. His candidacy was a long shot but, as one Vietnamese American journalist said, the Vietnamese are a "community on the move."

The legacy of April 30, however, extends beyond the Vietnamese people themselves. The course of events in neighboring Laos and Cambodia intermingled with those of Vietnam. Laotian nationalists had also overthrown their French rulers. Internal fighting then took place because North Vietnam supported the Pathet Lao to protect their supply route of the Ho Chi Minh Trail and the United States supported the Royal Lao. The Hmong and the Mien highland tribes were later recruited by the Central Intelligence Agency to conduct its secret military operations within Laos.

When the Pathet Lao seized control in 1975, 70,000 Laotians, 60,000 Hmong, and 10,000 Mien lost their homeland and were forced to seek refuge in the United States. Their adjustment to life here has been a difficult one. Many end up on welfare or in low-paying jobs. According to Professor Takaki of the University of California at Berkeley, it is especially common for the Hmong and Mien to feel "intensely lost in America" (1989, p. 463). They were subsistence farmers who, though it was not their sole crop, had cultivated opium. These traditional agricultural skills are ill-suited to the U.S. competitive farming economy, although efforts in this direction are notable in farming the fields of the Central Valley of California and Minnesota.

In Fresno County there are approximately 35,000 Hmong who have been attracted there by the mild climate and the availability of rental farmland. Pedro Ilic from the University of California Extension Service, formerly an adviser to Spanish-speaking farmers in the county, estimates that 40% of his potential clients are now Hmong, Laotian, Cambodian, and Thai. The Hmong, according to Ilic, have carved a niche for themselves in labor-intensive specialty crops. They grow almost all of the county's sugar peas, 80% of its strawberries, and half of its cherry tomatoes. They rent parcels of 5, 10, or 20 acres for $200 to $300 per acre per year, often in groups of families.

The Hmong, however, who would prefer to enter other occupations, sometimes feel trapped by the English proficiency requirements of programs designed to train people of the welfare system. The Hmong are from a preliterate society, and many must first learn to read and write in Hmong before even attempting English. Chong Toua Vang, for example, who wants to become a welder, was enrolled in welding classes at Fresno City College in 1987. However, his social worker made him leave the school and return to English classes.

The Mien now reside in the areas of Seattle, Washington and Portland, Oregon and in the California cities of Sacramento, Oakland, San Jose, and Long Beach. What does their future hold? Again, in Takaki's view, the older Mien as well as Hmong live much of their lives in sadness. As proud tribal peoples, they were "deeply and spiritually attached to the land they were forced to leave." Here in the United States they are displaced, perceived as backward, and often not accepted as full residents of this country (Takaki, 1989, p. 467–468).

The Vietnam War and the fall of Saigon also had tragic consequences for Cambodians. In April of 1975, the Khmer Rouge under Pol Pot overthrew the United

States-supported government of Lon Nol. The Khmer Rouge embarked on a mass extermination of all Cambodians affiliated with Lon Nol and the United States. One million Cambodians were murdered in the worst genocide since the Holocaust. It left the survivors scarred with unrelenting and traumatic memories. One survivor, Seang Seng, wrote this account:

> Death. It seems every part of my story ends in death.... Even water was hard to find, and there was almost nothing edible.... My youngest niece died first.... She had cried all the time because she had always been hungry. As for the older child, Vimol...I found a fish for him and put it into his hand to eat, but later that day he died, with the fish still in his little hand. I can't remember this without crying.... One of my sisters, the second one, tried to come home. They caught her. They tied her up for one day in the sun. I went to see her. She was swollen. I cry whenever I remember.... I can hardly bear to remember the deaths of my parents. The last time I saw my mother her chest was flat as if she had TB.... I tried not to cry. Somehow, the tears flowed incessantly. My mom begged me to stay and share her meager rice soup with her.... It was the last time I saw her. I often think of my dad, his dry skin and his fleshless body.... Within only 16 months of the Khmer Rouge takeover, all members of my family had starved to death except me and my younger sister, Sam Ang, who was 12 years old. We both were left behind in a world with no personal belongings...no free communication...no human rights.... Eyes full of meanness, glaring at us every second... (Seng, 1987, pp. 3, 7–9, 12)

Over 100,000 Cambodians were able to reach sanctuary in the United States. Many still hold hopes of someday returning to Cambodia. Subsequent events, however, have been confusing and disturbing to their plans. The Khmer Rouge were defeated by the Vietnamese in 1979. The Vietnamese then withdrew from Cambodia in October of 1989 as a step toward normalizing international relations. Until that time, the United States had been aiding the non-communist forces in their attempt to dislodge the existing leadership, which was accused of being a puppet of Vietnam. The Khmer Rouge, however, had been closely aligned with these non-communist forces. To some, the U.S. government had been dishonoring the slain Cambodians by helping to make it possible for the Khmer Rouge to return to power.

Most recently, in July of 1997, their plans were further complicated when a bloody coup by Hua Sen against Prince Norodom Ranariddh and the subsequent attempts at counter-resistance by Ranariddh's forces and Khmer Rouge guerrillas resulted in tens of thousands of Cambodian citizens streaming across the border into Thailand. As this book goes to press, Cambodia continues to experience political instability, intense warfare, and dislocation of its peoples.

The history of Southeast Asian immigrants and refugees is therefore laden with the death and destruction of war and the interference and intrusion of foreign powers. Life in the United States for them is not a wistful dream being fulfilled but a desperate retreat from a nightmare. In the United States, the Vietnam War divided the nation and wounded our pride. It also taught us lessons concerning human rights and how we treat our returning soldiers. But for the Southeast Asians, who now belong in the United States because they no longer have their ancestral homelands, the legacy of April 30 is the most pronounced and unforgettable episode in their lives. Their victimization as a culture envelops our notions of sorrow and grief and begs for a compassionate and patient response to their resettlement in this country.

Subjugated but Not Defeated

Native Americans have undergone a long travail of invasion, humiliation, subjugation, and displacement. This country's first inhabitants have endured numerous broken treaties, extermination campaigns, and military actions throughout U.S. history. There were many precursors to present day reservations, for example:

- In 1830, the Indian Removal Law required that all Native Americans in the south be moved to new lands west of the Mississippi. This "Indian Territory," in what is now the states of Oklahoma, Arkansas, and Kansas, was known then as the Great American Desert. It was assumed that no whites would ever want these lands.
- In 1836, 7,000 federal troops backed by state militia removed the Cherokee from Georgia. The ensuing migration of the Cherokee in the dead of winter became known as the Trail of Tears—this forced march to Oklahoma took six months and claimed the lives of one out of four Cherokee.
- In 1902, Congress moved to dissolve the land governance of The Five Civilized Tribes: the Cherokee, Creek, Choctaw, Chicksaw, and Seminole when lands in eastern Oklahoma were found to be rich in oil, coal, and natural gas. Through an "allotment" system, communally held tribal lands were broken up for individual ownership, "surplus lands" were sold, and town sites were established. Thousands of white opportunists raced to become "enrolled members" on tribal rolls, which was necessary to benefit from the allotments.
- From 1953–1962, "termination" was the federal American Indian policy, based on the belief that Native Americans should be assimilated into mainstream society. Thirteen tribes (the largest two being the Menominees in Wisconsin and the Klamaths in Oregon) were terminated, thus losing federal protections and services. In 1961, the National Congress of American Indians declared termination to be "the greatest threat to Indian survival since the military campaigns of the 1800s." The policy was subsequently outlawed during the administration of President Kennedy in 1962.
- In 1974, Congress passed the Hopi Land Settlement Act, which eventually forced the relocation of 12,000 Navajo in the Hopi–Navajo Joint Use Area. It became the largest Native American removal since the 1800s. Although the removal was ostensibly to settle a land dispute between the Hopi and Navajo, it removed those Navajo who were living over coal deposits coveted for stripmining by the Peabody Coal Company, the largest producer of coal in the United States (Nies, 1996).

Mistreatment and offenses against Native Americans are not just of the past. The injustices and exploitation of former centuries and decades rain down upon modern day Native Americans through condoning the deprivations of desolate reservation life, continuing the patronizing wardship and chronic dependency under the Bureau of Indian Affairs, displacing Native Americans into urban areas, affording tribes a complex quasi-sovereign status by the federal government, and ignoring ambiguous jurisdictional issues in the administration of justice in "Indian country" (Myers, 1996).

There are always exceptions. It would be a disservice to describe all Native Americans as downtrodden and displeased with their circumstances. Some prominent ones have entered into the larger society. Larry EchoHawk, a member of the Pawnee Tribe, for example, became the first Native American in U.S. history to be elected as a state attorney general. His victory in 1990 in Idaho was remarkable, as was his near election to the state's governor's office in 1994. Ben Nighthorse Campbell, a Northern Cheyenne from Colorado, was also elected to the U.S. Senate in 1992, the first Native American to serve there. Native Americans are, moreover, prospering from the gaming casinos established on reservation lands by attracting great numbers of non-Native American gamblers. The Flat Head Tribe in Montana has also benefited from its properties and holdings surrounding Flat Head Lake, a prime fishing and resort destination.

Joseph Myers, executive director of the National Indian Justice Center, left the Pomo reservation in Northern California, moved to Berkeley, and eventually graduated from the University of California with a law degree. His endeavors were seemingly rewarded and might have led him further away from the reservation at that point. Instead, Myers is among the forefront of those Native Americans who have honed their communication and legal skills and use them to work for cultural preservation, sovereignty, and cooperative relations with non-Indians. He knows that it is precisely because of the lack of opportunities *within* the reservation that individuals are forced to seek such opportunities outside, thereby severing ties with their culture legacy, social support network, and spiritual base.

Successes among Native Americans, in other words, only heightens awareness of what most Native Americans experience. They have, for example, the highest unemployment and poverty rates (three times the non-Indian population), highest suicide rate (four times the national average), lowest educational attainment, lowest per capita income, and poorest housing (U.S. Bureau of the Census, 1990). Native Americans who have relocated to urban settings often find themselves forced to live in "inner-city reservations." Many of the despairing faces of the men squatting on sidewalks or roaming downtown streets are Native American (J. Myers, personal communication, April 16, 1990). Perhaps if there were flourishing Native American reservations on which they would have pride, or to which they could return, or where they would have been nurtured before they left them, these men might have a far different existence and future (Walters, 1995, p. 3).

To attempt to understand Native Americans who are crime victims is, in other words, inseparable from understanding what all Native Americans have suffered. Romanticized caricatures of the "noble savage" and disparaging references to "drunken Indians," the deliberate isolation of life on reservations, and the general apathy of the dominant culture toward Native American rights and concerns have together resulted in *all* people in this country losing an essential part of our heritage. The Sioux chief, Luther Standing Bear, pronounced a half century ago what remains hauntingly accurate today:

> The white man does not understand America. He is too removed from its formative processes. The roots of the tree of his life have not yet grasped the rock and soil…The man from Europe is still a foreigner and an alien. And he still hates the man who questioned his path across the continent. But in the Indian the spirit of the land is still vested; it will be until other men are able to divine and meet its rhythm. Men must be born and reborn to belong. Their bodies must be formed of the dust of their forefathers' bones. (1933, p. 248)

Despite being removed from their ancestral homes and sacred places, Native Americans have been sustained by their strength as tribal peoples. The reidentification of Native Americans with a particular land, however, has been hindered on many fronts. Reservations, for example, are trust lands owned by the federal government. Native peoples are therefore in a dependency situation whereby they are deemed beneficiaries of Congressional laws and appropriations. The security of even this status has been assailed as certain reservations have been closed with the expressed purpose of integrating them but with the (intended) result of reclaiming lands.

There have also been efforts to abrogate treaties and dishonor the provisions for exclusive rights held by Native peoples to fish and hunt as well as to tap, harvest, or manage the natural forest, mineral, and water resources of their lands. In January, 1990, for example, The Wisconsin Counties Association tried to organize a national anti-treaty coalition at a conference in Utah attended by officials of nine other states. In the end, forming the coalition was delayed by the protest of tribal leaders and Native American activists. As Hilary Waukau of the Menominee Tribe stated:

> Indian treaties were made a long time ago by our ancestors, who were honorable people. Those treaties were made to stand for all time, as long as the sun comes up, the grass grows green and the water flows. (As cited in *The Tribal Court Reporter*, 1990, p. 13)

The battle for control of resources on the Hopi reservation in the high desert east of the Grand Canyon was also being waged in the 1990s. In the 1970s, the Hopi tribe began selling coal and water to the Peabody Coal Company, a British-owned firm, that supplies the means to power the lights of greater Los Angeles, Las Vegas, and Phoenix. Three-fourths of the annual tribal budget of $14 million was derived from this income. The agreement was controversial from the beginning, as older tribal members felt the sanctuary of the land was being desecrated whereas others sought to improve their standard of living on the barren and harsh landscape. Water, for the 10,000 Hopis, however, had been disappearing. Springs had dried

up, and the small river meandering through the reservation had slowed and
become salty. The Hopi Tribal Council decided to fight the coal company, which it
blamed for its dangerous depletion of water. Its chairman, Vernon Masayesva,
announced:

> We've been exploited enough. In a situation like this, a desert climate, it is
> insane to be using more than a billion gallons of water annually for an indus-
> trial purpose. Water is life here. Money is insignificant here. (As cited in Ake-
> men, 1990, p. 2)

The Tribal Council obtained lawyers, geologists, and hydrologists and lobbied
federal Indian and mining officials as well as Congressional leaders in order to protect the reservation's water. Rain dances and religious ceremonies were also performed to seek the intervention of spirits and gods. The Hopi have no word for war
or aggression. Their culture, the oldest continuously surviving one in the United
States, has traditionally been a peaceful one. But the survival of the Hopi themselves was at stake, and this had drawn them into a modern day skirmish with big
business.

In a collateral suit, the Dine Alliance, a Navajo organization of more than 500
traditionalists of Black Mesa, argued that Peabody's Kayenta strip-mine polluted
the air, contaminated ground water, killed their sheep, affected the health of Native
people in the area, and destroyed burial sites. In 1996, the federal court in Arizona
ruled that Peabody had ignored "the adverse effects mining has upon the lives and
well-being of Native Americans," and denied the company a permanent operating
permit (Nies, pp. 396–397).

Whether or not Native Americans will regain any semblance of their birthright
as the "first Americans" elicits more questions than answers. To some, like Myers,
there is a "steep mountain" of long-standing indifferences and historical injustices
that must be surmounted. There have been some attempts to scale this mountain
by means of dramatic demonstrations. On November 26, 1970, two hundred mili-
tants of the American Indian Movement (AIM) covered Plymouth Rock under a
ton of sand as a symbolic burial of the "white man's conquest." AIM members
Dennis Banks and Russell Means also seized control of the Mayflower II in Plymouth Harbor and declared Thanksgiving a day of mourning. And in 1973, over a
period of 71 days, 2,000 Native American men, women, and children occupied
Wounded Knee, South Dakota, besieged by an army of federal marshals and the
FBI. As Mary Crow Dog recounts:

> When I heard the words "Wounded Knee" I became very, very serious.
> Wounded Knee—Cankpe Opi in our language—has a special meaning for our
> people. There is the long ditch into which the frozen bodies of almost three
> hundred of our people, mostly women and children, thrown like so much
> cordwood. And the bodies are still there in their mass grave, unmarked except
> for a cement border.... [The] women and children were hunted down like ani-
> mals by Custer's old Seventh, out to avenge themselves for their defeat by

butchering the helpless ones. That happened long ago, but no Sioux ever forgot it…. Finally, on February 27, 1973, we stood on the hill where the fate of the old Sioux Nation, Sitting Bull's and Crazy Horse's nation, had been decided, and where we, ourselves, came face to face with our fate. (Crow Dog & Erdoes, 1990, pp. 124–125)

It is indeed remarkable that resentments among Native Americans are not more visible over the course of our history. This does not mean any resistance is absent. It means that, in apparent defeat, the energy and dignity to continue remains. Walter EchoHawk of the Native American Rights Fund, for example, led the campaign to close a burial mound of his Pawnee ancestors in Kansas. The bones had been discovered by amateur archaeologists on a farm, and the owner was charging tourists $3.50 for a peek into the exposed grave. The farmer insisted that he was caring for the bones by varnishing them frequently!

Anthropologists and archaeologists who study Native American peoples and their civilizations have also been criticized for denying Native Americans a voice in how their cultures are portrayed and how their artifacts are displayed, for holding a paternalistic view of safeguarding and preserving culture for the Native population, and for warehousing thousands of Native American remains as well as (stolen) sacred objects for study (Arnold, 1990, pp. D15–16). As EchoHawk has stated, "Desecrate a white grave and you get jail. Desecrate an Indian grave and you get a Ph.D" (Brower, 1997, p. 42).

Trivializing Native American culture as irrelevant, outdated, and of only historical significance must certainly be halted. In California, The Native American Heritage Commission established by the state legislature in 1976 is one notable attempt to protect and preserve Native burial grounds, religious sites, and cultural places. Something beyond the scope of commissions, however, is needed. In the words of Vine Deloria, Jr., a Standing Rock Sioux:

Who will find peace with the lands? The future of mankind lies waiting for those who will come to understand their lives and take up their responsibilities to all living things. Who will listen to the trees, the animals and birds, the voices of the places of the land? As the long-forgotten peoples of the respective continents rise and begin to reclaim their ancient heritage, they will discover the meaning of the lands of their ancestors. That is when the invaders of the North American continent will finally discover that for this land, God is Red. (1973, p. 301)

MINORITY FAMILY PATTERNS

The individual is "embedded" within a family that, in turn, is embedded within a diverse culture (Szapocznik & Kurtines, 1993, p. 406). Our ideas, therefore, about family must be informed by the differing definitions of family membership, dynamics, and responsibilities. Certainly the family forms an essential support base for crime victims. The nature, extent, and meaning of that support vary among racial and cultural groups.

Native American Children

In the spring of 1988 the legal case of Baby Keetso was given national media attention as a "bitter tug-of-war." A Navajo mother living in the San Francisco Bay Area desired to have her child adopted by a white couple. At issue were the intent of the Indian Child Welfare Act (ICWA) of 1978 to maintain the integrity of Native American families and its provisions that gave tribal courts jurisdiction over certain child custody cases. The Navajo court opposed the adoption and was considering instead having the child brought to the reservation.

According to Ray Moisa, a Navajo–Hopi writing in *News from Native California*, a wise and honorable resolution was reached when the tribal court finally decided to allow the adoption with the condition that the child be raised with awareness of her Navajo heritage. This satisfied the purpose of the ICWA to protect Native American parental rights and to ensure that Native American culture was not being lost through the placement of these children in adoptive homes (1988, pp. 10–11).

The ICWA was the result of the great concern and anguish felt by Native Americans for their families, who had undergone generations of disruption and dismantling. The Native American family is part of a kinship and tribal network; its strength is interdependence and group affiliation. A high value is therefore placed on preserving harmony and cooperation (Vace, DeVaney, & Wittmer, 1995, p. 187). This kinship, however, is more than a social–cultural structure based upon genealogy. Among the Sioux, for example, the religious dimension, a contract with *wakàn tànka* (Great Spirit), unites "all forms of being into an unbroken network of relationship." As DeMallie explains:

> [T]he Sioux define relationship in terms of a set of conceptual categories and the logical relationships among them based on proper "feeling" and behavior, rather than on concrete links of marriage and birth. Although these biological factors are at the basis of Sioux kinship, they are in fact de-emphasized by the system…Biological relatedness is frequently overridden by a plethora of adoptive mechanisms; although anthropologists generally relegate adoption to the category of fictive kin, for the Sioux, adoption constitutes genuine kinship. Through those mechanisms the tenuous network of genealogical relatedness is developed into a stronger, more secure system of relationship… For the Sioux…this transformation of natural relatedness into cultural relationship is an important criterion that distinguishes human life from mere animal existence. (1994, p. 142)

In the late 1800s, however, the federal government began systematically removing Native American children from their homes and kinship networks and placing them in boarding schools, often hundreds of miles from their tribal communities. Joseph Myers, executive director of the National Indian Justice Center, describes these boarding schools as really "acculturation programs" designed to "strip Indian children of tribal culture and tradition" (1981, p. 15).

Moisa reports that as recently as 1974 the Bureau of Indian Affairs (BIA) was operating 75 boarding schools with more than 30,000 children enrolled. He concurs with Myers and writes:

> While in school, many Indian children acquire a devastating cultural inferiority complex and belief in assimilation as the only path to survival. As a result, thousands and thousands of Indians grew up cultural orphans, feeling out of place in both the mainstream society that shunned them and in the traditional one from which they were torn. (1988, p. 10)

Reservation schools have also provided the opportunity for child molesters to prey on the Native American community. John Boone, for example, was a teacher hired in 1979 to teach on the Hopi Reservation. Fifty-eight Hopi boys were sexually molested by Boone during his tenure there. He was finally arrested in 1987 and was sentenced to life imprisonment in a North Carolina prison. On April 9, 1990, a $46.5 million lawsuit was settled by the federal government on behalf of the Hopi. This settlement is believed to be the largest awarded by the federal government in a child molestation case. Fifty-seven Hopi males who ranged in age from nine to 21 years, and the mother of one teenager who committed suicide as the result of his being molested, shared the award. A Congressional study revealed that such cases of sexual abuse have occurred on numerous reservations and that known child molesters have been inexcusably hired as reservation teachers by federal agencies.

After World War II the BIA formed a policy to relocate Native Americans from the reservations to major cities, where centers were established to provide them with vocational training and employment assistance. This government relocation policy has additionally wreaked havoc on traditional Native American cultures. Adjustment to strange urban environments, such as Los Angeles, Chicago, New York, San Francisco and separation from their tribes resulted in severe stress, alcoholism, and broken families. Under this policy, Native American children were again removed from their homes and placed in foster care.

On the reservations, Moisa states, Native American parents were often deemed unfit or neglectful, according to standards imposed by a system of social workers and judges "far removed from Indian reality." Native American children were therefore adopted out into non-tribal homes. A nationwide study in 1976, for example, found that compared to children of other ethnicities, Native American children were likely to be placed in white homes five times as often in Utah, six times as often in California, and 15 times as often in Wisconsin (1988, p. 10).

The ICWA is therefore of obvious historic concern to the Native American culture and family. Its implementation, however, has depended upon the cooperation of tribes, states, and federal agencies. There is at times either a lack of information concerning the ICWA itself or a resistance to follow its mandates. California, for example, requires by a Public Law 280 mandate that small tribes without the resources to sustain a tribal court system must relinquish jurisdiction to the local courts. Native American bands and rancherias, especially those within the interior of the state along the Sierra Nevada mountains are thus left without the protection of the ICWA.

The future of the Native American family undoubtedly depends on the abiding strength of individual tribal cultures to continue the shared attributes of respect for elders, communal responsibility for children, and the bond between and support of extended family members. As Crow Dog reflects:

> Our people have always been known for their strong family ties, for people within one family group caring for each other, for the "helpless ones," the old folks and especially the children, the coming generation. Even now, among traditionals, as long as one person eats, all other relatives eat too.... At the center of the old Sioux society was the *tiyospaye*, the extended family group...which included grandparents, uncles, aunts, in-laws and cousins. The tiyospaye was like a warm womb cradling all within it. Kids were never alone, always fussed over by not one but several mothers, watched and taught by several fathers. (Crow Dog & Erdoes, pp. 12–13)

The past and present situation of Native American children perhaps best represents the challenges for and emerging patterns of the Native American family. Reported abuse and victimization of their children must, in this regard, be evaluated and understood within their own cultural context. Supreme Court Justice Sandra Day O'Connor has reiterated that Native American nonadversarial methods or cooperative processes at problem resolution may be "particularly useful where family issues, particularly related to children, are involved, because...tradition provides a critical guidance for social behavior" (1996, p. 13). As Beth Binstock, the victim witness specialist in the U.S. Attorney's Office in the District of Montana, states,

> Being a Caucasian woman working with Native Americans, I felt it was extremely important for people to understand me and I wanted to understand them. I learned to share my life experiences and found people would share theirs. I truly listen to the children. Some have experienced a life-time of trauma and abuse; they have painful memories. Only if we listen, will we be trusted. During one particular case I met with several members of an extended family. It was heartwarming when I introduced myself and one family member stood and said, "I have heard of you—you listen." (1997, p. 2)

The Office for Victims of Crime (OVC) administers the Children's Justice and Assistance Act (CJA) of 1986, which provides funding for improving the criminal justice response to child physical and sexual abuse cases. After the CJA was passed, a number of multiple victim child sexual abuse cases surfaced in Indian country. The cases, totaling hundreds of victims, prompted the OVC to fund numerous tribal programs, including training for multidisciplinary teams, investigators and prosecutors, child advocacy and treatment services, and developing protocols. Recognizing the tribal and cultural base for assistance, the OVC's policy has been:

> The OVC defers to the needs and priorities of tribal communities, relying on tribes to identify the best allocation of resources. Decisions on hiring, types of training, case disposition philosophies, and treatment practices, to the extent they do not conflict with statutory provisions and regulatory requirements, are left to the tribes. (1997b, p. 2)

The practical and direct effect of the OVC's policy is exemplified in the case of a 13-year-old Navajo girl who was sexually assaulted by a relative. In addition to the medical services provided by the Indian Health Service, the family was offered compensation for the traditional healing ceremonies performed by a shaman (Sanders, 1997).

As the Native American family regains its traditional form as a source of nurturance within a thriving community, it will establish a positive identity and place for its children. Native children should therefore no longer be "leaving their ancestors" but should be "coming home." As Goodluck and Short summarize:

> Throughout the generations, Indian families have used the land cooperatively and productively, never seeing it as an individual possession to be bought and sold for personal gain. Similarly, the Indian does not view a child as personal property but belonging to the community as a whole. Attitudes toward the land base and toward children are parallel in that one does not terminate one's relationship with either, but provides support, sustenance, and nurturing to ensure continuity. (1980, p. 473)

Hawaiian Ohana

Group affiliation and sharing are also descriptive of many Pacific Island cultures. There was, for example, in old Hawaii, no concept of individual profit or ownership. Those who lived by the sea freely shared fresh or dried fish with those in the mountain valleys. They were in turn given the food staple called *taro*, fruit, and other goods. No one came empty handed, and no one left empty handed (Hazama, 1974, p. 25).

Native Hawaiian society was also governed by a hierarchical social structure of *alii* (chiefs), *kahunas* (priests and experts), warriors, and commoners. A *kapu* system of laws and protocol existed; one such example is the "rule of the splintered paddle" that offered special protection from harm to children and elderly widows. *Heiau* (religious sites) were constructed and rituals developed. In the early 1800s, nonetheless, Hawaiian society began to unravel from within after the death of Kamehameha I, who had unified the islands. At the same time, whalers, traders, and missionaries from the United States began descending on Hawaii. It was only a matter of time before the remaining vestiges of ancient Hawaiian life would be gone.

The family, however, remains the heartbeat of Hawaiian life and still carries with it much of the same meaning as it did before. The Hawaiian word for family is *ohana*, which is derived from the word *oha*, for taro, and *na*, signifying plural. Members of the ohana are like taro shoots from one root. The ohana consists of all those related by blood, marriage, or adoption. Hawaiians prosper as extended families and clans. The *hanai* is a system of informal adoption and acceptance that also guarantees that no child is "illegitimate" or unwanted. The older people regard all the children in the ohana as their own, to be treated with care and love. In return, not only are the *kupuna* (elders), both male and female, respected as the leaders of the ohana, but almost every older person is regarded with warmth and respect, whether technically a part of the ohana or not, is bestowed the title of "auntie," "uncle," or *tutu* (grandparent).

In Hawaii, it is the ohana which is at the center of any celebration, remembrance, and mourning. None of these occasions are lacking in food contributions, helping hands, or the family's supportive presence. The Hawaiian family functions through shared responsibility and cooperation. When a family member is troubled or troublesome, for example, the family may meet for problem-solving in a *ho'oponopono*, which means to "cleanse," "arrange in order," or "correct." At the ho'oponopono, all members have the opportunity to honestly and openly express their feelings and opinions. The purpose is not to insult, discourage, offend or condemn anyone. Solutions must be fair for all concerned and proper for the welfare of the ohana.

The status of present-day Hawaiian families is similar to that of Native Americans in the continental United States. There are serious issues of reparations for lost lands, the preservation of Hawaiian culture and language, and the sanctity of ancient burial grounds and sacred places in a state becoming saturated by resort development and military installations. The manner in which all of these concerns are addressed have direct bearing on the well-being of the Hawaiian ohana.

Strengths of African American Families

The African American family has been analyzed by sociologists and researchers from a number of perspectives. Earlier studies assigned pathological deficiencies and multiple problems as the cause for the widespread dysfunction and instability of black families. This view was based upon disparaging stereotypes, such as the need for matriarchal rule to compensate for emasculated males and absent fathers, moral ambiguity resulting from lack of behavioral norms, and inferior socialization stemming from racial discrimination and poverty (Billingsley, 1990, p. ix; Logan, 1990, p. 74).

There is little doubt that two hundred years of slavery and a century thereafter of struggle for equal social status and economic opportunity have levied an enormous toll upon the black family. But during the 1970s and 1980s, scholars began to reassess the black family's unnoticed and underestimated strengths, ties to African cultural traditions and values, and heterogeneity (Hill, 1972). Edith Hall and Gloria King, of the University of Alabama, for example, have summarized these strengths as:

- **Kin-structured networks** in which there is a close and supportive relationship among the individuals within a family and between families in matters of daily living and in crises.
- **Elastic households** which have the ability to adapt to external and internal pressures, such as the sharing of households with relatives or informally adopting the children of friends when personal or economic circumstances necessitate.
- **Resilient children** who learn "survival techniques" and are socialized to take part in the dominant culture while internalizing the values of their black heritage.
- **Egalitarian two-parent relationships** in which both partners share in duties and rights.
- **Steadfast optimism** that there will be better conditions for succeeding generations through the determination and aspiration of parents for their children. (1982, pp. 222–230)

The positive characteristics of the black family have also been emphasized by James Leigh and James Green of the University of Washington. They review the "well-defined principles of family organization" that existed in the cultures of West Africa, the area from which most slaves brought to America came. Families provided the complex network of ancestral lineage and cooperation between villages that "assured that the physical necessities of daily life as well as moral support in times of crisis would be available" (1979, p. 28).

Enslavement fractured the traditional pattern through a disregard for family relationships in favor of efficient plantation operations. Slave families lacked autonomy and stability because they were at the mercy of the individual whims, self-serving dispositions, and fiscal (and physical) appetites of their masters. Enslavement, however, did not mean that black family values disintegrated. Dispersal of family members, for example, forged kinship ties across plantations. This mitigated a sense of isolation and helplessness through the awareness of a larger community. Cushner stresses this about the African American kinship network:

> Africans arrived in America with an already extended sense of community, established in their highly structured, tribally oriented communal societies, where members depended on each other for physical protection and support, as well as assistance in economic ventures. In their new environment, a similar configuration developed—this time, however, predicated on skin color and experiential communality rather than tribal affiliation. The African American kinship network is thus multigenerational and regularly consists of relatives, friends, and neighbors. Through such a network, African American individuals and their nuclear family system are able to give and receive emotional, physical, psychological, and social support. (1996, p. 228)

There was, in other words, an energy that persisted then and continues to sustain the lives of African American families. External restraints by the larger society have not muffled the expressive culture of the black community in music, art, or literature. Racism and bigotry have not nullified the numerous efforts of African

Americans to foster identity and achieve dignity. And denial of admission into dominant institutions of power and influence have not precluded making inroads into native culture and developing relevant African American institutions. The lens through which black families are viewed, therefore, must not simply be the haze of slavery, poverty, and prejudice. Clarity must also come from seeing what strengths African American families have equipped and organized themselves with throughout history. Reinforcing and enhancing strengths is a far better perspective than offering help based on weaknesses (Billingsley, 1990).

It is this perspective which must undergird our approaches to the enormous realities that now face many black families. Sociologist Robert Hampton, for example, argues that the black family "ecosystem" is barraged by a number of negative societal and institutional forces (Hampton, 1987; see also McRoy, 1990). Marian Wright Edelman, founder and president of the Children's Defense Fund in Washington, D.C., more particularly states that the "crux of the problem facing the black family today is that young black women who become pregnant do not marry." In 1983, Edelman reports, 58% of all births to black women were out of wedlock. Among black women under the age of 20, the proportion was 86% (1990, p. 130). In a large part, the reason for the rising numbers of single-parent households, according to William Wilson of the University of Chicago, is the poor labor market for black males. Young black women are facing a "shrinking pool of marriageable (that is, employed, economically stable) men" (Wilson & Neckerman, 1987, p. 258).

The key to bolstering these young families, Edelman concludes, is improved education, training, and employment opportunities for both black males and females. She warns that we cannot await the outcome, only pondering whether the inadequacies of the black family produce its dire economic situation or whether it is the reverse.

> I am not going to spend time arguing about differing scholarly views. Nor am I able to resolve whether it is the change in black family structure which causes its desperate economic condition, or family destabilizing changes in the economy which have led to black family changes. I believe that poor female-headed households, male joblessness, and poverty are all parts of the same conundrum which we must act to pierce now, rather than just continuing to debate whether the chicken or the egg came first. Certainly, we need to understand as much as we can and thoughtful academic research and exchange on cause and effect are needed. But we cannot afford to wait for a precise disaggregation before we act to save another generation of black young. (1990, pp. 135–136)

La Familia

The Latino family in the United States is undergoing both reaffirmation and change. There are circumstances, for example, that allow for the steady infusion, teaching, and observance of traditional culture. These include:

- proximity of Latin American countries to the United States
- steady immigration of newcomers
- socialization within *barrios* (Latino neighborhoods)
- pervasiveness of the Catholic Church
- value placed upon *orgullo* (pride) in one's heritage, including the encompassing concept of "La Raza"

There are forces of stress, however, stemming from practices and norms in United States society, which confront the Latino family and cannot be ignored. Szapocznik (1995) and Rodriques and Casaus (1983) have highlighted these stresses as:

1. The emphasis in American society on **English as the primary language** compromises communication and reassigns roles, using children as interpreters and fostering negative self-esteem in non-bilingual members.
2. **Age segregation** in schools and same generation social activities shifts the focus from multi-generational interaction between family members to peer group influences.
3. **Veneration of youth** replaces *respeto* (respect) shown toward elders and creates a source of conflict.
4. The advocacy of social and economic upward mobility based on **individual successes and self-reliance** erodes the cultural value of cooperation and interdependence.
5. The orientation toward **individual competition** supplants the view that both group and individual are important because each contributes to the nurture and well-being of the other.

These same stresses, nevertheless, not only challenge the traditional pattern of Latino families, they can also serve as the catalyst for renewal and refinement. The practice of *compadrazgo* in Mexican American culture exemplifies this point, particularly in its application to group therapy for abused Latinas.

Compadrazgo is the custom of choosing godparents who become accepted members of the extended family. These *compadres* and *comadres* share in the rights and obligations of the family and offer significant and practical assistance. According to Beatriz Gandara, who was born in Mexico City and now counsels abused Hispanic women in the San Diego area, this custom has been a way for her clients to express their feelings and hurts to someone who is trusted and respected without shame or disclosure outside the family. For the Latina, in other words, her comadre prevents her from being isolated and alone in her difficulties and is a *natural* source of support (B. Gandara, personal communication, May 6, 1990).

Diane Lopez, originally from East Los Angeles and now living in Boston, has adapted and broadened the system of comadres into group therapy for Puerto Rican and Central American women who are victims of domestic violence. Lopez recalls the importance of her own comadre in her upbringing. Lopez's best friend currently fills this role. This friend is more than even a sister. They share *confianza*, feelings of security and warmth, in communicating with one another. From this personal experience, shared by many Latinas, Lopez has constructed a rationale and format for her counseling group.

The group meets as part of the program at a neighborhood clinic. Most of the Latinas in the group are in their twenties and thirties. The sessions are conducted in Spanish, which communicates to the women approval of their cultural heritage. The women learn to cope with being separated from their families and loved ones in Nicaragua, El Salvador, Guatemala, and elsewhere. They also share the emotional crises from being abused. What helps to sustain them is the circle of their *comadres*. Each woman is there because her family life was filled with pain. This family of Latinas gives them reason to hope and the experience of being cared for and understood.

FALSE CULTURE

Interaction with and service delivery to minority crime victims may include unfounded assumptions and incorrect generalities about cultural-based "interpersonal etiquette and participant burden" (Vega, 1992, p. 385). As these perpetuate, a "false culture" develops that influences both cross-cultural interaction and minorities' perceptions of themselves. The perceived male supremacy in Asian cultures and the popularized concept of *machismo* attached to Mexican culture are two illustrations of false culture and how they jeopardize attempts at understanding and assisting victims of partner abuse.

Asian American Patriarchies

Asian cultures have been characterized as having high "power distance," or a hierarchy of power distribution. Age, for example, is highly respected: information tends to flow from student to teacher, and from authority to subordinate (Cushner, 1996, p. 224). Nilda Rimonte, the executive director of the Center for the Pacific Asian Family in Los Angeles, argues that this favors a patriarchal system of male supremacy and rigidity toward women. The inference is that this sanctions violence against women. Rimonte, for example, outlines how this "power imbalance" creates the potential for abusive behavior. She states,

> A healthy family by Western standards has an open structure. Members are allowed to be individuals and to communicate their feelings freely. This ideal contrasts starkly with the controlled, conforming style of Pacific Asians, in which a high value is placed on one's strict accountability to the family. The Pacific Asian family has a closed structure. Communication is restricted and decision making is vertical. Power in the marriage is hierarchical.... Studies have shown that the more closed the system is, the more disordered and dysfunctional the family becomes. They also show that men's limited ability to express their feelings results in a continual state of explosiveness and possible violence. (1989, pp. 329–330)

Rimonte is primarily concerned that battered Asian women find the strength and support to speak out concerning their abuse. She qualifies her statements, however, by explaining that the Pacific Asian family is not by nature dysfunctional, only that it is "merely more responsive to the needs of men than to those of women." She adds that although a certain amount of violence directed at "women and children and other social inferiors" is accepted as rooted in Pacific Asian culture, this does not mean that the culture is itself the problem. It is of course the batterer who must be held responsible (pp. 330, 335).

This analysis by Rimonte is noteworthy but somewhat circuitous. It appropriately seeks to present the family context and cultural values that influence issues of domestic violence. The negative comparison of the Pacific Asian family to Western standards, however, is not only suspect, it is also misleading. Do we assume that there are more incidences of domestic violence in Pacific Asian families than Western ones because of the difference between a closed structure and an open one? Can one argue that the abuser accept *personal* responsibility for his behavior while remarking that it would "be ironic if the cultural concept of a strong family should become the very force that would cause the family to disintegrate?" (p. 337).

Asian cultures do appear to have well-defined gender roles. This does not necessarily mean that certain roles are subordinate to others or that females are subordinate to males. "Masculinity" and "femininity" in cultures, for example, does not necessarily refer to gender dominance but to the degree that certain values take hold (Cushner, 1996, p. 225). Masculine cultures are those that value assertiveness, task achievement, and the acquisition of goods. In more feminine cultures, expressiveness, empathy, and creativity are valued. Gudykunst and Gumbs (1989) add that cultures with a high value placed on masculinity perceive sex roles differently, whereas cultures with a low value placed on masculinity (and a high value placed on femininity) tend to have fluid sex roles. Hofstede (1980) also found that the more a nation or culture embraces masculine values, the greater the gap between the values of males and females and the more segregation there is in career choices.

The judgments and values a culture places on gender roles, in other words, makes it appear sexist or not. Equal value can also be given to the different roles of men and women. In Asian society, for example, children are considered the threads of the social fabric. Mothers are entrusted with their well-being and with inculcating proper respect for their elders. This responsibility is highly regarded. The mother's role itself is not subordinate. It is only when this role is diminished by either men or women, or when the right of a particular woman to exercise another role outside the home is disregarded or prevented, that sexism enters the equation. As David Levinson, in his study of the cross-cultural aspects of family violence, notes:

> The central premise of this study is that the concept of patriarchal society is too broad a notion for cross-cultural testing. Thus the strategy has been to define and conceptualize female status and power in very specific ways that are measurable with cross-cultural ethnographic data. When approached this way, it seems clear that there is no unidimensional relationship between female status and power and wife-beating. (1989, p. 84)

According to Levinson, the key indicators of wife-beating are related to inequality in decision making. If men unilaterally govern the family and have control over financial matters, and women are restricted in their freedom to divorce their husbands, the *possibility* of violence increases. In *all* cultures the absence of choice is a significant predictor of domestic violence.

Of course, persons, whether male or female, do not perfectly represent the ideal norms of their cultures, whether Asian American or another culture. There are Asian males who mistakenly assume that gender roles were established only for their advantage and not for the benefit of the entire family. In any family there should be the atmosphere of respect for tradition and the willingness to allow for changes based upon individual family preferences and circumstances.

Rimonte is correct when she suggests that Asians must learn to adapt to their new Western settings. There are pressures upon the Asian American family that test former customs and practices. Debbie Lee (1986), a women's advocate in San Francisco, concurs with Rimonte that cultural adjustment fosters an imbalance in traditional roles. Immigrant families, for example, may have both spouses employed out of economic necessity—a situation confusing domestic responsibilities. It may in fact be the collision of social and cultural values that has more to do with funneling frustrations and anger toward the incidence of domestic violence than any deficit of traditional mores.

When one emphasizes the Asian values of maintaining harmony and good relations in the home (and in the community) as well as the need to avoid direct confrontation and emotional outbursts, one begins to identify *nonviolent* aspects in gender relations. Asian cultures have been described as "collectivist" in that personal needs are secondary to members' interdependence with others (Cushner, 1996; Gudykunst & Gumbs, 1989). The self is defined by and attached to a network of others, particularly the family and extended family. In the Japanese language, for example, there are at least two words for the first person pronoun "I," depending upon one's status, gender, and whether it is used privately or publicly (Cushner, 1996, p. 221).

Asian cultures, like the dominant U.S. culture, in other words, are not inherently predisposed toward domestic violence, nor can they absolutely safeguard women from all abuse. Sexism pervades many cultures and is not simply or exclusively the bedfellow of so-called patriarchal systems. Indeed, no matter how urgent and compelling it is to bring an end to abusive relationships, it must be done so that no element of any culture can be portrayed as historically justifying insult or inviting injury to any one. All cultures are attempts to bring order, not disorder. All peoples are therefore accountable to this purpose.

Machismo

Ramon Salcido was raised in the town of Los Mochis, Mexico. His boyhood dream was to find a new life in *el Norte*. At age 18 he arrived in California, finding work first in the fields of the Central Valley and then in the vineyards of Sonoma County. It was there that he met Angela Richards, a shy and cloistered White girl. According to Berkeley journalist Shirley Streshinsky, Angela was "yearning to learn about life," and Ramon did not hesitate to teach her "things she did not know in the back seat of his Ford LTD" (Streshinsky, 1990, p. 11).

On November 28, 1984, Angela and Ramon, already expecting their first child, were married. They continued to live in Boyes Hot Springs with Ramon working as a forklift operator and Angela making use of her skills as a dressmaker. But life was not easy. The Salcidos lived in a cramped one-bedroom rented duplex and were burdened with financial worries. Ramon also drank heavily and began to be overly protective of Angela. Some time after their first year of marriage, Angela confessed to Ramon that he was not the father of their oldest child, Sofia. Ramon simmered in anger and humiliation. Over the next several years, however, the Salcidos had two more children, Carmina and Teresa.

Ramon's controlling behavior and alcoholic binges made Angela feel trapped in her marriage. She eventually began searching for a way out. At the encouragement of close friends, she enrolled in modeling classes to prepare for a career of her own. Friday, April 14, 1989, was the day of the photograph session for her portfolio, which was to be distributed to commercial agencies in San Francisco. She never reached the studio for her appointment. In the early morning hours of that day, the worst mass murder in Sonoma County's history occurred: Ramon Salcido initiated a "journey of destruction" (Bumerts, criminal trial opening statement, September 17, 1990).

According to Ramon's lengthy tape-recorded confession, he had arrived home after a night of bar-hopping, during which time he had consumed three bottles of champagne and ingested several grams of cocaine. He had been upset that he was recently served with court papers for child support from a previous marriage. He was further enraged to find that Angela was not at home. What Ramon apparently did not know was that she had left the house before dawn to walk the two miles to a bank teller machine to obtain cash for the day. But in Ramon's mind, she had secretly departed to meet a lover. With his daughters in tow, he set out to search for Angela. He drove around town for an hour without any success. The killings then began.

At an isolated quarry, Ramon slit each daughter's throat with a knife and hurled them down a steep embankment. Sofia, 4 years old, and Teresa, just one-year-old, died almost immediately. Carmina, 22 months of age, miraculously survived by bending her head forward to stop the profuse bleeding from her neck. She was found 36 hours later, sitting between her two slain sisters and eating small pebbles to stave off hunger. Leaving his daughters to perish, Ramon drove to Angela's parents' home. There he stabbed to death Angela's mother and her two young sisters. After ransacking the house, he found Mr. Richard's .22 caliber pistol— his new murder weapon. Returning to Boyes Hot Springs, he tormented Angela with the news that he has killed everyone in her family. He then shot Angela in the head, bludgeoned her with the gun when she did not quickly die, and then shot her once more.

Ramon's next intended victims were two winery supervisors whom he believed tried to have him fired. He intercepted one on the roadway and fired two bullets into his head, leaving him slumped in his car. He attempted to kill the other supervisor and his wife at their home but was only able to wound the supervisor in the shoulder. He then fled to Mexico. Four days later he was arrested and subsequently extradited to California.

The Salcido trial, which began on September 17, 1990, was held in the Superior Court of San Mateo County. Salcido's attorney, Marteen Miller, was granted a request for change of venue. Salcido had been charged with seven counts of murder and three counts of attempted murder. Prosecutor Peter Bumerts assisted by Ken Gnoss, presented the murders as deliberate and premeditated acts with malice of forethought. Salcido's attorney outlined an insanity defense based upon Salcido's supposed "paranoid personality of severe magnitude," "psychotic depression" and substance abuse (Samuelson, 1990, p. D-14). The defense argued that these factors contributed to a "rage reaction," precipitating the killings (K. Gnoss, personal communication, January 8, 1998). Salcido, however, was dutifully convicted and subsequently remanded to San Quentin to await his death sentence.

Northern Californians were confounded and horrified that Salcido could commit such predatory and wanton acts, especially against his own children. Particularly relevant for our understanding of how a "false culture" develops, nevertheless, is how the media and others have described Salcido. Was this horror "the collision of innocence and machismo, of inchoate yearnings and the American dream turned nightmare," as newpaper accounts portrayed it (Streshinsky, 1990, p. 9)? This reporter portrays Angela, through the accounts of her relatives and friends, as a woman held captive by "a hot-blooded Latin," who was not only prone to jealousy and violence but also gloried in *machismo*. She implies that Salcido's gruesome and repulsive crimes were committed because of raging passion toward an alleged unfaithful wife and her lover and a sense of powerlessness for not being able to forge a better life.

The employment of machismo to explain and contextualize such heinous crimes, however, is a distortion of a primary characteristic of traditional Latino male and female roles. There is no doubt that there are Latino men, perhaps some like Ramon Salcido, who use their machismo to argue for absolute male dominance and total female submissiveness. Not a few Latino spouse abusers have claimed that it is their "cultural birthright" to beat their wives and deny them the opportunity to seek outside educational and job opportunities. Fortunately, their argument is not legally acceptable, nor is it true to the proper meaning of machismo.

Insensitive representations by the country's media and negative stereotypes of the Latino culture in general have contributed to a limited and negative understanding of machismo. Accordingly, the term "macho" often is assigned to the male who is overly-aggressive, controlling, temperamental, and boastful. Alice Kahn, writing for the *San Francisco Chronicle*, in fact, warns the public that there is a resurgent masculine empire called "Nuevo Macho."

> Look out, old macho's back…. Crimes against women, from the most violent to the most bizarre, have been on the rise…. But I don't think the full effect of Nuevo Macho hit me until our old friend Jimmy came to town…. Jimmy turned to my husband and asked, "How about you? Do you ever want to slit Alice's throat?" (1990, p. 2)

Rodriquez and Casaus, however, describe a *macho* as "a man who meets his family responsibilities by providing food, shelter and protection for his wife, children and, in some cases, other relatives living with the family." The wife and mother in the Latino family, correspondingly, has primary influence in socializing the children and managing the family affairs of the home as a whole. The well-being of the family is thus based upon mutual *respeto* (respect) and interdependence. The man must show respect for his family, and he thrives on the respect given to him. He must be careful not to disrupt the family life by selfish and outrageous acts. The wife, in turn, is not rendered submissive but actively supports her husband in his role of provider and protector. In this manner, the dignity and strength of the family is maintained in the face of sometimes harsh social and economic realities (1983, p. 42; see also Sue 1981).

Latino culture itself, in other words, is *not* pathological, as has been assumed by those who have regarded machismo as promoting wife-battering. Misinterpreting or exaggerating elements of a culture can produce a "false culture," which Theresa Martinez, a University of Utah sociology professor, says, may serve "to justify excess and abuse and to eventually destroy the best in the culture itself" (T. Martinez, personal communication, January 8, 1998). Rogelio Tabarez, a Mexican family therapist in Los Angeles, likewise derides the tendency to attribute deviant social patterns such as domestic violence to ethnic characteristics like machismo. He sees the "culture of poverty," that is, low socioeconomic status, that is the plight of many Latino people in the United States, as a more pronounced factor. Violence in the family is therefore only culturally-related in that, as a symptom of stresses and maladaptations, it becomes *attached to* other elements of the culture (R. Tabarez, personal communication, April 9, 1990). Stresses, however, strike those of every class and race. Inability to cope and domestic violence are not restricted to the poor or certain groups. As Blackman has emphasized, "Violence in the family is no basis for cultural distinction" (1996, p. 15).

Indeed, it may very well be that the balance in relationships sought and nurtured within Latino families, that is emphasized in machismo and respeto, provides the safeguard *against* domestic strife. If so, then disparaging remarks and mistaken conclusions about Latino culture should be replaced with the effort to preserve some of its reasons and forms for fostering the hopes and dreams of family life. Ramon Salcido is an aberration of Latino culture, as is *any* criminal of *any* culture. His savage act—lacking in dignity of personal conduct, respect for others, and love for his family—was a failure to fulfill machismo, not an expression of it.

3
IMPACT OF CRIME ON MINORITIES

Bamboo
Japanese Family Crest

Family crests in Japan date back to the eleventh century. They were first used on formal attire for appearances before the Imperial government and the royal family. The emblems were refined and elegant, depicting floral patterns, such as wisteria blossoms, and birds, such as the crane.

In later periods, crests were adopted by warrior groups as battle insignias and by commoners to adorn their *kimonos* (traditional garments). Today, there are several hundred basic designs and several thousand variations of family crests, incorporating geometric shapes, plants, animals, implements, and natural phenomena. In the Meiji Period (1868–1912), however, any form of the chrysanthemum on a crest was prohibited because it symbolized the Imperial family.

There are a number of crests representing bamboo shoots, leaves, or stalks. For many Asians, the strength and flexibility of bamboo have signified resilience and adaptability to hardships. Folk wisdom has also imparted that bamboo groves are safe shelters during destructive storms and fierce winds. In like manner, a person finds the stamina to withstand life's storms through the support of family members.

Chapter Overview

- Minority Crime Statistics
- Vulnerability to Crime
- Cultural Misconceptions
- Cultural Response Patterns

All violent crime victims share their common suffering. Skin color and cultural values do not provide impenetrable armor against physical injury, psychological harm, or emotional wounds. Minorities, nevertheless, experience the trauma of victimization in unique ways. This does not mean that any particular group suffers more acutely or is more devastated than another. It does mean that there are cultural, socioeconomic, and situational factors to consider in understanding the impact of crime on minority victims. This chapter, in order to describe the nature of this impact, presents the reality of crime patterns in minority communities and shows their vulnerability to certain crimes, others' misconceptions of them as minority victims, and their (dis)similarities from the dominant culture in response to traumatic incidents.

MINORITY CRIME STATISTICS

The National Crime Survey (NCS) for 1994 reported an estimated 42.4 million incidents of crime victimization in the United States, excluding homicides and victims under the age of 12. Of this total, 10.9 million, or 26%, were classified as violent crimes such as rape/sexual assault, robbery, and simple or aggravated assault. Among the four regions of the country, the West had the highest personal crime rate, with 73.5 crimes per 1,000 persons, a figure 72% higher than the Northeast, which had the lowest rate at 42.7 (U.S. Bureau of Justice Statistics, 1997).

NCS data over many years have consistently shown that certain population groups—especially males, the poor, younger persons, single persons, and inner city residents—suffer higher victimization rates than others. Blacks are more likely than whites to fall in one or more of these groups. Fifty-six per cent of blacks, compared to 26% of whites, live in central cities (Bennett, 1995). The percentage of those with low family annual incomes (below $15,000) is 37.2% for blacks but only 13.9% for whites (U.S. Bureau of the Census, 1995).

Accordingly, for 1994, blacks had higher rates of violent crime victimization than whites (61.8 per 1,000 persons compared to 49.4) and received more serious injuries (U.S. Bureau of Justice Statistics, 1997). The NCS report for 1994 estimated that black females were prey to sexual assault almost 30% more often than the rate for white females (4.5 per 1,000 persons compared to 3.5). For the elderly, blacks 65 and older were more than four times more often the victim of crimes than their white counterparts (17.0 per 1,000 persons compared to 4.0) (U.S. Bureau of Justice Statistics, 1997).

The Federal Bureau of Investigation's Uniform Crime Reports, a compilation of information submitted from police departments and state agencies, furthermore, indicated that 21,587 murders were committed in 1995. The total number of black and white homicide victims was about the same. These numbers reveal that the homicide rate for blacks was thus nearly six times the rate for whites proportionate to population (Federal Bureau of Investigations, 1997b). The highest rates were for black males, followed by black females, white males, and white females, as shown below.

Black		White	
Male	7,913	Male	6,939
Female	1,781	Female	2,674
Total	9,694	**Total**	9,613

Even though black males ages 12 to 24 represent just 1.3% of the population, they experienced 17.2% of single-victim homicides in 1992. These young black males were almost 14 times as likely to be homicide victims as were members of the general population. Even the homicide rate for older black males was eight times that for the general population (Federal Bureau of Investigations, 1992).

Data for 1994 reveal that Hispanics experienced higher rates of violent crime victimization than whites (U.S. Bureau of Justice Statistics, 1997). This is partially explained by the Hispanic population having demographic characteristics associated with higher crime rates, similar to African Americans. These include being younger, poorer, and more concentrated in cities. Forty-five percent of the Hispanics, for example, are between the ages of 10 and 34, compared to 35% of whites. The median age for Mexican Americans is 24.6 years, for Puerto Rican Americans 26.9 years, and for Central and South Americans 28.6 years. One anomaly in this pattern of median ages is that of Cuban Americans at 43.6 years, because they are more similar to Anglos (Montgomery, 1994). In terms of annual family income of less than $15,000, the percentage of Hispanics in this category was 28.8% or 1.8 times higher than the percentage for whites at 16.3% (U.S. Bureau of the Census, 1995).

For 1994, Hispanics suffered violent crimes, including sexual and aggravated assaults, at a greater rate than non-Hispanics. This represented an average victimization rate of 59.8 per 1,000 persons compared to the 49.8 recorded for non-Hispanics. Sexual assaults committed against Hispanic women were 39% higher than the rate for those committed against non-Hispanic women (5.0 per 1,000 persons compared to 3.6). Aggravated assaults were, moreover, committed against Hispanics at a rate 46% higher than for non-Hispanics (U.S. Bureau of Justice Statistics, 1997).

The above statistics should be interpreted and applied with care. Some of the data are estimates based upon projections from known samples. Specific information on Asians, Pacific Islanders and Native Americans is also not readily available. These rates rely on prevailing census figures, which have varying degrees of accuracy for certain categories and populations. There is finally no intention to minimize the personal suffering that underlies all of these numerical summaries. The picture that does emerge, nonetheless, is that minorities, particularly blacks and Hispanics, are victimized by violent crime relatively more often than other groups.

We should avoid using these statistics to justify designating entire black or Hispanic communities as crime-ridden or overrun by violence, for this labeling casts unfair suspicion on all residents within these communities. Efforts by law enforcement to contain and reduce the problem of crime through such measures as the war on drugs, suppression of gang activity, and alliances with neighborhood groups through community policing are all essential and commendable. But as Alvin Poussaint of the Harvard University Medical School has written about black-on-black homicide:

> The Black community in particular is in dire need of homicide prevention centers with programs of prevention, research, and treatment.... If they are to be successful, these programs must help to bring about Black community justice in the broad sense, as well as crime control. (1983, p. 168)

Justice in "the broad sense," according to Poussaint, is the commitment to remedy the socioeconomic conditions associated with high crime rates, the willingness to address the psychosocial needs of self-respect and interracial cooperation, and the resources to correct the dismal level of victim services in minority communities.

VULNERABILITY TO CRIME

Murder on Twin Peaks

On January 25, 1990, there was a murder on Twin Peaks, the fog-shrouded hill overlooking the San Francisco Peninsula. The slain woman, only 23 years of age, was Felicia Stanberry, the mother of an adorable three-year-old girl named Lovely Precious. Felicia was black, unemployed, and an abuser of crack cocaine. Her death resulted from her courage and willingness to testify against three dope dealers who had shot and killed her friend in a dispute over drugs. Her bravery was rewarded with death.

Felicia was the third child and only daughter of Beverly and Charles Stanberry. She was described by her grandmother as "spoiled rotten" and a "happy little child." Girlhood friends remember her as having a "bubbly smile" and an outgoing personality (Seligman, 1990, p. A-1). She loved sports and cooking at family gatherings. When Felicia was in high school, her parents had separated. In 1985, Felicia entered the Job Corps, a federally funded vocational training program, and was stationed in San Diego. When she returned to San Francisco after the program terminated, she had difficulty finding employment.

Lovely Precious was born to Felicia and her boyfriend in 1987, but she was sent to live with her grandmother while Felicia tried to overcome her drug problems. In the summer of 1988, Felicia was arrested for selling rock cocaine to an undercover police officer. Her sentence included three years probation, a small fine, and substance abuse treatment. After violating probation she spent a brief time in jail. Upon her release, Felicia lived in one of the city housing projects. On January 6, 1990, she was there in a room with two men when there was a knock on the door. Mark Balinton and Kevin "Sinister" Hall, both 21, entered with guns drawn. After a heated exchange, Balinton shot Felicia's friend, 29-year-old Anthony Hunter, eight times. His lifeless body was then unceremoniously dumped into the hallway.

Felicia agreed to give a statement to the police at the Hall of Justice. Assistant District Attorney Thomas Norman hesitated to file charges because Felicia was an admitted drug user whose testimony would not be credible to the court. The *San Francisco Examiner* quoted Norman as saying:

> How can I put this one little lady with that background up there [on the witness stand]? They [the defendants] are just going to say they never saw her and they didn't do it. It doesn't matter whether I believed her or not. Could a jury of 12 have believed her beyond a reasonable doubt? (Seligman, 1990, p. A-1)

To Norman's credit he did listen to Felicia's taped interview and found it convincing. On January 22, police arrested the two suspects and another man, Joe Batiste, who was in the room at the time of the shooting. Barely 50 hours later, two shots punctuated the chill of the night air on Twin Peaks. At 8:30 P.M. Felicia's body was found with gunshot wounds in her neck and the back of her head. Although Balinton, Hall, and Batiste were still in custody at the time, there was no doubt why Felicia had been murdered. Her friends and relatives are resentful that she was not given any police protection. They insist that if she were white and lived in a classier neighborhood, Felicia would still be alive. The police responded that they had offered a hotel room to Felicia the night she had given her statement but that she had declined because she wanted to return to the housing project.

Balinton, Hall, and Batiste were released and charges against them were dropped because Felicia was the sole prosecution witness. There have been no arrests to date in Felicia's murder. To some, Felicia's errant life exposed her to dangers that could have been avoided if she had chosen a different course. But her close relatives have all said that Felicia loved her daughter and wanted to straighten out her life in order to be a good mother. She sought help, but jobs were scarce and the drug programs had no vacancies. Even her probation officer noted her sincerity and good intentions. It is ludicrous to believe that she would risk losing her life unless, that is, she was determined to live with self-integrity.

A victim's or witness's vulnerability to violent reprisals is a frightening prospect for minorities trapped in crime-infested neighborhoods. Criminals must obviously be accountable for their misdeeds. Felicia's uncle, nonetheless, feels that there are others who must shoulder the responsibility for the real-life drama of his niece's murder: "Where do you cast the blame? I think you blame the system…It's going to be harder to get people to step forward the next time" (Seligman, 1990, p. A-1). Indeed, there has been no one who has offered information regarding either murder, despite the $10,000 reward now being offered. The only hope is that there are other Felicia Stanberrys willing to stand up for themselves and their neighborhoods.

Asian Children

Teddy Unterriner was well-liked and trusted by many in the Southeast Asian community. He was a young, friendly American who worked tirelessly to assist Laotian and Cambodian refugee families in Berkeley and Oakland adjust to their new lives. He cared especially for pre-teenaged boys, who were eager to be with someone who would help smooth out the rough edges of growing up and being pinned between two cultures. Unterriner was an ideal big brother to the boys, providing them with companionship and counsel. His home was a place for them to find reprieve from feelings of insecurity and loneliness.

Unterriner's affection, however, was a sophisticated lure to attract victims for his voracious appetite for pedophilia. In the guise of unselfish regard for the welfare of Southeast Asian refugees, he deftly preyed upon the vulnerability of their children. His home was not a haven or clubhouse but a cloister of secrets and perversions.

Unterriner eventually aroused suspicions but managed to flee prior to being arrested because he was warned by one of the boys he had been molesting. Unterriner's trail led to Vancouver, Canada. While in a jail cell awaiting prosecution for molestations that he had committed there, a popular television program called *America's Most Wanted* aired his fugitive status. Even though Unterriner had changed his name, a fellow inmate recognized his face and reported the information to the jail guards. The warrant for Unterriner's arrest on 12 counts of sexual molestation in Oakland was filed by the Vancouver police. Unterriner was thereafter extradited to California.

Predators of Asian children like Teddy Unterriner are not uncommon. According to Glenn Pamfiloff, an inspector for the Juvenile Division of the San Francisco Police Department, there has been a rapid rise in child sexual assault cases involving children from Asia. The pattern is becoming predictable:

> Many [pedophiles] become trusted and honored family helpers. The families don't know America, they feel uncomfortable in this society, and what do they get? They get this wonderful guy, sent to them through a refugee organization they trust, who will teach their children the American way of life, who treats the family with utmost respect, buys the kids gifts that the family could never afford and completely wins their hearts. (Kortum-Stermer, 1990, p. 3)

Another scheme like the one described above ended with the arrest of one man sent by a refugee organization to teach English to one family's three young boys. For 18 months this man sexually molested the two older boys, ages seven and nine. A social worker became concerned about the amount of attention the man was giving to the children and asked the parents not to permit the man to be alone with the boys. The parents, however, continued to allow their children to go on outings with the man. They felt it would be difficult to hurt or insult him because they had known him for so long and he had been good for their sons.

After investigator Pamfiloff asked the seven-year-old boy if he wanted his five-year-old brother to have the same "relationship" with the man that he had, the boy began to cry and admitted what had been happening. By then, the man had already started to molest the youngest boy. As each brother had become "too old," he would switch to the next youngest in line. The boys were, of course, too immature to fully understand that they were victims. Their teacher had never beaten them, after all. He had instead lavished them with cookies and video games.

Pamfiloff can recite a litany of gifts and favors that child molesters have used to ingratiate themselves to Asian children and their families. Molesters have become afficionados of Nintendo, computers, pets, aquariums, movies, plus anything and everything that would gain the attention and interest of these children. One molester bought $150 to $200 skateboards to give to the 12- and 13-year-olds he met at a neighborhood park. Another would invite poor Asian children to his apartment to marvel at his array of electronic entertainment gadgetry. Yet another would sit in his parked van in an area where children mingled and persuade some of them to sit inside.

Pedophiles seem to be attracted to Asian boys for several reasons. These boys tend to appear younger than their age and are smaller in stature so that grooming and molesting them can take place over a longer period of time. Because these boys also lack bodily hair and possess smooth skins, they fulfill the fantasies of many of the molesters. Pedophiles are well aware that the refugee families are socially isolated, poor, distrustful of the police, and reluctant to share private and shameful matters with others. Infiltrating the refugee community and concealing their activities are therefore relatively easy.

A national and international network of pedophiles validates this conduct—(repugnantly) called "consensual intergenerational relationships." The North

American Man–Boy Love Association (NAMBLA), founded in the late 1970s, has 125 members in California and 600 worldwide. Members have been identified in Sacramento, San Francisco, Boston, the U.S. Military Academy at West Point, and elsewhere. The NAMBLA creed is that sex between a boy, even an infant, and a man is "natural" and that it is "misunderstood" by an oppressive and conservative society. There is also a loosely organized international ring, referred to as Club Ped, that schedules liaisons between pedophiles and Third World boys. Trips are arranged to Asian orphanages run by pedophiles as well as junkets complete with boy "tour guides."

Asian boys, however, are not the only targets of pedophiles. Korean girls adopted by American couples have been sexually abused. In one Hawaii case, a business owner not only molested his own adopted daughter but became an active member and leader of a support group for families with adopted Korean children. Trusted by the parents of this group, he selected other Korean girls that he could molest. His behavior remained undetected for many years because no one believed that a man so charitable to adopt an orphan from a foreign country could be so insidious.

In the city of Oakland, California, several Asian elementary school girls were molested by their teacher. The students were reluctant to come forward because their parents had always reminded them not to question the authority of a teacher or an elder. They were afraid that they would be blamed for what happened and for dishonoring the family. The teacher took full advantage of the girls' submissiveness and the deference that their parents gave to him. Fortunately, the girls' discomfort and difficulty with what occurred became apparent in their attitude toward school. The parents were unable to understand why their daughters had changed. Because of intervention by Asian Community Mental Health Services, the girls were able to admit to the molestation and receive supportive counseling. The teacher was eventually prosecuted and convicted.

Children of Migrant Farmworkers

Child abuse within the families of migrant farm workers is a blight infesting our nation's agricultural fields. It is believed that migrant children are between two and six times more likely to be mistreated than other children. This means that at least 10,000 are abused or neglected each year. Recidivism rates, moreover, are believed to range from 20–50%, indicating that many of these children are victims of more than one episode of abuse and that some parents are multiple offenders (ESCAPE, 1987, p. 2). As one farm worker through the Nuestros Hijos Project confessed: "I would always come home tired and drunk. I would argue with my wife and I began to beat her. Later, I began beating my 2-year-old daughter" (Sanchez, 1990, p. B1).

The state with the largest migratory and seasonal farm worker population is California, followed by Texas and Florida. Conservative estimates place the number of migrant children under age 15 living at least part of the year in California at over 400,000. The majority of migrants in the state are Mexican Americans, both established permanent residents and recent immigrants. Many speak Spanish as their primary language and derive strength from their cultural heritage and traditional religious beliefs. Most are hard-working individuals with strong family ties.

In general, parents who abuse their children suffer from poor parenting skills, alcohol dependency, negative self-esteem, and a history of being abused themselves. A report developed by Cornell University for the California State Department of Education, however, also concluded:

> The pronounced rate of maltreatment in the migrant population is to a large extent attributable to its extreme level of poverty and deprivation. Both result in stress, which may also arise from other characteristics of the migrant lifestyle, such as harsh living and working conditions, frequent travel, intermittent or uncertain employment, and economic insecurity. Social and physical isolation also increase the risk to migrant children. (As cited in ESCAPE, 1987, p. 14)

It is not surprising therefore that the predominant form of abuse among migrant children is physical neglect. The rigors of migrant work force both parents into the fields for long hours, leaving their small children unattended or with siblings who are themselves under 12 years of age. There is a dire shortage of day care facilities for migrant worker families and the alternative of bringing the children to the fields is dangerous. Each year, children are killed and injured by farm machinery or drown in irrigation ditches. There is also the substantial risk of exposure to toxic pesticides and herbicides.

Currently, there is a scarcity of social services nearby where migrant farmers either work or live, as well as a lack of Spanish-speaking providers. Clinic and agency hours also limit accessibility to services because they are not adjusted for the early morning to evening hours of field work. Effective service delivery is furthermore hampered by those in local communities and programs who are either unsympathetic to the plight of these families or feel that they are not entitled to the limited resources available. Special programs such as Nuestros Hijos are a partial solution. This program provides child abuse prevention services for Hispanics in the 18 California counties where most of the 800,000 farm workers labor.

Basic changes in work and living conditions, however, would help to alleviate some of the stresses bearing on migrant families. Farmworkers are a social underclass plagued by meager opportunities and public neglect (Rural Realignment Project, 1989, p. 18). Stopping the abuse of migrant children rests literally in the hands of their parents. Those hands, nonetheless, are calloused by a system of stoop labor that collects its bounty but offers little appreciation or understanding in return. Lessening the vulnerability of migrant children to abuse therefore necessitates not only direct assistance to individual families but also raising the overall status afforded to them.

Home Invasions

Five Southeast Asian youths, wearing hoods and gloves and armed with handguns, forced their way into a Vietnamese home near Sacramento, California. Over a period of three hours, they tortured and beat the couple who lived there in an attempt to locate hidden cash and jewelry. At one point, they poured boiling water over the woman's back and legs. After their brutality was completed, the youths calmly and arrogantly helped themselves to food and drink taken from the couple's refrigerator.

A wave of such home invasions has gripped Southeast Asian communities in California. Vietnamese youth gangs, for example, are well aware of the practice among their own people to stash money and valuables at home rather than rely on banks. Preying on their own people also gives these gangs a leverage of control because their victims are both fearful of reprisals and suspicious of the police. As Sacramento sheriff's detective Ed Ching states: "They think getting robbed is one thing. But getting killed, or one of their family killed, just to put someone in jail is something else" (as cited in Sylva, 1990, p. F-8).

Thuy Pham, a civilian community relations officer for the Sacramento Police Department, admits that the Southeast Asian community is an easy target for certain criminal activities. The criminal justice system in America is different from those in Southeast Asia. Pham explains, for example, that the practice of defendants being released on bail or probation is unknown in countries like Vietnam. Vietnamese, therefore, believe that bribery of the police must have occurred when they see criminals that were arrested here no longer being held in custody. Pham says his job is "very difficult" and although people listen to him politely and with respect, they are still not fully convinced that they will be protected if they come forward to testify.

From December, 1989, until April, 1990, there were 24 robberies and assaults in Southeast Asian homes in the Sacramento area, 30 in Stockton, and 36 in San Jose (Sylva, 1990). The actual numbers are almost certainly higher. Some of these invasions were linked to attempts to extort money from businesses. Marc Lee is a Hmong refugee who arrived in the United States in 1976. He now owns a market that stocks an assortment of Southeast Asian foods and merchandise. In the early part of 1990, Lee was victimized on several occasions by a Southeast Asian gang. The first incident occurred when four youths entered his home and held a gun to his wife's head, demanding money. The following month when Lee was returning home from his store, a gang member accosted him at his front door with a gun. Two months later, Lee was threatened over the telephone.

Lee, however, is atypical in that he is English-speaking, a U.S. citizen, knows how the American criminal justice system works, and is willing to cooperate with law enforcement. Still, Lee carries a gun on his person at all times to protect his store and his family, although, his adversaries may not be dissuaded by such bold behavior. Steve Harrold, a Sacramento deputy district attorney, remembers one youthful extortionist who looked him coldly in the eye and sneered: "If you think your jails are bad, you should see the refugee camps in Cambodia" (Sylva, 1990).

Many of the gang members are not only hardened survivors of the ravages of wars in Southeast Asia, they are also becoming more highly organized. These gangs, for example, are fluid in their areas of operation. When police in San Jose began winning community cooperation so that gang-related crime was curtailed there, gang members relocated their criminal activities to the venues of Sacramento and Stockton.

The vulnerability of the Southeast Asian community to gang violence and home invasions is being countered with outreach and educational programs given by police officers, community service workers, deputy sheriffs, and prosecutors. These officials amply acknowledge that the criminal justice system must introduce itself as a reliable ally from the outside. Gaining trust, however, ultimately rests upon the proven ability and long-term resolve of the criminal justice system to work with the Southeast Asian community despite the obstacles and challenges. Success at curtailing the menace of home invasions can establish the foundation for enduring and positive relations.

La Migra

The plight of undocumented residents, or illegal aliens, involves complex issues of personal prejudice and international politics. Sentiments among U.S. citizens regarding the clandestine migration of those, mostly from Mexico and Central America, who seek a better life here therefore range from compassion for the safety and dignity of those fleeing poverty and war to border vigilante hunts and savage beatings. It is estimated, for example, that 75,000 people have been killed in El Salvador, either in that country's civil war or by human rights violations. Among those living in the Washington, D.C. area, 76.6% of the Salvadoran refugees have experienced traumatic events, more than 50% know of someone who was murdered, 20% have witnessed a murder, 40% have been present when their homes or neighborhoods were bombed, and 40% have been forced to seek safety from gunfire (AYUDA, 1997).

Fleeing brutal warfare and great poverty, almost 1,185 people lost their lives between 1993 and 1996 in their trek to cross illegally from Mexico to the United States. The majority perished along the Texas–Mexico border, usually drowning in the waters of the Rio Grande, but also dying from exposure and dehydration in the intense desert heat or deep in the mountains, or being hit by automobiles when they were running across highways (Bailey, Eschbach, Hagan, & Rodriguez, 1996). Five men and one woman died, for example, trying to enter the country through an underground drainage pipe when a sudden storm sent a torrent of water through the pipe. Three other men, two women, and a two-year-old child survived by clinging to a ladder.

Many migrants who perish cannot be identified. They are the "floaters" found along the banks of the Rio Grande. Most of the ones who drown (about 50 per year) are male (94%) and young (55% are ages 20–39 and 13% are ages 10–19) (Bailey, 1996). In the words of Jacqueline Hagan of the University of Houston, there is a "legacy of unmarked graves along the border." Their deaths leave families worrying about what happened to their loved ones. They are simply *los desaparecidos*—the disappeared. These "silent deaths" are invisible to most Americans; they generate little attention and thus little concern (Verhovek, 1997, p. A4).

Many Americans honor others' yearning to improve their lives or secure the safety of their families. As Bishop Raymondo Pena, of the Catholic Diocese of Brownsville, Texas, has said,

A nation's responsibility to secure its borders may also need to be balanced with other matters of importance. For people trying to enter our country, legally or illegally, we must always apply our Judeo-Christian values of compassion and neighborly responsibilities. (As cited in Schiller, 1997c, p. 8A)

There are others, conversely, who focus on the social and economic impact the undocumented have on the quality of life of American citizens. During the 1980 Freedom Flotilla, Castro sent a large number of expelled Cubans to American shores. A number of these were found to have been incarcerated as criminals or were mentally ill. Subsequent riots at two federal detention centers helped to fuel the growing popular belief that immigrants (mostly illegal) were violent or dangerous (Marshall, 1997). Roger Hedgecock, the former mayor of San Diego, used this argument to initiate a "Light Up the Border" campaign in 1990. Hedgecock, as a radio talk show host, spurred hundreds of citizens to drive to the border and shine their car headlights on the illegal aliens attempting to cross. His message was that the border is "out of control" and that "a tidal wave of drugs, crime and violence" is inundating the United States soil. The police chief of San Diego and the Mexican consul were among those that accused Hedgecock of fanning ethnic hatred (Hecht, 1990c, p. B-1).

Pressure on the Immigration and Naturalization Service (INS) to halt the alleged flood of illegal movement into Florida and across our nation's 2,000 mile border with Mexico has been strong during the 1990s. Portrayals of one million Mexicans pouring across the border each year to take jobs from U.S. citizens and drive up welfare costs have been commonplace among politicians and social commentators. The INS has initiated numerous campaigns to halt immigration, including "Stay Out, Stay Alive" announcements on television and in newspapers in Mexico, "Operation Gatekeeper" in California, "Hold the Line" in El Paso, Texas, and "Operation Rio Grande" in south Texas. These and other "hardening the border" strategies have used blockades of Border Patrol agents standing at close intervals backed by glaring floodlights, the "militarizing of the border" by deploying Marines on drug surveillance patrols, and laying miles of concertina wire and erecting fences and walls. The Violent Crime Control and Law Enforcement Act of 1994 provided unprecedented Federal resources for these efforts (McDonald, 1997, p. 6).

Migrant advocates and opponents of such INS measures have stated that these only increase the chances of accidental deaths and vulnerability to "border bandits" as migrants seek more isolated or less traveled crossings. Undocumented migration into the United States involves a human cost that, they say, is being largely ignored (Bailey et al., 1996, p. 1). Eluding the Border Patrol means that migrant women, for example, are easier prey for criminals who target them for sexual assault. The following is a common occurrence:

A 17-year-old girl from Mexico was assaulted in broad daylight Tuesday afternoon as she tried to sneak around the agents by climbing through weeds and wading across the river about a mile east of town.... Border agents discovered the girl bleeding and partly clad about 4 P.M. as she and three companions emerged from the river. (Schiller, 1997b, p. 4A)

The shooting death of 18-year-old Esequiel Hernandez, Jr. on May 20, 1997, in West Texas by a Marine patrol has also intensified the controversy. Hernandez, a high school student in the small farming community of Redford, was herding his goats when he encountered the four Marines. Hernandez was carrying a .22 caliber rifle to protect his goats from predators and for target practice. The Marine who shot Hernandez claimed that he fired his M-16 rifle in self-defense when Hernandez aimed at another Marine. A Presidio County grand jury did not return indictments against Corporal Clemente Banuelos, age 22, or the other Marines. A civil rights investigation, however, has been initiated by the U.S. Department of Justice.

The actual numbers of illegal immigrants, despite nativist rhetoric, may be far fewer than previously suggested. The first formal migration study by the Mexican and United States governments concluded that the number of undocumented Mexican workers who settled in the United States between 1990–1996 is only about 630,000 or 105,000 per year (Dillon, 1997). The Binational Study on Migration, commissioned in early 1995, brought together 10 Mexican and 10 U.S. demographers and scholars for two and a half years of research, field work, and analysis. The Mexican-born population in the United States, according to the study, numbers 7 to 7.3 million, of whom 2.3 to 2.4 million are "unauthorized residents" (Dillon, 1997). In the 1980s, some U.S. demographers had overestimated the number of undocumented from Mexico at 5 million to 6 million.

In 1995, U.S. law enforcement authorities detained 1.3 million aliens from all countries trying to enter the United States illegally at the Mexican border. This figure has been used to project widely divergent images and characterizations on the undocumented. Forty-one percent of the illegal immigrants, in fact, enter the United States legally at airports and other entry points and "overstay" their visas (McDonald, 1997). The top four countries illegal immigrants emigrate from include Mexico, El Salvador, and Guatemala, but also Canada. Most of the illegal immigrants reside in California, Texas, New York, Florida, and Illinois (INS, 1997b).

The so-called "explosion" of undocumented Mexicans, in other words, appears exaggerated. Mexican migrants are also no more likely to receive welfare than poor Americans. Many local governments may pay more in services to Mexican-born households than they receive in taxes, but this stems from migrants earning less and, accordingly, paying less in taxes. Money that migrants send home to Mexico, moreover, is $2.5 billion to $3.9 billion each year—equivalent to one-half of the direct foreign investment in Mexico (Dillon, 1997b, p. 6).

Whether attempting to enter the United States or already here, the undocumented are easy targets for victimization. The National Institute of Justice reports that "a wide range of predators victimize illegal immigrants":

Guides and organized gangsters have robbed, raped, and killed them; abandoned them in the desert; tossed them overboard at sea or out of speeding cars under hot pursuit; or forced them to work in sweatshops or prostitution rings to pay off the cost of the trip. Bandits prey upon them during their journeys. Xenophobes and hatemongers terrorize them. Some employers cheat them of their earnings. The fact that illegal immigration is a crime makes the immigrants particularly vulnerable because they are unlikely to seek the protection of the law. (McDonald, 1997, p. 4)

Immigrant smuggling, for example, from free-lancing "coyotes" to sophisticated operations constitutes a multibillion dollar business. One of the largest rings, transporting up to 500 immigrants per month, was based in Dallas, Texas. Some of the immigrants from Mexico were "moved like cargo packed in the holds of U-Hauls or 18-wheelers with nothing but a jug of water to drink and another jug to urinate in" (Holt, 1997a, p. 10A). Once in the United States, inhumane treatment may continue. For example, undocumented Mexican laborers, many from rural Indian villages where Spanish was not even spoken, were paid $1.00 an hour at a Ventura County, California, flower farm surrounded with barbed wire. They worked 16 hours a day, lived in filthy barracks, and were silenced by threats of deportation. Marco Antonio Abarca of California Rural Legal Assistance describes the conditions as slave labor:

They controlled these people through a regimen of psychological abuse and terror.... You shave their heads when they arrive, then you work them all the time. You don't let them sleep. They're too tired to eat. You scream at them constantly. You hit a person here and there. Then you scare them with stories of how they will be picked up by Immigration. (As cited in Associated Press, 1990a, p. A-10)

The owner of the flower farm eventually agreed to plead guilty to corporate racketeering and to pay $1.5 million in back wages to 300 former workers, the stiffest monetary judgment ever levied in a U.S. immigration case (Kelly, 1992, p. A1).

Direct physical assaults against individual Mexican males also occur, as in the following example. A 20-year-old enters a small San Diego market to purchase groceries. He is one of many unregistered workers who, early each morning, stand on the roadway in front of the market waiting to be hired for field work or yard clean-up. The store's proprietor and other business owners in the area have become increasingly hostile to the presence of the workers. They claim that white female employees and customers have been harassed and annoyed by leers and catcalls. This time, while the young worker is in the store, several white males decide to demonstrate their resentments. They begin by throwing a plastic grocery bag over his head, knotting it tightly around his neck so that he has difficulty breathing. They then punch and kick him repeatedly.

Gasping for air, the young man staggers through the doorway and retreats to the safety of the nearby hills. There he has erected a make-shift shelter for his home. What are his choices? He is reluctant to go to the police because he does not have an immigration green card. He is afraid to return to the roadway the next morning, but he must if he is to find work for that day. He has no money to seek medical attention. He is angry at his attackers but must hold back what he feels because *La Migra,* the INS, is to be avoided at all cost.

The vulnerability of Latinas may be even more pronounced. AYUDA, a community-based agency providing legal, advocacy, empowerment, and educational services for low-income Latino and foreign-born families in the Washington, D.C. area, describes how immigrant and refugee women "become more inextricably caught in the domestic violence web."

> They are new arrivals in a foreign country, traumatized by the life-threatening experiences that caused them to flee their homelands, separated from their families, living under the threat of deportation, and often dependent upon the financial resources and language abilities of an abusing spouse. Fearful of seeking legal or other assistance, they remain marginalized and alone, with no traditional cultural support. (AYUDA, 1997, p. 3)

Alfonso Lopez was born and raised in Tijuana, Mexico, and serves as a victim counselor in Los Angeles. Lopez believes that there is an epidemic of sexual assaults committed upon young, undocumented Mexican women. Their assailants, some of whom are Mexican males, know the illegal status of the women and are confident that their crimes will go unreported. For many of the undocumented women, there are no adequate support services and there is no legal recourse. Street justice by brothers or by male cousins and friends of the victim then becomes an alternative. This of course exposes *them* to law enforcement officials and possibly other authorities. How else does one right a wrong when there appears to be no safe access to the criminal justice system? How does one reconcile the need for justice with the fear of arrest and deportation?

Even agents of the INS are known to prey upon these women (see also Kahn, 1996). One Los Angeles agent, for example, was charged for separate incidents of kidnapping, rape, and assault of four women. When each woman refused to offer proof that she was a legal U.S. resident, the agent would handcuff his victim, take her to his apartment, and rape her at gunpoint (Associated Press, 1990b, p. A6). Former guards at the INS detention facility in Bayville, Texas, the country's largest immigration camp, alleged in a lawsuit filed in 1992 that female detainees were routinely sexually assaulted by supervisors. The former guards stated they were fired after reporting the incidents (Associated Press, 1997, p. 1B).

An emotional quandary arises, however, when both the offender and the victim are of the same family. In Chula Vista, California, I heard the despair of a father and mother whose daughter had been raped by her older brother. The girl, confused and ashamed, disclosed the incident to a school counselor who, in turn, reported the incident to Child Protective Services. The girl was temporarily removed from the home until legal proceedings against her brother were completed. The boy, who was 18 years of age, was found guilty after a change of plea and was sentenced to six years in prison.

As a result of his early release on parole, the INS ordered the boy's deportation to Mexico. Such action by the INS often occurs when an illegal alien who has been convicted of a felony is released from incarceration. All the members of the family had been previously granted temporary residency in the United States under the amnesty provision of the Immigration Reform and Control Act of 1986, but they were awaiting the results of their applications for permanent residency when the rape was reported. The parents were distraught. They believed that their son had been punished enough for what he had done. The daughter, seeing how upset her parents were, became anxious and guilt-ridden. Now that he would be deported, the family would be separated from one another.

From one viewpoint, it can be said that the brother deserved the consequences of his actions and, for the safety of the sister, it was desirable that he be deported. From this family's perspective, however, they had been hurt enough by what had occurred and deportation would only make matters worse, not better. A Latina counselor listened to the parents' concerns without making judgments and referred them to a legal clinic that handled immigration matters. Their daughter was fortunately already in a group for sexually abused girls in the same agency where her mother and father were attending a group for parents of sexually abused children. There was thus immediate support for the feelings experienced by this family and sensitivity for helping with the problems ahead.

Through community outreach meetings, and early in their contact with individual victims, Latino service providers strongly emphasize that the criminal justice system is separate from *La Migra*. The immigration status of victims is *not* customarily reported to immigration authorities, although offenders who are undocumented are frequently brought to the attention of such authorities for possible deportation hearings. Criminal laws, these service providers explain, protect not only U.S. citizens but also anyone who resides here or visits from another country. Some victims are suspicious that this is just a ploy by *La Migra* to ferret out the undocumented. There is a mistrust of authorities that must be carefully bridged. Persons like Alfonso Lopez, who has family ties to Mexico, create and reinforce these bridges. Twice a month Lopez crosses the border *into* Mexico to visit his father in Tijuana. When he returns, he realizes that he has the freedom to do so and the opportunity to help those who do not.

MISCONCEPTIONS

Black Girls Are Not Good Girls

Rape is an extreme violation for any woman. Its brutality extends beyond sexual violence to include an assault on a woman's perception of personal safety, self-image, and sense of control. Not only are a woman's physical and social defenses forcibly overcome, but also her relationships, lifestyle, and career may be severely altered (Ogawa, 1988).

The rape victim, however, is almost never seen as a true victim. The seriousness and authentication of her ordeal is judged by her "contribution" to what occurred, the intensity of her "resistance," or the credibility of her character. Without doubt, all women suffer needlessly under varying layers of sexism in such an evaluation. But for women of color, this screening may include an additional checklist of racial stereotypes and degrading myths.

Is the rape of a white female, for example, considered in the United States to be more horrifying or of greater concern than that of a black female? Who derives more sympathy from society at large? Schwendinger and Schwendinger found that "racism and the rape laws are unquestionably inseparable" (1983, p. 110). Giddings reports that well into the twentieth century, laws "stated that women who worked outside the home, or whose race had a history of sexual exploitation, were outside the realm of 'womanhood' and its prerogative" (1984, p. 49). The law implied that black women were not legally capable of being raped.

Certainly our laws do not (any longer) differentiate based on color. But in actual practice there is disturbing evidence that rape victims of African American heritage are not afforded equal access to either the criminal justice system or appropriate treatment providers. There is an incongruity, argues Belknap, "between high victimization rates and low validation rates for women of color" (1996, p. 133). Dr. Darnell Hawkins, a sociologist in the Black Studies Department at the University of Illinois–Chicago, states that black victims of crime in general are not treated seriously, particularly if the offender is also black. "Society," he continues, "has this outdated notion that good girls don't get raped and most Black girls are not good girls" (as cited in O'Brien, 1989, p. 9; see also Madriz, 1997).

Attitudes toward black women and the nature of their sexuality are rooted in the long period of legalized slavery in the United States and proliferated by current prejudices. Black women were the sexual property of white slave masters. Because they had no rights to resist or protest, there was no definition of rape to protect them and thus no legal recourse. As Alice Walker chronicles:

> Within days we were in sight of land, the young women among us pregnant by force and too young to know it, or to know that because we were delivered to our new owners already pregnant we earned a bonus for the master of the ship, many of whose sons and daughters—for he was a violator, with the rest of his crew—entered into American slavery with us, long before they actually issued from our bodies. The slavers did not care. Color made their own seed disappear to them; the color of gold was all they saw.... (1989, p. 70)

Many black women assume that they will be treated unfairly by police and prosecutors when they do report rape. Wyatt (1992) discovered, for example, that African American women were far more likely to not have disclosed incidents of sexual assault to anyone until years after the event. They were also less likely to have reported the incident to the police (McKean, 1994).

Any rape case in which there is a lack of strong corroborating evidence, such as physical injuries, and there is only the woman's word to substantiate the charges against the defendant, presents a challenge. When the woman, however, is black, there appears to be increased reluctance by legal authorities to proceed beyond investigation. The standard of "guilt beyond a reasonable doubt" requires that judges and juries are provided sound testimony and convincing argument. There are some in criminal prosecution that have decided that both testimony and argument are handicapped when a black woman is the victim. Lafree, in fact, studied 38 jury trials of sexual assault cases in Marion County (Indianapolis), Indiana, and found that "jurors were less likely to believe in a defendant's guilt when the victim was black" (1989, p. 290). Interviews with jurors suggested that stereotypes regarding the sexual behavior of black women influenced some jurors (McKean, 1994).

Rape victims need validation. They deserve to be believed and reassured that the rape was not their fault. But the black woman is often prone to sexual stereotyping about her promiscuity and "readiness" for sex at all times. She is viewed as a sex object and sex solicitor. Young (1986) expands the negative and damaging categories assigned to black woman into the following four:

- **the amazon**—inherently violent and capable of protecting herself
- **the sinister sapphire**—vindictive, provocative, and not credible
- **the mammy**—stupid, passive, and bothersome
- **the seductress**—sexually driven and not credible as a victim or professional

Evelyn White, in *The Black Women's Health Book*, recites this list of paradoxical caricatures:

> We are considered evil but self-sacrificing; stupid but conniving; domineering while at the same time obedient to men; and sexually inhibited yet promiscuous. Covered by what is considered our seductively rich but repulsive brown skin, black women are perceived as inviting but armored. With all the mixed messages about us, society finds it difficult to believe that we really need physical and emotional support just like everybody else. (1990, p. 94)

These views "neutralize" African American rape victims and make them "legitimate" targets of sexual assault, denial of injury, and blame. It follows, according to McKean, that "their assailants are thus pursued, prosecuted, and punished with less zeal" (1994, p. 118). According to Joan Crear, who directed the Rosa Parks Sexual Assault Center in South Los Angeles, these stereotypes have permitted the impact of rape on black women to be largely ignored. Crear's steadfast message to black women is therefore, "Sisters, we've been silent long enough!" (J. Crear, personal communication, 1990). Davis (1981) discusses how it has been difficult for African American women—whose husbands, lovers, and family members are victims as well—to be active in the anti-rape movement (led largely by Anglo women), given the harsher treatment of black men than white men charged with rape. The voices of black women need to be heard, not only by the criminal justice system and the dominant society, but also by those most closely related to these women. Byllye Avery, founder and director of the National Black Women's Health Project in Atlanta, presents an unsettling portrait:

The number one issue for most of our sisters is violence—battering, sexual abuse. Same thing for their daughters, whether they are twelve or four.... When you talk to young people about being pregnant, you find out...that most of them got pregnant by their mother's boyfriends or their brothers or their daddies. We've been sitting on that. We can't just tell our daughters, "Just say no."...we need to talk to our brothers. We need to tell them, the incest makes us crazy. It's something that stays on our minds all the time. We need the men to know that. And they need to know that when they hurt us, they hurt themselves. Because we are their mothers, their sisters, their wives; we are their allies on this planet.... We need men to stop giving consent, by their silence, to rape, to sexual abuse, to violence. You need to talk to your boyfriends, your husband, your sons, whatever males you have around you—talk to them about talking to other men. When they are sitting around womanizing, talking bad about women, make sure you have somebody stand up and be your ally and help stop this. (1990, p. 8)

The Rosa Parks Center, founded in 1984 as a program of the Martin Luther King Legacy Association, is named after a black woman who chose not to remain silent. Rosa Parks, in the words of Taylor Branch, "crossed the line that in polite society divided Negroes and niggers" by refusing to relinquish her bus seat to a white passenger in Montgomery, Alabama, in 1955. In doing so, she risked "not only stinging disgrace among her own people but the least civilized attentions of the whites" (1988, p. 129). Parks persisted, however, and sparked the civil rights movement, that gave new dignity to black women. A tribute to her courage to face these challenges is offered in the poem "Stand Up Rosa" by Adele Dutton Terrell (p. 67).

The courage of Rosa Parks is thus a moving symbol for the Center that serves the Los Angeles Police Department's southern bureau precincts, an area where there are the highest number of reported rapes in the city. The Rosa Parks Center is one of the few places that a rape victim from the area's black community finds acceptance, understanding, and respect. The staff members themselves contribute the fortitude and aspirations necessary to debunk stereotypes and fashion a new, more truthful image for black women.

More Than Shame

Mei had just arrived at the rapid transit station on her commute home from the city. It was evening and the rush hour crowd had abated an hour before. As she crossed the parking lot, she sensed that she was being watched. Hurriedly, she found her car, unlocked its door and was about to enter when she was grabbed from behind, punched, and thrown inside. Her assailant sexually assaulted her and then fled. Passersby heard Mei's cries for help and called the police.

A suspect was later apprehended. He was eventually charged, brought to trial, and convicted without any major setbacks or delays. Mei's emotional recovery also seemed uneventful. She was a second generation Chinese American woman, single and 46 years old. The victim advocate described her as a quiet, withdrawn woman who did not ask for counseling and chose not to tell her family members

Stand Up Rosa

Adele Dutton Terrell

I was with Rosa on the bus that day;
I whispered in her ear—sit down Rosa
and by sitting down, she stood up for me.
> I was with Rosa on the bus that day;
> though I was too young to understand
> my future cried out for someone
> to stand up for me.
I too was with Rosa on the bus that day;
although I was busy, bent-over my work
and did not know anyone cared enough
to stand up for me.
> I was also with Rosa that day;
> Somehow I found the courage to
> whisper—sit down Rosa; though I was old and battered
> and far too weary to stand up for myself.
So Rosa sat down on the bus that day;
And by sitting down,
stood up for me.
> You don't hear much about what Rosa did;
> most of the credit goes to those who preached,
> and to those who led and those who wrote about it.
But Rosa was the first one to stand up for me.
And when she sat down she set the tone.
She did not shout, she did not fight,
she merely sat down on the bus that day.
> And by sitting down, stood tall and proud for me.

about what had occurred. The advocate had offered, through several telephone calls and letters, to assist Mei in whatever way she needed. Mei did not request any assistance except to ask the advocate that, if she was going to be at the trial, she would appreciate their meeting at the courthouse on the day of her testimony.

The advocate had learned from readings and conferences that Asian women feel a great deal of shame when they are victimized. She thus believed she understood Mei's reluctance to seek services because of the fear of others knowing, especially her parents. She also knew that Asian women hide their feelings, are not verbally expressive, and are concerned with privacy and confidentiality. The advocate, accordingly, did not push any services upon Mei and accepted her minimum participation in the prosecution of the case.

Undoubtedly, there was the factor of shame in what Mei was experiencing after being sexually assaulted. Many rape victims lapse into self-blame, withdrawal, and fear concerning how others look on them. For Mei, however, shame was only a part of what she was feeling. In Chinese culture there is a strong emphasis placed on one's sense of obligation toward others. This applies to parent–child, friendship, and teacher–student relationships, as well as how one reciprocates a favor or service given.

Frequently intertwined with the practice of obligation is carefully avoiding causing discomfort or trouble for someone else. Telling someone your problems may not only obligate them to respond in some manner, it may also result in pain and worry for them. Mei chose not to tell her parents about the rape, in part because she did not want to reveal the "dirtiness" she felt and the "foolishness" in failing to prevent it. But she was also concerned that her elderly mother would become highly upset and would feel compelled to travel from her home hundreds of miles away to be with her daughter. Mei did not want to bring unnecessary suffering into her mother's life because she felt it was *her* time in life to take care of her parents and not the reverse (anonymous, personal communication, 1990).

These same principles of obligation and not imposing oneself on others can also apply to asking for help from service providers. Mei was an educated woman and was aware of the general availability of services in the community. The rights to these services, however, are seen by Chinese in the context of being conservative in how one appropriates obligations. Mei did not want to say a blunt "no" to the offer of services by the advocate because that might have hurt the advocate's feelings. But she also did not want to obligate herself by freely accepting every service offered. Instead, she chose a service that she would appreciate and that would not cause the advocate a great deal of inconvenience—court accompaniment.

The advocate, in other words, was culturally sensitive in appreciating her client's sense of shame. By not being fully aware of other cultural elements, though, she missed a variety of ways she could have been more helpful. She could have picked up from the hints what else was present when Mei returned her calls and apologized for disturbing her busy schedule. Most advocates are, of course, extremely busy. But if the advocate conveys too often the difficulty of scheduling an appointment to a person like Mei, then the requests for services by the victim will be very few.

The advocate, moreover, could have approached the meetings for trial preparation by asking Mei the favor of assisting *her* so that Mei would have had a specific means to "repay" the advocate. The advocate would then be communicating that Mei's participation would ease and not increase the "burden" of providing assistance in the case. Finally, the shame Mei felt was probably both a matter of self-image (how she evaluated herself) and of disgracing the Chinese people (how she evaluated herself as a Chinese woman). Asian cultures, in general, stress social relationships and group loyalty. Individual achievement and failure are judged by how they reflect on one's family or group or race. Mei's isolation protected her because she felt "out of place." An effort to share with her that women from every race and walk of life have been victims of sexual violence may have lessened her perception of "being different."

The assault on a 19-year-old Korean female college student in Texas also illustrates that the concept of shame is multifaceted in Asian cultures. Helen Thueson, director of Victim Services at the Waco Police Department, described a call to the scene of a knife attack (H. Thueson, personal communication, 1997). It was a campus apartment, and there were two victims—a 19-year-old woman and a 20-year-old man—both Korean. They had been assaulted by the young woman's estranged boyfriend. The female victim, Sunja, had recently broken off the relationship because she had become increasingly uneasy with his temper and jealousy. He was furious at her and told her he would never allow her to dishonor him in that way. Frightened, Sunja had gone home for the weekend to be with family in Houston. She had returned to Waco reluctantly because of final examinations. Fearful of being alone, she had asked a male friend to accompany her back and to stay with her until she could leave school.

Early Monday morning Sunja was ready to leave for classes and her friend was just beginning to stir on the couch where he had spent the night. Her ex-boyfriend suddenly arrived and began banging on the door and yelling for her to let him in. She yelled back for him to leave. He peered through the window and through a small crack in the blinds got a glimpse of the friend. He became furious. He kicked in the door, cracking the door frame despite two deadbolts, a handle lock, and a chain lock. He ran in and attacked Sunja's friend, eventually grabbing a knife from the kitchen and cutting him several times. Sunja tried to intervene but was punched in the face and thrown to the ground. The police were summoned by neighbors.

Thueson remembers that the victims were very hesitant to give a statement. They would say little and would not answer questions. They would only say how sorry they were for the trouble and just wanted to forget it. They were worried that their families would find out and be ashamed of them. Thueson said she kept telling them they were victims and had nothing to apologize for. She told them that their families would want to know and that they would understand. It was then that Thueson began to realize that her ideas about shame were limited.

The young man told Thueson that he was living with his uncle in order to go to school in the United States and that if his uncle found out what had happened, he would send him back to Korea. He wanted to apply for crime victims' compensation because he had no money for medical treatment but did not want the forms sent to his house. Thueson respected the victim's wishes and mailed the compensation forms to another friend's home. She refrained from overemphasizing that it was not their responsibility for what had happened—this was counter to their own sense of contribution—and instead stressed how important it was to cooperate with authorities, since laws against forcible entry and assault needed to be enforced. She also stopped putting any pressure on them to inform their families.

> This approach worked perfectly. They seemed to feel so relieved and thanked me for understanding. They gave good statements. They told us that the Korean comments (muttered by the defendant upon arrest) had been death threats. He told them he would have them hunted down in their hometown and killed. I arranged for them to follow-up with a special officer assigned to the Asian detail back in their home city. (H. Thueson, personal communication, 1997)

Just Another Day

The newspaper headline announced: "Just Another Day in South Central." Yet another gang-related slaying involving drug dealers, automatic weapons, and bullet-ridden bodies had occurred in this embattled district of Los Angeles. The familiar scenario of young black males—this time hard-core members of the vicious Eight-Trey Gangster Crips—and violent reprisal for a cocaine buy gone awry are present. But there is an alarming difference. The victims in this instance are two innocent teenage girls, one age 13 and the other age 18. This is *not* "just another day" for their parents, loved ones, and classmates (N. Johnson, personal communication, 1990).

Jeanine was in the seventh grade and her friend, Cindi, had just graduated from high school. Their families lived next door to one another in a neighborhood of modest homes with manicured yards and wide streets. The community lies in the shadows of the black middle-class enclave of Baldwin Hills but also escapes from the stark existence of central Watts. Jeanine's mother was employed in an office, and Cindi's parents owned their own small business.

One late summer afternoon, Jeanine and Cindi were returning from the market where they had just made purchases for that evening's dinner at Jeanine's home. They were driving in Cindi's red compact car, which had been a graduation present from her proud parents. Both girls were looking forward to what was unfolding in their lives. Jeanine was excited about starting to sing in the church choir and Cindi was preparing for college. The two girls were totally unsuspecting as two vehicles were fast approaching them. Five heavily-armed gang members had just sprayed one nearby house with gunfire. They were now searching for a red compact car driven by the sister of a dope dealer who had cheated them of $15,000 worth of cocaine by substituting two pounds of ordinary white flour. They planned to kill the sister in retaliation. Spotting Cindi's car, which they mistakenly believed was the one for which they were looking, they gave chase.

Jeanine and Cindi must have been terrified as the two vehicles descended on them and began ramming their car. Cindi tried desperately to drive away, but her car was forced to a stop after several blocks. The sound of bullets piercing steel and flesh punctuated the air. Less than one block away, Jeanine's mother heard the shots as she was busy in the kitchen. A neighbor ran to her doorway and cried out, "Doesn't your daughter wear corn rows [braids in her hair]?" Horrified, Jeanine's mother ran from her home to the street corner and to Cindi's car. She went immediately to the passenger side and saw Jeanine slumped over and bleeding. By now the police and paramedics were arriving. They nudged her to the side as they proceeded to render aid. She expected her daughter to be placed in the ambulance and rushed to the hospital. Instead, Jeanine and Cindi were covered with sheets. They had both died instantly of multiple gunshot wounds (anonymous, personal communication, 1990).

A veteran police officer was quoted in the newspapers two days after the mistaken murders as saying: "Well quite naturally it's depressing. But for us it's not unusual—unfortunately." An elected public official of the black community was also quoted as stating: "It's not extraordinary for us to hear about our children being killed" (N. Johnson, personal communication, February 14, 1990). For Jeanine's mother Cheryl, however, life will never be the same. Even before her daughter's death, she never accepted the gang violence and the fear it had brought to her neighborhood. Although such violence is tragically commonplace, to Cheryl that will not ever mean being numb to its disastrous effects. She is upset by the notion she thinks white people hold—that blacks have built "a tolerance to crime" because it is such an everyday part of their lives. The day her daughter was murdered was not "just another day" (anonymous personal communication, February 14, 1990).

Neither are the three most difficult days of each year now for Cheryl—the date Jeanine died, Jeanine's birthday, and Cheryl's own birthday. Her birthday is especially painful because Jeanine would go to extra lengths to make her mother happy on that day. Her daughter would "make a big deal out of it," said Cheryl. Now as she gazes at Jeanine's photo, taken only one week before her death and placed prominently on the fireplace mantle in the living room, Cheryl remarks that a "life sentence" has been imposed upon her. Twenty-five years from now, she says, she will wonder what her daughter would have looked like (Anonymous, personal communication, February 14, 1990).

For too many mothers of black children, Cheryl's experience is all too common. If it was "just another day," then the anguish would be less. The pain, however, may or may not be initially evident. Helen Thueson of the Waco Police Department in Texas, for example, recalled her first homicide case (personal communication, 1997). A young African American male had been fatally shot in a public park. A large, noisy crowd had gathered and Thueson had a difficult time locating the young man's family members in the midst of the confusion. People were sobbing loudly, screaming, and fainting. Thueson finally found the victim's mother, who was silently standing by the side.

Thueson introduced herself and began her textbook approach to the situation and the mother's grief. The mother listened quietly and expressionlessly. Finally she said, "Honey, you're very sweet, but I'm okay. The number one cause of death for young black males is murder. We live with that reality. You always hope it won't be your son, but you know that the risk is real. My best friend had her son murdered last year. She'll be there for me. God will get me through it. I don't need anything else." Thueson's reaction:

> I was speechless. I had been trying to "normalize" what I had interpreted to be her state of shock, but instead it may have been acceptance. I was offering help from the perspective of a white, young female. Murder, from my perspective, was unimaginable. This was not her experience. (H. Thueson, personal communication, 1997)

Acceptance of the reality of the high incidence of homicide plaguing the African American community does not, again, mean acquiescence or absence of hurt and suffering. It does mean that mothers in this community desire and deserve to imagine another future for their children.

CULTURAL RESPONSE PATTERNS

Brick in the Purse

The morning after her daughter was murdered, Cheryl was visited by Norma Johnson, the victim counselor for the 77th Precinct of the Los Angeles Police Department. Norma had been alerted to the incident by one of the homicide detectives and realized, as a long-time service provider in the black community of South Central, that she needed to be ready with practical suggestions and straightforward answers. She found Cheryl distraught and in shock. Cheryl was faced with the immediate and unavoidable responsibility of arranging for Jeanine's funeral, but she was too confused to know where to begin.

Norma offered emotional support and information on mortuaries that had designed funerals to match the state criminal injuries compensation guidelines. Cheryl did not want "charity" and felt ashamed that she did not have the insurance or financial resources to meet the funeral obligations. To that, Norma succinctly explained the compensation system and the rights of all victims to receive its benefits. She then escorted Cheryl to the mortuary to select a casket and plan the services. Norma's encouragement and presence helped to assure Cheryl that she was doing the best for her daughter.

Norma also extended her assistance in an unusual way. Cheryl wanted to know if her daughter's face had been badly disfigured by her injuries. She was also concerned how Jeanine's body would be treated during the autopsy. Norma promised her that she herself would go to the coroner's office to witness the autopsy while it was being performed. She knew that the only way Cheryl would continue to trust law enforcement authorities was if someone she trusted could provide her with first-hand knowledge.

The prosecution proceeded very slowly over several years. Norma continued to keep Cheryl informed. There were many times that Cheryl wanted to go into court with "a brick in my purse to beat them [the defendants] up so they'll be dead." She lost one job because her employer could no longer accept her periodic absences as she tried to monitor the court process. She was afraid that, if she relaxed her watch, some sort of expedient plea bargain would be reached. It was her belief, commonly felt in the black community, that if the victim and the defendant(s) are both black or minorities, the case is more apt to be settled for less than the original charge and penalty (anonymous personal communication, 1990).

Cheryl's imagined solution of the "brick in the purse" is symbolic of the true feelings that she harbored but not the more constructive actions she chose. She carried the emotional weight of her daughter's murder daily. There were sleepless nights and the dread of morning. Cheryl knew that she would no longer awaken to help her daughter get ready for school. At the end of the workday, she would come home somehow expecting Jeanine to lift her spirits by her smiling welcome at the door. Instead, she was rudely reminded that that would never happen again. She even missed the way Jeanine would routinely annoy her by her loud renditions of rap songs and accompanying body gyrations. The absence of her daughter's voice and exuberance made the quiet of the house deafening and unbearable.

Cheryl did not literally carry a brick in her purse into the courtroom, however. She was fortunate to have been referred by Norma to a homicide survivors group called Loved Ones of Homicide Victims. Cheryl knew she needed help coping, but she could not afford therapy and did not want to be labeled crazy because of the grief and difficulties she was experiencing. Mental health clinics and professionals have usually been looked on with suspicion by the black community as a means for the white majority to exercise control over blacks through misdiagnosis, institutionalization, and medication. The homicide survivors group in her community thus offered Cheryl a non-threatening and accessible alternative to receiving emotional and psychological support (see also Cantrell, 1993).

Cheryl began attending the group two weeks after her daughter's death. Seeing other black mothers there, her sense of being alone lessened. She knew that she had to go on with her life despite her loss. The group has helped her to learn how to do just that. At meetings held twice a month, each person has the opportunity to share her pain. The group also plays a greater and more useful role. The emphasis on listening and reaching out to others includes finding something positive for each member to do in her life.

At first for Cheryl, just making it through each day was an accomplishment. But the Christmas holidays challenged her to do more. She was extremely anxious about facing that first Christmas without Jeanine. She knew that, in spite of having two other children and a boyfriend with whom to celebrate, she would not even feel like cooking a Christmas meal or shopping for gifts. The group, however, wanted to have a Christmas party for its many children. Someone was needed to buy presents with the $2,000 a benefactor had donated, and Cheryl was enlisted. She not only descended on the toy stores with a fervent mission and bought all the presents, but she also wrapped each one of them.

An even greater challenge came later to Cheryl. The California Youth Authority requires an "impact class" for those juveniles about to be released. This class stresses the serious and damaging effect of criminal behavior on the lives of victims. Cheryl was invited to be the speaker at one class. She brought with her the photo of Jeanine being carried in a casket to the grave site. She informed the juveniles: "This is my last memory of my daughter." She then demanded of them: "Do you want this to be the last memory of your sister or your mother?" Her message conveyed the personal account of her own suffering as a mother and the grim reality that any criminal not wanting to follow rules "on the outside" will, ironically, encounter even more rules while serving a prison sentence. For Cheryl, speaking to these young people was a way to help keep other mothers from experiencing a hurt similar to hers. She hoped that the "brick in her purse" would "knock some sense" into at least some of the juveniles she confronted.

Although Jeanine's death is something Cheryl can never erase from her mind, belonging to the homicide survivors group has given her a bond with other parents and a way of living *with* hurt. Cheryl hesitates to talk to her own sister about Jeanine because it is hard for Cheryl to see her sister cry. The group, however, has a "buddy system" in which members call one another between meetings to lend encouragement. There is also a common link of suffering that has dissolved barriers. Several black men and a white couple who travel from Whittier, for example, are now coming to the group. As the white woman began to cry at her very first meeting, she was comforted by the black woman who sat next to her with a hug and the words: "We all cry." The death of a loved one has pulled members of the group closer and made gender and racial differences not disappear but obviously seem less important (anonymous, personal communication, 1990).

Verbalization and Demonstration

Differences in cultural background between spouses may result in seemingly conflicting ways of responding to a crime. Linda, for example, is a white woman who was born in the Midwest. Her parents moved to California when Linda was in her early teens. Peter, her husband, was born in Mexico and came to the United States when he was a teenager also. Linda and Peter met at a high school party, began dating, and after Peter served in the military, they were married.

A home in the suburbs, a middle-class lifestyle, a vacation cabin in the mountains, and five daughters were the fruits of their labor of love over 15 years. But it took just one night, in only a matter of a few minutes, to nearly destroy the dreams and successes of the Ruiz family. While spending the night at a neighbor's house, Linda and Peter's nine-year-old daughter, Tiffany, was raped by her girlfriend's father. Awakening during the assault, Tiffany began squirming and crying, causing her molester to stop. She was then able to run to the telephone and stammer to her parents that she wanted to come home. Her girlfriend's father grabbed the telephone and insisted that Tiffany had merely been having a nightmare. Peter, however, immediately went to the neighbor's house and brought his frightened daughter home.

Tiffany sobbed hysterically as she told her parents what had happened. Peter, bristling with anger, loaded his hunting rifle to confront his daughter's assailant. Linda somehow managed to stop him from leaving the house and convinced him that they should instead call the police. After the police officers arrived, they interviewed Tiffany, Linda, and Peter, and arrested the neighbor.

Tiffany's ordeal was prolonged by a series of maneuvers by the defense that delayed the court proceedings over two years. When the trial eventually did take place, it resulted in a hung jury. During this time, Peter's Hispanic heritage came to the fore. As a father, he was to be the protector of his family. His guilt for having failed his daughter weighed heavily on him. He told Tiffany that what had occurred that night was not her fault. Instead he blamed himself.

Carrying this burden in silence, sedated by alcohol, Peter refused to discuss anything related to his daughter's assault. He only told his parents about the incident months afterwards because his mother persisted in asking him what was troubling him. He participated only minimally in the legal proceedings, and then only when he was subpoenaed to testify in court. He ignored visits to his home by the district attorney. He did not seek counseling nor was he involved in the counseling sessions attended by his daughter and wife. He also became more restrictive concerning his children being away from the home. He believed that if he had followed two years ago the Mexican tradition of centering the family on the home, he would not have allowed his daughter to spend the night elsewhere, and she thus would not have been molested.

On the other hand, Linda wanted her daughters to experience slumber parties and visits to friends' homes, as she had when she was growing up in the Midwest. She wanted to talk openly with her husband about what had happened to their daughter. She needed his support and Tiffany, she felt, needed his guidance. She saw Peter's initial anger turn to withdrawal and what she considered denial. She had been taught to verbalize problems. She had forthrightly told her parents about the molestation, had gone to counseling, and had actively cooperated with the prosecution.

This crisis in the Ruiz family has heightened the cultural differences that had not been tested in the same manner before. Obviously, the protracted criminal justice process did not help the situation. All of the therapists had also been white females, who demonstrated little understanding of the Hispanic culture or the role of the Hispanic male. What helped this family to cope was Peter and Linda acknowledging that the differences between them in responding to life problems were cultural and not the degree of caring. They realized that they shared a commitment to the welfare of their children.

Linda began to appreciate that Peter demonstrated his love by renewed efforts to make life at home more enjoyable for his daughters. He built a walk-in sized playhouse for them in the backyard complete with glass windows, kitchen sink, electricity, and wooden shingles. He landscaped the garden area with a pond and constructed a tree house. Communication for Peter was other than the spoken word. Indeed, it is not the father's place in a Mexican home to talk to his daughters about sexual or "female matters."

According to Nydia Eva Rosales, a therapist in San Francisco, in Latino families closeness between husband and wife is seldom achieved through "mutually shared confidences of each other's inner truths, insecurities, or vulnerable, hidden thoughts and feelings." The Latino male is instead known through a sense of "mutual responsibility," "shared experiences of joys and sorrows," and "the subtle process of the interpretation of non-verbal cues, body statements, and covert expression of moods and feelings." In this relationship, the woman generally avoids confrontation that threatens the male's dignity (1989, p. 37).

Knowing that Linda was preparing for the interview with me, Peter wanted to tell his side of how the family was handling their daughter's sexual molestation. He chose not to participate directly in the interview but instead conveyed beforehand to his wife why it was difficult for him to talk about what he was going through. This provided the opportunity for some initial conversation and a better understanding between Peter and Linda. At the end of the interview, the names of several bicultural Latino therapists were given to Linda to discuss with her husband. Their dissimilar responses did not have to keep them apart. They just needed to see them as differences from which both of them could grow.

Who Suffers?

In the family orientation of Asian cultures, the suffering of the victim is not an individual experience or the sole consideration. Mary, for example, was a six-year-old Vietnamese girl who was raped by her 26-year-old male cousin in the bathroom of the apartment in which their family lived. Her cousin warned her not to tell anyone and bribed her by giving her a new box of color crayons. In the days that followed, Mary had nightmares in her sleep and would awaken screaming. She then began to have severe pain in urinating. Her mother took Mary to a community medical clinic, not realizing the cause of her daughter's suffering. The doctor who examined Mary found a gonorrhea infection and, therefore, evidence of the rape. A report was made to the police and an investigation ensued.

The manner in which Mary's parents reacted to the discovery that their daughter had been raped shows how the victim's needs can be supplanted by other issues facing the family. Mary's mother had graduated from a French-instituted high school in Vietnam. During the war, she was jailed by the communists for three years. Upon her release, she married a fisherman, primarily because he owned a boat, which became their eventual means of escape to Indonesia. From there, they went to Guam and then to Northern California. Mary was the first-born of five children.

Mary's father, because his family's traditional livelihood had been fishing, did not receive any formal education and was illiterate even in the Vietnamese language. Once he settled in the United States, he accepted the responsibility to look after his brother's only son by allowing him to live with his family. This young man worked so that he could send money back to Vietnam for his parents. It was this same young man that raped Mary.

There is little question that Mary's parents care for her and her siblings. Mary's mother blamed herself for what had befallen her daughter and had thoughts of suicide because she felt Mary's loss of virginity has ruined her future prospects for marriage and a normal life. At the same time, she told Mary not to talk to her about what happened because she did not want to hear about it. She allowed Mary to receive therapy with a Vietnamese social worker soon after the rape had been brought to the attention of authorities. Therapy, nonetheless, has discontinued because of transportation difficulties and because both parents believed that something is *lost*, not gained, in seeking help from outside the family.

Mary's father was also placed in a dilemma. His brother depended on his son to help support the family back in Vietnam. Now that the rape had occurred, Mary's father felt ashamed that he did not guide his nephew firmly enough to avoid trouble. He was therefore unable to discuss the matter with his wife, except to plead with her to tell the court that he did not want his nephew imprisoned. He was not placing his nephew's well-being above that of his daughter's. It was his way of trying to fulfill the promise to his brother *and* allow his daughter to recover without unnecessary family disruption.

The sexual assault, in other words, caused suffering on many fronts. Mary's physical and emotional trauma undoubtedly had to be addressed. Mary's parents also suffered, knowing that their daughter had been raped by her own cousin. The rape severely affected both the immediate and extended family structure, including their adherence to past obligations and future relationships. The educational and social background differences between Mary's father and mother, moreover, have rendered them incompatible and unable to support one another in relating to an unfamiliar U.S. justice system and equally foreign "mental health" issues to solve problems.

Fortunately, the Vietnamese social worker understood the family's predicament. She placed primary emphasis on establishing trust with Mary's parents. She knew that this was the only way she could continue the opportunity to assist Mary. She also communicated the circumstances of the family to the legal authorities. This was one reason that the defendant was sentenced to probation without incarceration, but with the conditions that he undergo sex offender treatment, maintain employment, and live in another city. As more of the encircling family issues were acknowledged and respected, in other words, the possibility for meeting Mary's needs correspondingly increased.

A Better Life

As a single parent, Rosa had been proud that she had raised four children on her own without government assistance or welfare. When she arrived in the United States from Guadalajara, Mexico, with her husband twelve years ago, she was determined to make California a home for her family. Her husband, however, was soon discouraged by the life here, especially the prevalence of drugs on the streets. He decided that this was not a place to raise children and wanted to return to Mexico. Rosa insisted on staying. Although it meant divorce from her husband, she believed that life was better here.

This belief sustained her for many years as she worked six days a week cleaning houses, taking her children faithfully to the Catholic church on Sundays, and living frugally in a small and sparsely furnished one bedroom apartment. There were the fun times of going to community fiestas, movies, and buying ice cream cones for the children on the walk home from Sunday Mass. But everything changed dramatically for Rosa when her oldest daughter, Carmelita, age 17, was shot and killed. Carmelita's murderer was her boyfriend, a *cholo* (gang member), who was upset because she had made the decision to leave him. In the past, he would beat Carmelita to prevent her from leaving, but this time he fired a rifle bullet into her back.

Rosa cries often. The pride and strength she had felt over many years in raising her children have been replaced by grief and confusion. Her self-esteem as a mother was badly shaken by her daughter's death. Rosa has difficulty now thinking about the future. She is afraid that her next oldest daughter, Tina, now age 15, may also be killed by some boy she meets. Rosa blames herself for not protecting Carmelita well enough from danger. If she had raised Carmelita correctly, she feels, her daughter would never have had anything to do with a cholo. She wonders if she was foolish not to have followed her husband back to Mexico.

Rosa's contact with the criminal justice system has unfortunately added to her distress. On the day of the shooting she was notified by an officer, who spoke little Spanish, that her daughter had been in an *accidente* and was at the hospital. The officer told Rosa to come to the police station first before going to the hospital. Rosa went to the station and waited for over an hour before she was shown a photograph by which to identify her daughter. She was then told that Carmelita was dead.

Rosa did not want to believe what the officer was saying. She wanted to see her daughter. She was finally allowed to go to the morgue but could only see Carmelita from a distance for a few brief moments. Rosa was warned not to go near her daughter or touch her because fingerprints had not yet been taken from Carmelita's body. Rosa could not understand why she could not have been with her daughter at the hospital, why she had to wait at the police station so long, and why, as in Mexican custom and as a mother, she could not caress her deceased loved one.

The prosecution of Carmelita's killer was not resolved for almost a year. He received the eight years maximum in prison because he was a minor. Rosa refused to accept this as fair. Thankfully, she has been assisted by a Spanish-speaking advocate who visits on Mondays when the children are in school. The advocate provides information and the only opportunities for Rosa to talk about what she is feeling and to cry freely. Her sisters and friends tell her *not* to cry because she will become sick. They tell her to think about other things. She has told her priest that her daughter's violent death disturbs her greatly. The priest has told her to pray to God for help, that others have experienced suffering also, and that she will have "no more bad luck!" Her children worry when she cries, so she holds back. She has not been able to go to counseling because she cannot afford it, she has no car to drive to a free clinic, and her work and home schedules do not allow time for regular office hour appointments.

Carmelita died at the time she was leaving her boyfriend to return to live with her family. She had told her mother just one week before her death that she was going back to high school and was giving up the life of a runaway. Rosa's last conversation and personal remembrance of her daughter, in other words, affirmed the strength of their relationship. In spite of the pain she suffers, Rosa knows how her other children have provided her with hopeful and uplifting moments. Her youngest child, Lupe, just five years of age and fathered by a man with whom Rosa had been engaged, makes her smile every time she crawls up and nestles into her lap to watch cartoons on television. Tina, an older daughter, assures Rosa that she will not get serious with a boy until she has completed her education to become a teacher. These daughters give Rosa the courage and determination to continue to seek a better life.

Oklahoma City Bombing

On April 19, 1995, at 9:02 A.M., a 4,800-pound bomb concealed in a rented truck exploded in front of the Alfred P. Murrah Federal Building in downtown Oklahoma

City. There were 168 people killed and 674 others injured. The blast, the single most destructive act of domestic terrorism in our nation's history, also damaged or destroyed 325 buildings, set cars ablaze, and shattered windows in a 10-block radius (The City of Oklahoma City, 1996, p. ix). Broken also was the sense of safety and security many Americans had taken for granted. Karen Huggins Lashley, an initial crisis responder and psychologist working with survivors and their families, describes the bombing as a microcosm of massive trauma and intervention (1998).

The immediate response by rescuers, crisis intervenors, and ordinary citizens to this tragedy in the heartland of the United States established the "Oklahoma Standard," a measure of the efficient and remarkable teamwork that ensued:

> The community's response was as instantaneous and as overwhelming as the act which precipitated it. The wounded and severely shaken survivors came out of the buildings in the core of the blast area to be met by citizens rushing to offer support, first-aid, and rides to hospitals. Men and women of all callings went into the rubble of the Murrah Building to search for the living and comfort the dying. Fire, police, and emergency medical services units self-dispatched, responding to the sound of the blast. They were guided to the site by the column of smoke that towered over the city.... Initial commands were established, units were assigned to search each of the buildings...and triage centers were set up.... Rescuers on the ground formed human chains to bring the wounded out of the rubble.... A name has been given to the selfless devotion and untiring commitment of those working at the site and the community's response to and support of the workers, the survivors, and the families of the victims. That name is the "Oklahoma Standard." It is a unique combination of training, dedication, and professional excellence rooted in and nourished by the caring and compassion of the community. (The City of Oklahoma City, 1996, pp. ix–x)

For nearly two weeks following the bombing, moreover, violent crimes in Oklahoma City virtually stopped. The devastating effects of what had occurred had not only stunned the city but had also launched a massive rescue and crisis response that riveted the city's attention and brought citizens together. Almost every person in the city seemed to know someone injured or killed in the blast. Many experienced the impact of multiple losses on their lives (Lashley, 1998).

Ninety-one percent of those who were in the Murrah Building at the time of the explosion were killed or injured. Of these 163 were killed or died of injuries. There were four deaths and numerous injuries in other buildings or outside (The City of Oklahoma City, 1996, p. 80). Almost 75% of those killed in the bombing were white and over 20% were black. Of those injured over 35% were white and 11% black, but the majority, over 50%, were of unknown race. According to the Oklahoma State Health Department (1997) the racial backgounds of those killed in the bombing, excluding a nurse later killed by falling debris, were:

Race	Number	Percent
Asian	2	1.20
Black	35	20.8
American Indian	1	.6
Pacific Islander	1	.6
Unknown	5	3.0
White	123	73.8
Total	167	

The Oklahoma State Health Department (1997) listed the numbers of those injured as follows. (Note that the large number of injured of unknown race is the result of data collection methods.)

Race	Number	Percent
Asian	4	.6
Black	78	11.6
American Indian	5	.7
Pacific Islander	2	.3
Unknown	348	51.6
White	237	35.2
Total	674	

Two notable ways the Oklahoma City bombing revealed both the diversity of the citizens and the striving for inclusiveness were the memorial services held for the victims and survivors and the pilgrimages to the site of the bombing. When the First Lady of Oklahoma, Kathy Keating, organized a memorial service that was televised, a black choir from a Baptist church provided the music and song that touched the hearts of those grieving all across the nation. Oklahoma, as a state, has the second largest concentration of Native Americans, particularly Cherokee, in the nation. Many of the other memorial services and ceremonies therefore reflected the meaningfulness and symbolisms of this heritage (see also Young, 1994, pp. 23–25).

On May 7, for example, just weeks after the bombing, the Good Medicine Society, an intertribal Native American association, conducted a special ceremony of healing and recovery. Traditional Native American dances and blessings of smoke were offered to the victims and survivors, rescue workers and volunteers, and the community. People of all races came together. Tim Tallchief, an Osage and director of the Native American Center for Excellence at the University of Oklahoma Health Sciences Center, recalls the Dance of Fall Fest '95 held within several blocks of the former Alfred P. Murrah Building. Rescue workers and others involved in the grueling task of search and cleanup were invited as special guests. Iola Hayden, a Comanche, suggested that the dancers do a Round Dance (sometimes called a friendship dance) and invited everyone to join in the Circle of Life movement of the dance with the honorees in the center. Tallchief remembers that the circle was so large that it filled the mammoth room of the Myriad Center. As part of the ceremony, people came forward to place money in the hands of the rescue workers— an offering of thanks. The rescue workers, in turn, passed on the money to be donated to the Red Cross and other organizations to help with the work left to be done in the aftermath of the bombing (K. Lashley, personal communication, 1997).

Another ceremony was conducted at the Miami Tribal Headquarters in Ottawa County, Oklahoma. During this intertribal powwow, 19 small cedar saplings (a tree sacred to many Native American people) were brought into the circle of dancers—one for each child who had died in the bombing. The trees were blessed and then given to 19 children who were present that evening. The children were instructed to take the trees home with them, to plant them, and to care for them as living memorials to the lives of those children who perished in the blast. The Ponca Tribe, in another symbol of interracial honor and remembrance, named a tribal building after a HUD worker, a non-Indian, who died in the bombing. The Susan Farrell Building stands as a tribute to this woman who had worked hand in hand with tribal members and had earned their admiration and respect.

Across the street from the bombing site, a small, open-air worship center, The Heartland Chapel, was erected on the grounds of the First United Methodist Church, whose sanctuary was heavily damaged by the blast. Through the donations of corporations and individuals and the interdenominational support from the Islamic and Jewish communities, the chapel serves as a place of quiet meditation and prayers as well as special services. The altar is made from native stone and granite from the remains of the Murrah Building. Well-wishers and visitors from all over the world come to the chapel 24 hours a day.

The most remarkable single occurrence stemming from the bombing, however, is the spontaneously-erected living memorial to the victims and survivors surrounding the blast epicenter. A simple chain-link fence was placed for security and safety around the Alfred P. Murrah site after it was leveled, and grass was planted in early June of 1995. This fence has become an international symbol of not only the destruction of the bombing but of the tremendous outpouring of support and care. Hundreds of thousands have come to the fence from every state and many countries to confirm the horrors of what happened and also to express sympathy. Attached to almost every inch of the fence are flowers and wreaths, stuffed animals, prayers, poems, letters, and notes. Baby blankets; high school and college sport teams' tee-shirts; ceramic angels; crucifixes; photographs of the men, women, and children who perished in the blast; and countless other mementos are left by family members, residents, and visitors. Each day, irrespective of the hour or weather conditions, people of all ages, social and ethnic backgrounds, states, and national origins walk silently or in soft conversation along the perimeter of the fence. Some take photographs, some pause to offer prayers, some stare in disbelief, others cry. The fence has become a monument that has allowed diverse people to come together to create a national place of healing (Lashley & Ogawa, forthcoming).

For Tony Du the fence has been particularly poignant. Mr. Du left Vietnam in 1979 at the age of 20. In 1984, he was sworn in as a United States citizen in the Murrah Building. As a refugee and Oklahoma City resident, Mr. Du is shocked by the bombing. Although he witnessed much death and destruction living in Vietnam, his conception of the "American dream" and the orderliness of our society has been rocked. "You would expect buildings to be blown up in war-torn Vietnam," Du stated, "but not in downtown Oklahoma City. I am made numb by the children killed so senselessly" (as cited in Lashley & Ogawa, forthcoming).

4

RACISM AND HATE VIOLENCE

I Have a Dream

Martin Luther King, Jr.

I Have a Dream

The marvelous voice of the Reverend Dr. Martin Luther King, Jr. was stilled by gunfire in Memphis, Tennessee, on April 4, 1968. Dr. King was a preacher whose congregation had been humanity and an orator with a dream, not imaginary, but visionary.

Had this voice carried a superfluous message or words disengaged from personal sacrifice and courage, then that voice would now be lost and forgotten. But King was a prophet of our nation who was there at every painful step of the civil rights movement. He was at once a black minister, a nonviolent soldier, a captivating leader, and a philosopher–activist.

As Taylor Branch describes it, King's famous "I Have a Dream" speech went "beyond the limitations of language and culture to express something that was neither pure rage nor pure joy, but a universal transport of the kind that makes the blues sweet."

Chapter Overview

- Rising Conflict of Differences
- Us against Them
- Racism and Crime

Racial and ethnic minorities have experienced long histories of discrimination and hostility. Racial boundaries and disparities in socioeconomic status have created tensions not only with the white majority but also between minority groups. The pendulum of race relations, some believe, is veering from uneasy coexistence toward growing distrust and intolerance. A central factor contributing to our failure to live more in accord with one another is our miserable habit of killing our prophets of change. Dallas, New York, Los Angeles, and Memphis—cities in every part of our nation—have reverberated with gunshots assassinating our heroes whose reason and conciliation guide our nation.

This chapter describes the hate violence and conflict of differences in the United States, and offers portraits of the ways we are dividing ourselves against one another based on culture and race. The connection between racism and crime is also viewed through three illustrative criminal cases.

RISING CONFLICT OF DIFFERENCES

Bias-Motivated Crimes

It has been called "an explosion of racism and intolerance unprecedented in recent history" by Paul Igasaki, Washington, D.C. representative of the Japanese American

Citizens League (1990, p. 5). It is a problem of "growing severity," confirms Eugene Mornell, executive director of the Los Angeles County Commission on Human Relations (LACCHR, 1990, p. 2). Hate violence is on the upswing in the United States. The assessment by those most closely monitoring such activities is that such violence is not just the outbursts of extremists or traditional racist organizations such as the Ku Klux Klan, White Aryan Brotherhood, or neo-Nazi skinheads. Many observers believe that it reflects a magma of widespread prejudice brewing below the surface of our society.

Resistance to rapid demographic change due to large-scale immigration of those with different skin color, language, and customs has conjoined with long-standing racial bigotry against minority groups, especially black Americans. The effect has been to produce a "social greenhouse." Whether or not the prevailing climate of racial tensions is an aberrant episode which will eventually subside as adjustments are made to form a more pluralistic society, or whether increased polarization will occur, is unknown. The signs are not altogether encouraging.

In 1995, there were 7,947 incidents of hate crimes reported to the FBI. Sixty-one percent were motivated by racial bias and 10% by ethnicity/national origin bias. There were in total 9,895 separate offenses with 8,433 known offenders and 10,469 victims. Seventy-two percent of the crimes were categorized as crimes against persons, including 20 murders. The states with the highest number of hate crimes of all categories were (in rank) California (1,751 incidents), New York (845), New Jersey (768), Michigan (405), Massachusetts (333), and Texas (326) (FBI, 1997).

Hate crimes include not only physical violence but intimidation (41% of the 1995 total) and damage/destruction/vandalism of property (23%). The Reverend Cecil Williams of Glide Memorial Church in San Francisco was the target of one such incident. Williams was in Atlanta to mark the birthday of Martin Luther King, Jr. While he was away, racist posters were attached to his house and car. William's Chinese neighbor, disturbed by this display of bigotry, spoke out in front of television news cameras. The next day, obviously in reaction to his statements, he received a telephone call, recorded on his answering machine, which said, "Screw that nigger. Free James Earl Ray" (the latter referring to King's convicted assassin).

The extent to which hate violence exists is much greater than the reported amounts. The 1995 FBI report, for example, covered only 75% of the U.S. population—not all states or law enforcement agencies were able to supply information despite assiduous efforts by the FBI. Bryan Levin, legal director of KLANWATCH, a division of the Southern Poverty Law Center that monitors hate crimes, estimates that the actual number of hate crimes is five times as high as the FBI's numbers. Levin notes, however, that the passage of the federal Hate Crime Statistics Act of 1990, together with the U.S. Supreme Court's 1993 ruling that hate crime laws are constitutional, have encouraged "greater recognition and acceptance by law enforcement of this type of crime" (American Psychological Association [APA], 1995, p. 1).

Hate crime laws—which have higher penalties for crimes motivated by bias—are in place in more than 40 states. A number of victims, however, are not even aware that the acts committed against them are considered criminal. Law enforcement officers themselves continue to need training on the proper identification of such crimes. The San Francisco Police Department, for example, began recording hate crimes more systematically as early as 1988. Formal classes were held covering relevant state statutes, newly incorporated departmental general orders, and historical information on racism. A checkbox to indicate prejudice-based crime was also added to incident reports. Despite such efforts, many jurisdictions throughout California and the United States have not yet formalized methods or guidelines to collect such data.

The federal Hate Crime Statistics Act was introduced by the House of Representatives in 1989, passed by the Senate, and signed by President Bush on April 23, 1990. It also requires all law enforcement agencies to identify and report criminal acts that "manifest evidence of prejudice based on race, religion, sexual orientation, or ethnicity." The Attorney General has established guidelines for the collection of data, and these are annually reported. A confidential telephone hotline has been operated by the Community Relations Service of the U.S. Department of Justice since May of 1990. Complaints of incidents motivated by prejudice can be reported by calling the toll-free number 1-800-347-HATE. The task of compiling national statistics had previously fallen to private groups such as KLANWATCH, the Anti-Defamation League of B'nai B'rith, and the National Institute Against Prejudice and Violence (NIAPV).

The emphasis on accurate statistics is justified, according to experts on hate violence, because such information is the basis for alerting public safety and community agencies to the seriousness of the problem and for providing the justification necessary to formulate effective public policy. There are others, nonetheless, in minority communities who believe that too much attention is being placed on gathering statistical data when more proactive efforts should be supported. They are weary of studies and procedures that endlessly discuss problems and divert resources instead of directly addressing what can never be fully described or counted.

One study that has attempted to both quantify incidents and measure their impact on victims was the National Victimization Survey conducted from April through June of 1989 by the National Institute Against Prejudice and Violence. The sample consisted of 2,084 individuals: 929 self-identified as white, 1,013 black, and 167 others. One-third of those interviewed, 726 individuals, reported being directly victimized by crimes, including those that were motivated by prejudice and those that were not. In analyzing the black subgroup, it was found that in 23 out of 25 comparisons, victims of hate violence experienced greater trauma than other victims. Those who were crime victims suffered an average of five behavioral and psychological symptoms, whereas victims of hate violence, or *ethnoviolence,* averaged 12 such symptoms. The preliminary conclusions of the survey stated:

> The substantive character of these responses is quite serious, ranging from psychophysiological problems indicative of great stress (higher levels of depression and withdrawal, increased sleep difficulties, anxiety and loss of confidence) to an extraordinary percentage reporting serious interpersonal difficulties with friends and significant others. The post-traumatic stress of group violence could not be more dramatically documented. (NIAPV, 1990, p. 6)

These findings lend credence to the statements of Monsignor William J. Barry, chairperson of the California Attorney General's Commission on Racial, Ethnic, Religious and Minority Violence, who stated that there is a "qualitative difference" between victims of ordinary violent crime and victims of hate violence. All victims suffer injury to their dignity and honor, but victims of hate violence are singled out because of *inherent characteristics* and robbed of their *essential self-esteem.* The concern for statistical evidence is thereby warranted. So also is the urgency for an immediate response to assist these victims, for they cannot await numerical precision and final tallies while the situation worsens (Attorney General's Commission on Racial, Ethnic, Religious and Minority Violence, 1987, Appendix p. 25).

Levin further cautions that hate crime laws can only do so much. "This isn't a problem that is limited to the criminal justice system. We're just on the verge now of sending a clear message that status-motivated violence is intolerable in our society, but we have a long way to go" (as cited in APA, 1995). Levin asserts that education is crucial in this endeavor. Ironically, there is racial hostility taking place where we would least expect or desire: at our colleges and universities. These centers of learning have become some of the new centers of racial friction. From 1988 to 1990 there were hate crime incidents reported at 250 campuses nationwide (National Institute Against Prejudice and Violence [NIAPV], 1990). At the University of Mississippi, arsonists burned the school's first black fraternity house before its members were even able to move in. At Temple University and the University of Florida, undergraduates formed White Student Unions to promote "white pride" and combat affirmative action programs. At California State University–Chico, Native American students were taunted with war whoops and pushed by other students who sought to disrupt their heritage festival. At the University of Texas, Austin, a black student returned to her dormitory room to find "Die Nigger Die" scrawled across the door. At University of California campuses, derogatory fliers attacking blacks, Jews, Asians, Hispanics, and gays turned up often on bulletin boards and in mail boxes.

According to the National Institute Against Prejudice and Violence (1990), one out of every five minority college students will be victimized by racism at least once during a single academic year. The reasons given for this upsurge are the general lapse of support for civil rights in the country since the idealism of the 1960s, the competitive nature of college entrance that has generated efforts to abolish affirmative action as unfair "preferential treatment of minorities," the lack of leadership in minority affairs by college faculty and administrators who do not themselves reflect racial diversity and are ill-prepared to cope with the increasing numbers of minority students, and the backlash by white students against the campus activism of their minority peers.

Hopwood, et al. v. State of Texas, et al. is a case in point. White students who were denied entrance into the University of Texas at Austin Law School filed suit, claiming they were discriminated against because of the affirmative action policy of the university. The Fifth U.S. Circuit Court of appeals ruled in 1996 that race and ethnicity can no longer be considered in admissions decisions at Texas public higher education institutions. Dr. Mercedes de Uriarte, an associate professor at the University of Texas, notes that minority applications subsequently dropped sharply. This is alarming, states de Uriarte, because within the next 25 years when today's students reach their career peak, this nation will have no racial or ethnic majority in the forefront of their careers. Yet the Eurocentric perspective—often too narrow—provides "almost all of the interpretive tools with which we struggle to understand one another." Fewer minority students translates into fewer minority professionals and leaders, she notes (de Uriarte, 1997, p. 19A).

In contrast, University of Texas law professor Lino Graglia, speaking on affirmative action, stated that, "Blacks and Mexican Americans are not academically competitive with whites in selective institutions. They have a culture that seems not to encourage achievement. Failure is not looked upon in disgrace" (Roser, 1997, p. A1). A furor resulted from Graglia's remark. De Uriarte, however, appears not to be surprised by such bias. Without non-white faculty or their encouragement, minority students do often lack inspiration to succeed. Nationwide, for example, fewer than three percent of all college professors are Hispanic. Of the 58,000 tenured professors, only 255 are Latinas, and only four of those are at the University of Texas at Austin, the flagship higher education institution in a state where half the population will be Hispanic in twenty years.

Alongside institutionalized racism on campuses, there is also blatant insensitivity. The campus newspaper at Central Seattle Community College, for example, published a cartoon strip featuring a character named "Ding Dong" who had slanted eyes and spoke broken English. In it he was described as a "token geek." Short thereafter, graffiti on campus appeared that said, "Speak English or die, squinty eye." The Asian Pacific Islander Student Union protested, but they were told by the Dean of Students:

> In a democracy, things don't always work out the way we like. The cartoon is demeaning, something we don't want to see at the college. But neither I nor any other administrator can decide what students can publish. ("Caricature," 1989, p. 1)

Most of the persons who commit hate crimes are juveniles and young adults. What does that portend for the future? If prejudice is not simply what was stereotypically deemed the province of uneducated and paramilitary bigots, but rather is festering in the very institutions from which our leaders and professional elite will matriculate, how prevalent or in vogue will racism be in the decades to follow? Any act of hate violence is inflammatory in its potential to create a climate of conflict. At anytime, each one of us could be the victim of someone else's bigotry. The methods we now formulate and the resolve we now summon can only benefit us all. No one segment of or institution in our society can be expected to single-handedly root out intransigent racism or to lessen the separation between peoples. Only if there is a universal insistence that racial hatred is unacceptable will we manage to reverse any trend toward greater intolerance and violence.

Racial Uniforms

The phrase "racial uniforms" was coined by University of Chicago sociologist Charles E. Parker to describe each race's distinguishing physical traits (Takaki, 1989, p. 328). European immigrants could always shed much of their distinctiveness from the whites around them through changes of name, dress, language, and customs. Bernie Schwartz thus became Tony Curtis (the film actor) and Edmund Marcizewski became Ed Muskie (the former Congressman). Non-European racial minorities, however, cannot discard or conceal their identity in the same manner. The shape of their eyes, the color of their hair, and the complexion of their skin can never be fully bleached or perfectly tailored to fit the dominant American model.

Racial uniformity rather than diversity is favored by many in our society. Interracial marriages and mixed-race offspring are regarded by them as an unnatural mingling of the races and a stain upon the purity of a specific lineage. The terms *mestizo, mulatto,* and *half-breed* therefore convey a "tattered" racial uniform. This view has been vociferously advocated in the past (Takaki, 1989, p. 328).

In 1930, for example, a white person, testifying before the House Committee on Immigration and Naturalization, declared that Filipino men were a "social scourge" because they dated and married white women. He was alarmed to see at an automobile show in Washington, D.C. a Filipino male walking with a "nice white girl." This man felt compelled to follow the couple to make certain that he was not mistaken. The government, another person testified, must take official measures to shield white women from such "hot little rabbits" (Takaki, 1989, p. 328). In 1936, *Time* magazine quoted San Francisco Municipal Court Judge Sylvain Lazarus as stating, "It is a dreadful thing when these Filipinos, scarcely more than savages, come to San Francisco, work for practically nothing, and obtain the society of these [white] girls." V. S. McClatchy, in further congressional testimony on Filipino immigration, emphasized that California "is seeking to protect the nation, as well as itself, against the peaceful penetration of another colored race" (as cited in Takaki, 1989, p. 329).

By 1980, despite such attempts to quarantine the races from normal relations and communication with whites, the rate of marriages to whites in California by Filipinos was 24%. The rates for other Asians included Japanese 32%, Koreans 19%, Vietnamese 15%, and Chinese 14% (Takaki, 1989). Anti-miscegenation laws are no longer formally sought. Nonetheless, an interracial relationship today is often strongly discouraged, socially rejected, or only grudgingly received. Only time, it seems, can dispel the false notions and fears that substitute skin tone for moral character in measuring a person's worth.

Yuri Hosoi, for example, was born into a prominent Japanese family in Hawaii. The Hosoi Mortuary, the family's long-established business, was known throughout the islands. When Yuri met a black serviceman, Flipper Fairchild, at a USO dance in Honolulu in 1943 and fell in love, her parents and relatives were aghast. Even in the generally race tolerant atmosphere of Hawaii, relationships with blacks were uncommon, in part because of the relatively small number of blacks who lived in Hawaii. Thus, when Yuri and Flipper later announced their plans to be married, Yuri was disowned by and ostracized from her family. She was, in fact, forced to sign away all rights to an inheritance.

The Fairchilds moved to the Crenshaw area of Los Angeles. As Yuri recalls: "Though no one supported me back home, black people have a big heart for all the strays that want to come in. So they accepted me" (as cited in Njeri, 1990, p. E-1). The Fairchild's youngest son, Halford, however, now 41 and a former president of the National Association of Black Psychologists, remembers a period not entirely without conflict.

> In the junior high school years, people are at the height of their unfriendliness toward each other. Kids talk about people being fat or skinny, light or dark. My own racial background and physiognomy made me the target of that kind of adolescent chiding and abuse. I think I was scarred by some of that for a long time. (p. E-2)

The "cold war" between Yuri and her family finally thawed in 1970. By an interesting twist of fate, she met her brother, a wealthy physician, at a party given by a relative too young to know that she had been cast out from the family decades before. Her brother realized that Yuri had made a good marriage. At the time of his death, he left everything he owned—a palatial mansion and a vast collection of Asian art—to his sister. The rest of the Hosoi relatives have now also reconciled because, as Yuri only half-jokingly remarks, "Who would want to kick out a wealthy heiress?" (p. E-2).

When condemning intermarriage exerts an influence within the criminal justice system, however, it is usually more intractable. In a California county, for example, there was a vicious assault upon a young woman by her drunken husband. His violent behavior had flared sporadically throughout their marriage, but the most recent attack resulted in severe injuries. Because the woman needed medical attention in a hospital emergency room, the police were prompted to respond. Their report of the incident was routinely forwarded to the prosecutor's office for screening. The original charge of a felony was eventually reduced to a petty misdemeanor because of insufficient evidence. An undocumented factor in the final determination was that the woman was white but her husband was black. In other circumstances in which the victim is white and the offender is black and they are unrelated to one another, a felony assault would likely have been filed. But the back room comment by the white deputy district attorney who handled the case was: "She deserves it because she married a *nigger*" (R. Garrett, personal communication, 1990).

In the mind of this particular prosecutor, in other words, any white woman who is in an intimate relationship with a black male (and perhaps any other minority male) has somehow forfeited her rights to ordinary sympathy and legal protection. His attitude universally degrades a woman and marks *any* black male as a second-rate and dangerous partner. When such personal prejudice invades sound judgment, it subverts not only the specific criminal proceeding involved but also blurs the entire concept of justice.

As an additional consequence of the above-mentioned case, a black female district attorney in that office felt the intense betrayal when she became aware of her fellow prosecutor's indefensible remark. She was insulted that a woman could be regarded as somehow "deserving" of abusive treatment, enraged on behalf of her own African American husband, and stunned that another prosecutor alongside whom she had worked—even socialized with for a number of years—would harbor such bigotry toward persons of her race. Because of the political "intricacies" of the office, however, she felt that she could do nothing to express her feelings or seek a remedy (anonymous, personal communication, 1990).

The force of such discrimination has reawakened the need for a sense of racial pride among minorities. As Mary Crow Dog writes:

> I have white blood in me. Often I have wished to be able to purge it out of me. As a young girl I used to look at myself in the mirror, trying to find a clue as to who and what I was. My face is very Indian, and so are my eyes and my hair, but my skin is very light. Always I waited for the summer, for the prairie sun, the Badlands sun, to tan me and to make me into a real skin. The Crow Dogs, the members of my husband's family, have no such problems of identity. They don't need the sun to tan them, they are full-bloods—the Sioux of the Sioux. (Crow Dog & Erdoes, 1990, p. 9)

None of us can afford to be less than accepting of our own and others' distinguishing racial features.

Offensive or Funny?

Humor is one of life's cherished endowments. A side-splitting laugh, a demure chuckle, or a wisp of a smile lightens the heart and brightens the moment. But when it comes to matters of what is termed "ethnic humor," our nation seems to be choking in poor taste, insulting portrayals, and inane remarks. In the mass media and the entertainment industry, minorities are the brunt of jokes that are being justified under everything from the First Amendment to comedic license to good old healthy catharsis. A few examples follow.

The Pulitzer Prize-winning columnist Jimmy Breslin of *Newsday* calls a female reporter of Korean descent "a slant eyed yellow cur" because she criticized one of his articles as sexist. Breslin is reprimanded by his editors but lashes back with the quip that this is not a totalitarian state and that he can say anything he (expletive) pleases. He then telephones a New York radio personality and "humorously" asks him—on the air—if the uproar means he cannot attend his nephew's pending wedding to a Korean woman. Breslin neither acknowledges nor realizes that the emotional violence he caused to reporter Ji-Yeon Mary Yuh cannot be lightly ignored by claiming free speech or attempting to be witty (Associated Press, 1990b, p. A-14).

One of the hottest comedians on stage and screen in the United States in the late 1980s and early 1990s was Andrew Dice Clay, referred to as "the Dice-man." He was a foul-mouthed, chain-smoking, gutter-brained protagonist of wretched humor aimed against gays, women, the disabled, and minorities. He referred to

Asian immigrants as "urine-colored" and as being singularly able to use dental floss for blindfolds. He asserted that women enjoy having "rough sex." He lampooned gays for contracting AIDS because who else, he deadpans, could not deduce that having one's private part covered with excrement might be harmful. Dice insisted that it's all an act—that he should have received an Academy Award—and that he was not ruining Western civilization with his all-American male bravado (Goldstein, 1990, p. 35). Most disturbing, Dice believed he was merely saying out loud what most other people in the United States were really thinking. Drawing fame and fortune from the undercurrents of racism, homophobia, and sexism somehow nullified the painful injury he was inflicting on others.

John Callahan, a 38-year-old cartoonist in Portland, Oregon, draws two Ku Klux Klansmen, draped in their white sheets, setting out to commit some atrocity. One turns to the other and says, "Don't you just love it when they're still warm from the dryer?" (Ellerbee, 1996, p. 5). Callahan insists that the cartoon is meant to be both offensive and humorous. He points out that people don't want to "accept the suggestion that simple humans like us, concerned equally with creature comforts, wore those sheets and committed those crimes." Callahan strangely has tried to humanize those whose purpose is to dehumanize others (Ellerbee, 1996, p. 5).

Bruce Hilton, director of the National Center for Bioethics, states that the penchant for racial jokes is a "grim slide back" for the United States. The fundamental struggle of any harassed and oppressed group, he reminds us, is to be taken *seriously*.

> And there was a while, after the vision of a burning Mississippi, that we were ashamed to tell racist jokes. For a while we could see that the beatings, the fatal rifle shots and even the grinding daily poverty could exist only in a society that refused to take the victims seriously. That seems to have been a temporary conversion. (1990, p. D-16)

The appropriate venue for taking minorities seriously, however, may be arguable for some. Consider the comment of Harvard Law School Dean Robert Clark on efforts to diversify the school's student body and faculty. In 1988, Clark, prior to becoming dean, is reported to have said: "This is a university, not a lunch counter in the Deep South" (Griffin, 1990, p. A-23). The reputed liberal institution has had a history, along with many other major centers of higher education, of only slowly diversifying. It has made considerable progress in doing so with its student enrollment but lags far behind in its tenured faculty. Derrick Bell, the first African American to receive tenure as a professor at the school, has stated:

> There is a strange character to this black achievement. When you have someone that reaches this high level, you find that he is just deemed exceptional, and it does not change society's view of all the rest. (As cited in Drummond, 1990, p. 5)

The question that must be asked of all ethnic humor is precisely what purpose it serves. Linda Ellerbee writes that our sense of humor as Americans is "constipated" because we don't know how to laugh at ourselves anymore and we can't afford to laugh at others. We are so uptight that we call everything racist or sexist or fascist or "just plain cruel." She argues: "Funny is what keeps back the dark." Our periodic foolishness and our painful experiences cry out to be relieved through our funny bone. "When you're standing on the gallows (and we all are), gallows humor makes good sense" (1990b, p. 6).

What brings Americans to the gallows or keeps us groping in the dark, however, may be that we are laughing *at* too many others rather than *with* them. Humor can be a balm to soothe hostilities as long as it does not send shrapnel into the parity minorities are trying so hard to achieve. What purpose does it serve for a Virginia radio station to label acclaimed TV personality Connie Chung as Connie "Chink"? Chung, a native of Maryland and former newscaster in Los Angeles, has made her way to the very top of her profession. She has been a respected New York-based journalist and media star. Was calling her "a chink" a way to remind her that despite her success she was still *only* an "Oriental"?

Howard Ehrlich (1989), writing in the *International Journal of Group Tensions,* states that verbal insults under the guise of humor plague the U.S. workplace. He tells of a janitor who was referred to as the "Black Sambo" by the building manager. The personnel officer similarly addressed his minority employees as "you people" and "your kind." This minority individual was thus robbed of personhood and seen primarily as a member of a group, with all of the accompanying prejudices attached. Ehrlich adds that minority persons not only "disappear" as individuals but are also treated as "invisible."

Ehrlich recalls a literal case of invisibility in which the newsletter published by a firefighters union carried a photograph of the fire chief standing with 23 firefighters who had been cited for heroism. Charles Johnson, the only black in the group, did not appear. His face and upper body had been airbrushed out of the photo though his shoes and part of his legs were still noticeably visible (1989, pp. 74, 77). Removing Johnson from the firefighters photograph was intentional, and it may have seemed humorous to the other firefighters. They certainly demonstrated their disapproval of his presence within their ranks by reminding him that his outstanding performance would still not be enough to warrant inclusion within their circle.

An incident in which unintentional remarks were made, but suitable apologies offered later, occurred on the December 3, 1989, San Francisco radio program hosted by sportscaster Bob Costas. The guest was Art Donovan, a football star in the 1950s, who was also regarded as a "naturally comic ex-jock." As Donovan mentioned his World War II combat experiences, he used the terms familiar to him— "Japs" and "Gooks." Costas says he cringed when he heard the terms, and his show's producer was stunned. Nevertheless, they made the decision to proceed with the program live rather than interrupt and correct Donovan. In response, the station received many telephone calls from irate Asian American listeners to whom the station indeed replied apologetically ("NBC Sportscaster," 1990, p. 1).

The foibles we all make as humans are fair game for humorous jabs. The clumsy and absurd ways we sometimes conduct ourselves at love, work, or play are a fertile source of jokes. But racial caricatures do not have to be assigned to these moments and mannerisms. At its best, ethnic humor is both offensive and funny—it is rarely just funny. Minorities may laugh, but it may be a nervous or ambivalent laughter. At its worst, such humor is strikingly cruel. Though it is out of vogue to make willful and outright racist comments that crack through the veneer of racial tolerance, ethnic humor may be used as a convenient camouflage for expressing intolerance. When this happens, it is no laughing matter.

US AGAINST THEM

We are prone to partition the human race into assemblages of "us" against "them." These divisions have been erected for an infinite number of reasons. Some cast back to national and political affiliations, social and economic hierarchies, or religious and legal dogma. The most perennial, however, may be those associated with race and culture. Introducing these ingredients almost always seems to vilify others by the differences by which we categorize one another.

The Homeless

Many Americans, for example, find it difficult to sympathize with the plight of the homeless. Thirty years ago when most of the homeless were white, over the age of 45, and winos who had dropped out of society, we were more understanding of the misfortunes and broken spirits that they had suffered. But today most of the homeless are minorities, under the age of 45, and outside the mainstream of U.S. culture bearing a wide assortment of problems. As Ferguson reports:

> As the population shifts, the stereotypical image of the old skid row bum meekly extending his palm for change has been replaced by young African-American and Hispanic men, angry at the lack of well-paying jobs, often taking drugs or selling them—or demanding money with a sense of entitlement that passers-by find enraging. (1990a, p. 13)

As the homeless are becoming more numerous and belligerent, Ferguson believes, a class war is brewing. Indigents huddle in the doorways of stores and businesses, stake out ramshackle encampments in city parks such as New York's Tompkins Square and public areas such as San Francisco's United Nations Plaza, and infiltrate crowds of office workers in Atlanta and Washington, D.C. Merchants and ordinary citizens are increasingly annoyed and losing patience. Merchants see their customers being intimidated, and citizens must choose to glance away from the accusing stares of the homeless or must sidestep, even flee, from their advances. Government officials have responded by ordering police sweeps and massive cleanups of public spaces occupied by the homeless.

Ironically, those who have advocated and lobbied the most for the rights and dignity of the homeless, and those who have organized and staffed shelters and programs, have themselves become the primary targets of the disgruntled homeless. Mike Neeley, founder of the Homeless Outreach Project in Los Angeles, explains:

> All too often, services and events are developed by white, middle-class people. But when you look out there, the majority of the homeless are black or brown and have never been middle class and are never gonna be. (As cited in Ferguson, 1990b, p. 14)

"It's almost sublime," says Jim, one of 500 people lined up to receive trays of rice and hot dog casserole in the basement of an inner city San Francisco church. "It's like they want to keep you here—to keep you down" (p. 14). The homeless themselves have therefore begun to organize and assume leadership positions. They are beginning to speak out for houses instead of shelters, jobs instead of welfare, control instead of charity. But some of those who have been at the forefront in the past caution that single homeless men, *especially* young and demanding minorities, are not going to move congressional hearts or generate public outcry.

Fortunately, the chasm between power brokers and homeless minorities is not absolute. The bridges, nonetheless, are both splintered by stop-gap measures and retrofitted by advocating possible long-term solutions. In Oakland, the Dignity Housing Project was opened through the efforts of county officials and federal funds, to the cheers of prospective residents. But in California's richest county, Marin, a proposed system of motel vouchers for the homeless has proved only a temporary solution. Cynics observe that poverty in the U.S. is too visible when the homeless are on the streets where middle-class people travel, shop, and work. By having *inner city* shelters and housing projects, poverty is less glaring and noticeable and therefore more easily forgotten and ignored. Mark Forrester, who gives the homeless a voice through a monthly newsletter, has written:

> They are obvious and that makes us uneasy. When we see them, we see mirrored our failure, failure in a system we insist is fair and humane…and, most distressingly, failure in our personal claims of caring and sharing. The sights mirrored in our homeless do not flatter us… (1990, p. 26)

George Carlin, the counterculture comedian, once asked on stage why houses could not be built on prime land rather than in deteriorated neighborhoods. He pointed to the thousands of meticulously landscaped and maintained golf courses scattered on magnificent sites across the country. Carlin deadpans, is our curious obsession to repeatedly hit a tiny ball into the air with a stick, chase after it, and then knock it into a small hole more important than giving the poor decent homes on decent land? The question, he knows, has already been answered.

It is no wonder that when the homeless are victimized by crime there is generally pity at best—we blame the victim for being unnecessarily vulnerable—or even a sigh in relief at our own sense of safety. There is little empathy or compassion engendered. When the serial murders of vagrants in Los Angeles occurred in the

1980s, for example, it raised minimal concern because the killer confined his activity to *that* population in *that* area of town. It was deemed terrible that a murderer was running loose. But it was gratifying for many others to know that he was only targeting *them.*

One of the most haunting criminal cases I have ever encountered was the rape and murder of an elderly bag lady. This woman had plied her trade of collecting junk, discarded items, and rags from her home base near Third and Broadway streets in Los Angeles. She was a familiar sight as she routinely pushed her worn-out shopping cart everywhere, muttering unintelligibly as lyric accompaniment to the squeaky sounds of her cart. I was a deputy coroner in behavioral analysis at that time. I was horrified when the police related to me that they found this woman murdered in an abandoned tenement. She had been dead for three days. The police, however, had to pry five men off her decomposing body because they were still sexually assaulting her.

Yes, this bag lady lived among those we regard as the dregs of our society. She was defenseless on the streets and perhaps could have found a better life. We do not know what she thought or how she felt about her circumstance. And that is troublesome. We have only to imagine the loneliness and terror that she experienced as she was viciously killed and repeatedly attacked before *and* after dying. But then, she was simply a strange old woman with an unknown minority heritage.

Korean Merchants and Black Customers

In 1960 there were approximately 10,000 Koreans residing in the United States. By 1990 there were 799,000 (U.S. Bureau of the Census, 1997a). The largest concentrations are in New York City, with a population exceeding 74,632, and Los Angeles, with 145,431 (U.S. Bureau of the Census, 1992). These recent immigrants have come mostly from the college-educated middle class, as *yimin* (settlers) rather than sojourners, along with their families. They have come "to breathe the air of freedom" and begin a "new destiny" away from the deterministic tradition and history of their old country (Takaki, 1989, p. 437).

Although many of these immigrants were professionals and white-collar workers in Korea, the United States presented limited opportunity for them to continue in their occupations. Seung Sook Myung, for example, had been a pharmacist in Korea, but became a knitting machine operator in a Los Angeles plant where 90% of the low-wage workers are Korean. A number of physicians are now on staff at big city hospitals, but others are restricted to being orderlies and nurses' assistants. Social scientists have become gardeners and house painters. Salespersons are now gas station attendants and television repairers.

Koreans have also become small business owners and shopkeepers at a remarkable rate. A striking illustration of this fact is that Koreans in 1983 comprised 75% of the 1,200 greengrocers in New York City. As you drive along a stretch of Olympic Boulevard, festooned with Korean signs and bustling with Korean patrons, you will experience being in Seoul instead of midtown Los Angeles. Even in El Paso, Texas, Korean businesses have flourished among the mostly

Mexican American population (Hamann, 1996). Nevertheless, only a very small percentage of Korean immigrants had actually been proprietors in their home country. In the United States, because other areas of employment were not forthcoming, Koreans combined the monetary resources brought from their country and the labor pool of family members to enter into retail and wholesale enterprises. As Takaki comments:

> Korean newcomers have become shopkeepers at a very opportune moment. Middle-class whites have been fleeing to the suburbs and abandoning the inner cities to blacks and Latinos, and older white merchants have been closing their businesses to retreat from the growing ghetto or to retire.... A niche in the retail economy has developed for Koreans to fill. Ironically, they had left white-collar jobs in a modernized economy in Korea and had become old-fashioned shopkeeping capitalists in America. (1989, p. 442)

The particular niche that Koreans have filled, however, has at times brought out violence with members of those communities. Blacks, in particular, have complained that Korean merchants have treated them with disdain, viewing them merely as hoodlums or "welfare queens." They allege Korean shopkeepers refuse to hire them as employees, exploit their neighborhoods through high prices and poor service for quick financial gain, and use excessive force against them when misunderstandings or alleged shoplifting occurs. Blacks also resent the encroachment of Korean shopkeepers when they themselves have difficulty securing loans to start or refurbish their own businesses.

Koreans, on the other hand, point to the vandalism and firebombing of their stores as well as the armed robberies and murders that have occurred against them. Most of their businesses do not hire any outside employees, black or others, because they are dependent on family members for their operation. To open their shops, they sold their homes and possessions in Korea. Their stores therefore represent their dreams but also their vulnerability to fears of failing. This keeps them on guard and quick to respond to any perceived or existing threat, including from those who enter their premises.

This climate of tension has escalated into acts of violence over many years. Attempts by black community leaders and Korean associations to resolve issues have been only periodically successful. Recurring hostilities signal real and obstinate problems. In the Flatbush section of Brooklyn during the spring of 1990, for example, a Haitian woman claimed she was beaten by a Korean grocery store owner. Although the owner denied the charge, a boycott by black residents of the store and another store owned by a Korean were launched. Loud and aggressive picketing, which lasted months, prompted a court ruling barring demonstrations within 50 feet of the stores. In a related incident, a young Vietnamese man was chased and assaulted because he appeared to be Korean.

There are those who believe much of the conflict arises from the language and cultural differences between the Korean people and U.S. blacks. Many of the Korean store owners have limited English-language skills and, because they are first generation immigrants, have not become acculturated to ways in the United States. But others believe that economic rather than cultural factors are the source of friction. There is, they argue, a class disparity between the more educated and prospering Koreans and the majority of their black customers, who lack jobs and are caught in a downward spiral of frustration.

Both perspectives are legitimate. Mistrust often results from miscommunication. When one group is viewed as foreign and unapproachable and the other is viewed with suspicion and disrespect, barriers are cemented. The common ground between Koreans and blacks, however, does exist. Each has been prematurely thrust into interdependence because of larger socioeconomic forces, including racism. For now, blacks must rely on the goods and services of Korean businesses, and these businesses must seek to identify with and not siphon from the communities in which they are located. Korean immigrants, who as a group are strongly motivated to sacrifice for their children by working the long hours demanded by their stores, have faced their own discrimination in the U.S. labor market. They have been pushed into opening shops in low rent and high crime areas, and are caught up in the same ambitions as most blacks. Likewise, blacks desire a means to support their families, are too often excluded from rewarding and fulfilling employment, and know they deserve the same opportunities as others. Each group must stop victimizing the other, for the issues that have been interpreted as separating them are really those of minority status and economic condition, the very conditions that have brought them physically together.

White Straight Males

He is a veteran police officer in his 40s. Thoughtfully, without any rancor in his voice, he states his irritation with continually being the brunt of virulent tirades about white, heterosexual males who cause all others to become disenfranchised. Changes within the makeup of the police department have left him bemused. He now accepts the presence of female, minority, gay, and lesbian officers because, he admits, they have generally proven themselves in the field and are assets in relating to members of "their own group." At the same time, he is nervous that he will blunder by saying an off-color joke that will appear sexist, racist, or homophobic. He is concerned that minorities will be given preferential treatment in promotions and therefore "leapfrog" the years of service he has recorded. He wonders about his personal future as a member of a dwindling group.

There is no doubt that the United States is in a volatile period of social change. White supremacist groups are attempting to forcibly move our nation toward a form of apartheid in which white males will rule, no matter how racially diverse we become. They are bellwethers of fear and hysteria. Their crude and unabashed tactics include arson, physical violence, terrorism, and demagogy. They seek to permanently establish racial separatism by any means necessary. Tom Metzger, a television repairman in Fallbrook, California, for example, is a former Ku Klux Klan grand dragon and founder of the White Aryan Resistance. A civil suit was brought against him for inciting the fatal beating of Mulugeta Seraw, a 27-year-old

Ethiopian who was killed in Portland, Oregon, on November 13, 1988, by three neo-Nazi skinheads. During his trial, Metzger testified:

> I tell the entire white working class of this nation figuratively and literally that they are going to have to kick ass just like our founding fathers did. I make no apologies for that. (Associated Press, 1990c, p. D-14)

A more subtle strategy to retain control, however, has come from some of the bastions of U.S. political and corporate power. This has been particularly evident in the historic underrepresentation of Hispanics in elected government positions in California. Through contrived means to dilute their vote and gerrymandering to preserve the seats of favored incumbents, political officials have restricted Hispanics from fully participating in the electoral process, both as candidates and voters. In 1879, for example, California rescinded an earlier mandate that official documents be published in English and in Spanish. An English-literacy requirement, which was first adopted in 1894 to prevent Asian Americans from voting, was also revived and directed against Mexican Americans in the 1950s and 1960s. "After all," states Joaquín Avila, a key attorney in the Mexican American Legal Defense Fund's advocacy for Latino voting rights, "the very first elections were intended for white males only.... Voting laws [thus] have a long history of exclusion" (as cited in Torres, 1990, p. 20).

The federal Voting Rights Act of 1965 removed many of the obstacles that minorities faced. A 1982 amendment, moreover, allowed those election systems that had a discriminatory effect to be legally challenged. In June of 1990, U.S. District Court Judge David Kenyon not only ruled that prejudice existed but also that the Los Angeles Board of Supervisors had the intent to discriminate in the manner in which district boundaries were drawn. Latinos constituted 36% of the nearly 9 million residents of the county. The Board, however, had split the concentrations of Latino votes so that the dominance of white male supervisors, which has existed for 115 years, would continue as long as possible. Richard Martinez, executive director of the Southwest Voter Registration Project, characterized the actions of the supervisors as one in which "five kings got together and drew the lines to determine their own incumbency" (Hecht, 1990, p. A1).

UCLA demographer Leobardo Estrada, lead counsel Richard Fajardo, Joaquin Avila, and others devised an equitable reapportionment plan and submitted it to the federal courts. Now that the Hispanic community has the opportunity to affect its own destiny and significantly contribute to solving the crucial issues neglected in their neighborhoods, the 1990s are seen by many as the decade of Latino empowerment (as cited in Brazil, 1990, p. A-2).

The higher echelons of the corporate world have also been primarily the reserve of white males. Although the country's work force will be more than half women and minorities by the year 2000, the CEOs, board presidents, and top management of major businesses may very well remain the same. Minorities are "like a fly in the buttermilk" according to some observers (Figuero, 1990a, p. A-25).

As Takaki has written, the United States in the twentieth century is locked in an "iron cage" by huge, bureaucratic corporations. These corporations preach a culture of "individualism" and "meritocracy," which comfortably and intentionally separates races into manageable and competing entities (1987, p. 250). As each person, group, or race thus scrambles to climb the ladder of upward mobility, in the culture of the iron cage, there is the compulsion to weaken or remove the lower rungs rather than joining in manufacturing a sturdier ladder for all. By also being designated and showcased as "model minorities," specific groups have been manipulated to resent one another. There is, however, for these model minorities (such as the "hard-working" and "conformist" Asian Americans) the ever-present glass ceiling through which plum positions can be viewed but rarely reached.

There is little ultimate reward in engaging too far in white male bashing. The way we dismantle the systems and institutions in which injustice is rampant sets the precedent for how any new system or fledgling institution will itself be treated and reformed. But to shy away from accurately depicting the current state of affairs and forthrightly embarking on solutions also benefits no one. The popular journalist Linda Ellerbee beseeched Nelson Mandela—the soul and inspiration of the African National Congress (ANC) and now President of South Africa—during his historic visit to the United States in June of 1990:

> We have this little problem here in America. It's called racism. Or, put another way, hatred. . . . We have black people hating Koreans. We have Hispanic people hating Vietnamese. And, of course, we have white people hating everybody. . . . [I expect] more than hope. More than words. I expect action. Leadership. And I'm not getting it. Not where racism is concerned. . . . but the words of Nelson Mandela, in America *on* America, are just the kind of action we need. Remind us, Mr. Mandela, where it was we intended to go. And why. And soon. (Ellerbee, 1990, p. 6)

Mandela is a commanding symbol of enormous personal sacrifice for the cause of his people. Arrested and imprisoned for 27 years in South Africa for his anti-apartheid stance, he remained courageously steadfast. As Mandela proclaims, "Imprisonment, torture and mass killings shall not undo flames of resistance burning in our hearts" (Hecht, 1990b, p. A-12). Following his unexpected release from a life sentence on February 11, 1990, he continued to speak out for political and economic sanctions against the South African government and its racist policies. He did so without compromise but also with a remarkable absence of bitterness. Mandela and then South African President Frederik de Klerk forged a cooperative union that eventually led to the needed reforms toward democracy.

Although Mandela has not directly addressed racism in this country, he did state during a visit to Harlem:

> The kinship that the ANC feels for the people of Harlem goes deeper than skin color. It is the kinship of our shared African experience and our kinship as victims of blind prejudice and hatred. (As cited in Hinckle, 1990b, p. B-7)

If Mandela and other black South Africans can manage to peacefully achieve parity with the white minority and are able to structure a stable and prosperous government, the symbol for African Americans will be overwhelmingly powerful. Mandela himself, as an internationally respected black African, brings pride and hope to black Americans. As his movement develops into a united and strong South Africa, African Americans will be able to identify positively with a great nation of their homeland.

The pace of social, economic, and other change, whether in South Africa or the United States, however, has always been set according to an intricate formula between the vested interests of those in control and the strivings of those seeking to improve their circumstances. One of the variables in this formula is how far apart we judge ourselves from others. For example, when the AIDS crisis first appeared in the United States and was thought to affect mostly promiscuous gays and needle-using drug addicts, it was slighted by many as the consequence of their immoral and reprehensible lifestyles. AIDS victims acutely felt the impact of suffering with an incurable disease *and* the lack of others' sympathetic response.

Seeing their loved ones wither and perish caused AIDS activists to demand funding for enlightened care, hospice centers, acceleration of research, and public education to allay fears and provide factual information. To many, however, it was apparent that only when increasingly numbers of innocent white children, blood transfusion patients, the famous, and heterosexuals were diagnosed as HIV-positive or having AIDS, and also began to die, that our country's leaders admitted their mistake in minimizing the epidemic and stopped condemning those who contracted the disease.

For some activists, even this conversion has not been enough. "Outing," dragging prominent gays out of the closet and exposing their homosexuality to the public, has become a sensational yet dubious method to slice through hypocrisy. Though recalcitrant to expose their homosexuality, those in the corporate, political, and entertainment world, who have the power to act in a large and immediate fashion but have not exercised it, are being rudely summoned to come forward—or else. For some, this amounts to the "psychological rape" of homosexuals who should be allowed to announce their orientation by choice and not by coercion. To others, desperation calls for confrontation and even rioting to make known the urgency of combating AIDS.

Still, the most visible AIDS activists are white, even though a disproportionate number of AIDS victims are people of color. It is estimated that 18% of AIDS patients are Hispanic and 35% are black (Center for Disease Control [CDC], 1997). The adult/adolescent and pediatric rate of AIDS cases per 100,000 persons by race/ethnicity in 1996 was 89.7 for blacks, 41.3 for Hispanics, 13.5 for whites, 10.7 for American Indian/Alaska Native, and 5.9 for Asian/Pacific Islanders (CDC, 1997). It is also believed that 55% of the women with AIDS are black and that 60% of the AIDS pediatric cases are black children (CDC, 1997). Beth Richie, a New York health educator, offers this sobering commentary:

> Premature death is not a new trend among African-Americans. AIDS, in many ways, is like every other health, social and economic crisis that black people

have faced for generations. What is alarmingly different about AIDS is the severity of the infection and the particularly repressive political timing of the emergence of the disease. The combined effect of all these elements leaves the black community in an extremely vulnerable position. AIDS has the potential to cripple black people in a way that few other health or social forces have since slavery. (1990, p. 183)

Too many Americans are satisfied that minorities remain crippled. The spectre of minorities occupying positions of influence over their lives has often generated fear and disgust. Resistance has come through a labyrinth of programs. The powerful prefer, in other words, to chide the disenfranchised to quit moaning about being victimized and rely more on their own wits and diligence. Shelby Steele (1990) in his book, *The Content of Our Character*, has espoused a similar message. Steele argues that blacks must halt the "fixation" on their own victimization that leaves them with an identity that is at war with their best interests, magnifies oppression, and diminishes the sense of possibility. He calls upon blacks to master their own fate and to support social policies that instill values of self-reliance.

Blaming the disenfranchised for having spurious and self-deprecating alibis for not achieving, however, does little to remove the antecedents of racism and discrimination. There must be a concerted effort by both the powerful *and* the disenfranchised to correct *whatever* impediments exist to a more equitable determination of worth in society.

Homophobic Panic

During his childhood, Rafael's mother would admonish him to refrain from overtly responding to the taunts of other children. "Don't fight, we're Chinese," she would insist. "We don't want to cause any further problems" (San Francisco Human Rights Commission, 1990, p. 256). Now, as an adult living in San Francisco, Rafael has little choice as to whether or not to fight back. He and other minority gays and lesbians experience a double dose of prejudice and violence because of their sexual orientation and racial heritage. Even in the touted liberal atmosphere of the city, lesbians and gays have been the repeated targets of hate-motivated verbal and physical attacks. Skin color and gender preference in intimate relationships have become the insignia of victimization. Rafael is indeed fighting back—with rousing speeches to public officials and commissions and through his active leadership role in the Gay Asian Pacific Alliance. The only problems he is eager to cause are for those who condone gay-bashing or commit ethnoviolence. As Jewelle Gomez agrees:

It's very important that all our voices be heard. Everyone asks why do we have to talk about homophobia? Why can't we be quiet about it? The fact that we have to talk about it means that a whole lot of people don't want to hear it. And as soon as there is something they don't want to hear, it's very important that we say it. I learned that as a Black person. (Gomez & Smith, 1990, p. 212)

Kevin Berrill, director of the Anti-Violence Project of the National Gay and Lesbian Task Force, describes the growth of gay and lesbian activism over the last several decades (Herek & Berrill, 1992, pp. 2–4). In June of 1969, for example, a New York City gay bar called Stonewall Inn was raided by the police. Patrons of the bar interpreted the raid as yet another tactic of police harassment. The riot that ensued is generally regarded as sparking the modern gay rights movement. One of the largest civil rights demonstrations in U.S. history, in fact, was the 1987 march on Washington for Lesbian and Gay Rights. Berrill recounts the march as a drama-tization of gays and lesbians stepping out of the closet of "isolation, suffocation, and self-hatred" to unapologetically acknowledge their identity. Some have called this activism a "flaunting of sexuality," but such visibility has been more a matter of survival in the face of pervasive anti-gay prejudice. To remain hidden is to be denied a positive sense of self and community (Berrill, 1990, p. 1).

Speaking out does incur a cost. There are those who are annoyed that lesbians and gays have broken the political and social code of keeping their lifestyle clos-eted. The AIDS epidemic, moreover, has fanned what Berrill terms a "second epi-demic" of anti-gay violence. The spread of AIDS has led some in our society to unfairly label the openly gay presence in our population as no longer just a "moral problem" but as a deadly menace. Homophobia has increasingly developed a bru-tal dimension. A U.S. Department of Justice study reveals that among the most fre-quent and probable victims of crimes associated with bigotry are homosexuals. The National Gay Task Force estimates that more than 40% of gay men and women have been threatened with violence and that at least 20% of gay men and 10% of lesbians have been physically assaulted. In the San Francisco Bay Area alone, one survey recorded an astonishing 45,000 incidents of hate violence directed against the homosexual population (Berrill, 1985, p. 1).

The majority of homosexuals therefore realistically fear for their safety—and their lives. In Bangor, Maine, a young gay man was assaulted by three teenagers and thrown off a bridge to his death. On Staten Island, New York, another gay man was verbally ridiculed by two assailants and then fatally stabbed. In San Francisco a gay man was killed by a band of ruffians, amid shouts of "faggot" and "queer." In North Carolina three men perceived to be gay were murdered execution-style by members of a hate group.

Violent acts against lesbians are, moreover, riddled with unmistakable sexism. In one incident, a woman in Northampton, Massachusetts, was sexually harassed by three men sitting on a porch of a house diagonally across the street from the home that she shared with two other lesbians. The three men were suspected of dousing a mattress with gasoline and igniting it next to the women's home later that night. The women barely escaped death. In Oakland, California, a woman was sav-agely raped and repeatedly slashed with a knife by a neighbor who ingratiated him-self with her but who concealed that he was a "dyke-buster." He wanted to punish the woman for her "infidelity" to men. In May of 1988, two women hiking on the Appalachian Trail in Pennsylvania were stalked and shot by a male who was enraged at their "blatant lesbianism." One woman died. The murderer reportedly justified that he shot the women because he was ensnared and prompted by their repulsive behavior.

The murders, battery, and rape of lesbian women, according to Jane Caputi of the University of New Mexico and Diana Russell of Mills College, not only fall to the extremes of "homophobic panic" but also exist as forms of "sexist terrorism." They offer the term "femicide" to describe the murder of women by men "motivated by hatred, contempt, pleasure, or sense of ownership of women" (Caputi & Russell, 1990, p. 34). A telling example of femicide was the rampage of Marc Lepine at the University of Montreal on December 6, 1989. Lepine targeted feminists as causing his application to the school of engineering to be denied when those of women were approved. In a half-hour murder spree, he killed 14 female students and wounded nine others in revenge for this particular humiliation and for his overall life failures. As Caputi and Russell comment:

> His [Lepine's] response to the erosion of white male exclusivity was a lethal one. It was also an eminently political one.... *Whether individual hate killers are demented is beside the point.* In a racist and sexist society, psychotics as well as so-called normals frequently act out the ubiquitous racist and misogynist attitudes they repeatedly see legitimized. (1990, p. 34.)

When homophobia intersects racism, the margin of safety becomes even more tenuous. In the words of Joan Weiss, former executive director of the National Institute Against Prejudice and Violence, victims of hate violence are "always vulnerable." They are at risk and never completely safe because they are selected as victims *because of who or what they are* (NIAPV, 1990, p. 1). Minority gays and lesbians are thus susceptible to being cast as inferiors because of "abnormal" gender orientation *and* "faulty" pigmentation. In a peculiar mixture of homophobia and xenophobia, for example, General Motors Corporation produced a promotional video for executives, car dealers, and the media to showcase their 1991 automobile lineup. In the portion meant to highlight the advantages of GEO trucks, a farmer being interviewed described a Japanese-made truck as "that little faggot truck." The slur was clearly intended to depreciate what was "foreign" and "strange" (Figueroa, 1990b, p. A-2).

Concurrently, within their own ethnic communities, homosexuals may encounter hostility based on the erroneous assumption that for homosexuals race is no longer a primary loyalty. Barbara Smith, however, provides a necessary clarification:

> One of the myths that's put out about Black lesbians and gay men is that we go into the white gay community and forsake our racial roots. People say that to be lesbian or gay is to be somehow racially denatured.... We are as Black as anybody ever thought about being. (Gomez & Smith, 1990, p. 212)

Being minority *and* homosexual therefore requires the balancing of the concerns of both of these identities. For minority lesbians and gays, the rights and protection afforded to them must not only reflect the colors of their cultural heritage but also the color purple.

Right to Go Anywhere

Yusuf Hawkins lay dead of gunshot wounds on the corner of 20th Avenue and 69th Street. He was just 16 years old. Only a short while before on that night of August 23, 1989, Yusuf and three friends had come by subway to the New York City neighborhood of Bensonhurst in hopes of buying a used car. But Yusuf and his friends were black. There were no passports issued for their free entrance into this tough, white middle-class area, with a large Italian American population. There was also no easy exit permitted. Thirty white youths, some with baseball bats and golf clubs, attacked the four black teenagers without mercy until they had extinguished Yusuf's life.

In the aftermath, African Americans held a march through Bensonhurst. They were greeted with jeers and curses by the white residents who lined the sidewalks and brandished watermelons. Months later, when Keith Mondello, a 19-year-old defendant, was acquitted on murder and manslaughter and convicted of lesser charges, a second protest through Bensonhurst was staged. The marchers demanded "Justice for Yusuf" and "Death to Racism." Diane Hawkins, Yusuf's mother, was present that eve of Mother's Day because she wanted to see where her son was murdered. Hundreds of Bensonhurst residents shouted back, "White Power" and "Go back to Africa" and carried signs that read, "Do the White Thing" and "Free the Boys from Bensonhurst" (Hinkle, 1990a, p. B-7).

To some, these marches merely heightened tensions and allowed another forum for the ugliness of this country's racial relations. For others there was an overriding need to demonstrate the right of people, including African Americans, to go *anywhere* in the city without fear or harm. David Dinkins, the first black mayor of New York, urged citizens to build a city of "peace and dignity" (Diamond, 1990b, p. A-7).

The murder of Yusuf Hawkins is one of a series of incidents that have placed New York at the front line of interracial warfare. In December of 1986, for example, Michael Griffith, an African American, was chased onto an expressway by a gang of white youths in Howard Beach and killed when he was struck by a car. This brought the attention of the nation to the drama of New York's racial scene.

But New York is not unusual. As Adele Dutton Terrell of the National Institute Against Prejudice and Violence explains, "New York is no better or worse than anywhere else. It's just that you have demographics in New York that throw people into conflict more often" (as cited in Smith, 1990, p. A-10). These demographics reflect the sheer numbers that have inundated the city. Likewise, they show the development of prejudicial attitudes since the 1960s of U.S.-born generations of European immigrants who have attempted to distance themselves from the tide of black and Hispanic emigration from the south, the Caribbean, and Latin America. Communities such as Bensonhurst are efforts to recreate the old lifestyle for the white residents. John Mollenkopf of the City University of New York explains:

They see blacks and Puerto Ricans as having invaded their old neighborhoods and fear the same for their new communities. There is an anger that the old world they struggled for and made is now passing and that they are just not a powerful force anymore. (French, 1989, p. 31)

There is of course a vitality to ethnic neighborhoods that deserves some preservation. Homogeneity of language, customs, and mores is in many ways essential. Bensonhurst itself is a place where the elderly speak in Italian, where young adults gather at dozens of Italian social clubs, and where generations of family members live just down the street from one another. But neighborhood segregation can also obliterate any possibility of meaningful social contact between races. The likelihood increases thereby for misunderstanding, discord, and violence. As the Reverend Vincent Termine, a Catholic priest, has witnessed:

The blacks in the Marlboro project [city housing on the fringe of Bensonhurst] and the white Italian homeowners had never talked to each other. If you don't talk to someone, then you don't know what they are like. (As cited in Diamond, 1990a, p. A-8)

In the gym of Reverend Termine's church, therefore, the Flames youth basketball teams hold practices. The Flames were originally an all-white team that did not win a single game until its coach, Gerard Papa, who had been raised in Bensonhurst, recruited boys from the Marlboro Project. At first there was trouble. The black players were attacked by mobs of white teenagers as they walked the short block and a half from the project to the gym. Papa was often reminded by white Bensonhurst residents that it would be difficult to coach basketball from a hospital bed. Papa, however, refused to quit.

The number of Flames teams grew to 30 with 300 players between the ages of 8 and 20. Prejudices between the Marlboro and Bensonhurst youth have been replaced by teamwork and new understanding. White team members no longer view their teammates as "muggers on welfare," and black members are less resentful of those they had once believed had it easy. There has also been a ripple effect. In the words of Reverend Termine: "First it was the kids on the team getting to know each other. Then it was the parents who went to see the team and interacted with each other. People got to know each other as people" (p. A-8).

Unfortunately, such efforts did not prevent the killing of Yusuf Hawkins. Decades ago Emmett Till, a 14-year-old, was lynched in Mississippi because he supposedly whistled at a white woman. In Bensonhurst many claim that the passions of the white youth were similarly inflamed to murder Yusuf Hawkins because a Bensonhurst girl—referred to by one Bensonhurst woman as a "tramp with her spandex pants with holes in them"—began dating blacks and Hispanics. In other words, as long as blacks "stay in their place" in their housing projects, on the basketball courts, and among "their own kind," there is no problem. But if they venture beyond these limits, they "invite" hostility and even death.

Discrimination and racism, however, are not confined to blue-collar neighborhoods such as Bensonhurst. Polarization exists across the United States and may be worsening. The movement of blacks out of ghettos, for example, has lagged in all regions of our country, in part because the black underclass is growing as a percentage of all blacks and in absolute terms. In this regard, Morton Kondracke has queried:

> The source of the growth is not precisely clear: To what extent are more Blacks being absorbed into the underclass as they become poorer and are caught up in the culture of illegitimacy, drugs and joblessness and to what extent are children simply being born into the underclass and failing to escape? (As cited in Terrell, 1989, pp. 3, 6)

Poverty is not the sole reason that blacks remain segregated from the rest of society. Since 1960, the number of middle-class blacks has nearly tripled. About 1.5 million blacks are managers, business executives, and professionals. Nearly 7,000 hold elected public offices, although this represents only 1.4% of all such officials. One-half of all blacks also own their own homes. But as Michael Woodard of the UCLA Center for Afro-American Studies explains, the black middle class is not happy: "We've done all we were supposed to do. We got educated, we've been frugal and hard-working and still [we're] subjected to discrimination based upon race" (as cited in C. Jones, 1990, p. 6).

A study of the 60 largest U.S. metropolitan areas by University of Chicago sociologist Douglas Massey and researcher Mitchell Eggers did, in fact, find that affluent and middle-income black Americans tend to live in poorer neighborhoods than their non-black counterparts. This means that all blacks, from the affluent to the poor, are more or less clustered together. In San Francisco, for example, according to Jim Jefferson of the Black Chamber of Commerce, blacks of all economic levels live in the Western Addition. The highest concentration of low-income blacks is found in Hunter's Point, but this is also where the highest proportion of black home ownership in the city is located (as cited in Lewis, 1990, p. A-12).

In other words, segregation in housing persists. Although the United States as a whole is becoming increasingly pluralistic, our individual neighborhoods are only slowly reflecting this change. Upward mobility does not spontaneously equate to outward mobility. As Terrell states, the minority underclass and middle class are prevented by prejudice from "buying or renting our way out of inner city neighborhoods" (1989, p. 6). For the white defendants in the Bensonhurst case, African Americans did not have the right to go just anywhere. Apparently, for many others, they also do not have the right to *live* just anywhere.

Yellow Peril Revisited

In 1924 Ogawa Masanobu, 17, arrived in Seattle aboard the steamer *Hawaii Maru*. He had left the town of Kochi, on the island of Shikoku, to seek adventure and a life beyond the social and economic bonds of Meiji-era Japan. With youthful spirit,

Masanobu set out to leave an indelible mark on the "land of promise." He naively dismissed the fact that the *Hawaii Maru* was the last ship permitted entry from Japan following the Asian Exclusion Act passed that year. For the many Japanese pioneers that had preceded him, 1924 was not the year of new beginnings but instead one of discovering the hardened edge of long-standing racial hostility and prejudice.

The Issei (first generation Japanese in the United States) had suffered countless indignities over the more than 30 years since their arrival in the late 1800s. They were denied citizenship and land ownership because they were officially declared "clearly not Caucasian." They were driven into ethnic enclaves because of scorn from the larger society but were then castigated for being clannish and "resistant to assimilation." They were considered the "most dangerous" of all races even though they had contributed immensely to U.S. agriculture by having "moistened the land with their sweat" and having turned wilderness and desert into fertile fields "pregnant with crops" (Takaki, 1989, p. 211).

When the 1924 Exclusion Act was passed, the Issei felt betrayed. The most admirable tradition of the United States, they believed, was the welcoming of all people to its shores. But because they were, in Takaki's words, "strangers from a different shore" than Western Europe, their race was being barred from further immigration. The alleged menace they posed was remarkable considering that the Japanese at that time constituted only one-hundredth of one percent of the U.S. population. Takaki captures the mood of the Issei:

> The 1924 law was a turning point in the lives of the Issei generation. They saw the handwriting on the wall: they had no future in their adopted land, except through their children—the Nisei. The Issei could see that they had been doomed to be foreigners forever, their dreams destroyed and their sweat soaked up in an expanse called America.... Like the carp, which they admired for its inner strength and intrepid spirit, the immigrants had swum against the currents of adversity; still, struggling upstream and climbing waterfalls in search of a calm pool where Japanese might live peacefully in America, they found themselves driven backward. (1989, p. 212)

The young Masanobu, however, stepped seemingly unrestrained into the vast potato fields of the Northwest. Despite his small stature—he was barely five feet tall and weighed just 110 pounds—he grappled with heavy bushels and carried 100-pound bags. On numerous occasions the exertion wrenched muscles and caused blood spots in his urine. Unswayed, Masanobu continued to work his way down the West Coast through Washington and Oregon, into Sacramento and the Central Valley of California, and then to the wholesale produce markets in Los Angeles. The grime and noise of downtown were more appealing to him than the stoop labor and crowded living quarters of migrant work. This new job also offered more individual recognition. Accordingly, because few could pronounce his name, Masanobu was renamed George by his fellow workers.

By the mid-1930s, George had become the produce manager of a Southern California grocery chain called Robert's Markets. At one of the stores he met and courted Tsutako Alice Tanaka, a demure vegetable clerk, who was born and raised in Montebello. They married in 1936, moved to Santa Monica, and opened a "mom and pop" market on the corner of Fourth and Pico, complete with butcher shop and fruit stand. By this time, George had been given yet another American name, Frank, because there was another Japanese employee at Robert's who had already been renamed George. Two Japanese with the same name would create too much confusion for the non-Japanese workers!

As a bachelor, Frank had earned a reputation of living a *bon vivant* lifestyle— driving a Ford roadster, wearing zoot suits, and dating flirtatious women. He now settled into a more expected pattern of thrift and responsible behavior. He and Alice built a modest home in Santa Monica after years of scrimping and saving. Then Japan and America went to war. The despair that the Issei had experienced in 1924 was now even more acutely felt in 1941 by all Japanese Americans. Frank would never again recover the sense of independence and freedom that quickened his heart when he came to the United States as the upstart Masanobu. When he was 17, the doors to this country had been closed *behind* him. Now, coincidentally and ironically on the 17th anniversary of his arrival in the United States, the only doors opening for him were the sentry gates of an internment camp. Ten relocation centers, located in the remote and desolate areas of seven states, including Manzanar in California, became the prisons for 120,000 persons of Japanese ancestry for an indefinite period. As a syndicated columnist for the Hearst newspapers wrote:

> I am for immediate removal of every Japanese on the West Coast to a point deep in the interior. I don't mean a nice part of the interior either. Herd 'em, pack 'em off and give 'em the inside room in the badlands. (As cited in Takaki, 1989, p. 388)

The Ogawas were transported with 10,000 others to Manzanar, a compound of spartan barracks, communal latrines, and mess halls surrounded with barbed-wire and policed by armed soldiers. The internees could bring only as much as they could carry. They were given only a matter of days to evacuate, and many of their businesses, farms, homes, and treasured belongings were lost, never to be recovered. With the brief stroke of a pen, the signing of Executive Order 9066 cancelled the achievements of decades of patient sacrifice and silent suffering. Despite today being known as the "worst wartime blunder" by the United States and the "greatest abridgment of constitutional rights" in U.S. history, the internment was at that time justified on the flimsy basis of military necessity and protection of the civilian population. Present, but not always stated, were the economic interests of others who benefited from the removal of the Japanese, especially in the fishing and truck farming industries, and an outpouring of extreme racial hatred.

Japanese Americans survived the internment and, after the war, began the arduous trek to rebuild their lives. The median age of Issei males at that time was nearly 60, the women 50. For many, the setback was thus too much to overcome. But others set about enduring the racial epithets, housing discrimination, and subservient roles as gardeners, maids, and waiters. Their purpose was not only to pursue individual and familial dreams but to reverse the prevalent negative attitude toward Japanese Americans (Wilson & Hosokawa, 1980, pp. 286–87). Frank and Alice left Manzanar and returned to Santa Monica with two sons born in camp, Masaaki Dennis and Kenji Brian. My father worked as a dishwasher, learned to cook, and eventually became a French chef. My mother found work as a maid, shuffling between the homes of wealthy attorneys, actors, and businessmen to iron their clothes, feed their children, and mop their floors. After many years, she became an assembly-line worker at an electronics plant.

My parents' lives were thus forever altered and their livelihood as independent store owners brought to a halt by the internment. Although my father became a naturalized citizen in 1954, I do not think he ever completely healed from the deep wounds that had been inflicted on his spirit. Before he died in 1988, he absorbed himself with visiting his birthplace and keeping abreast of the latest news stories from Japan. It was as if his aging and failing heart found solace in a distant homeland. My father's most loyal and productive years were rooted in the soil of this country. But the bedrock of racism underlying much of that soil would not allow a firm planting. The United States had displayed its preference for the seeds of only one race.

My parents believed, nevertheless, that perseverance for the sake of their children, *kodomo no tame ni,* would mean a better life for the next generation. Japanese Americans indeed have proven themselves to be dependable citizens, and Japan has developed into the steadiest ally of the United States. At least these were the impressions that once prevailed. The climate of racial tolerance in this country, however, has again revealed its seasonal shifts.

Just as lives were intertwined with the state of relations between Japan and the United States in 1941, the "Japan bashing" of the 1980s and 1990s has had Japanese Americans nervous. As Cressey Nakagawa, former president of the Japanese American Citizens League, stated, many people here cannot or do not distinguish between a Japanese national and a third or fourth generation Japanese American. The Japanese are once more looked on as perilous to the well-being of the country. A *New York Times*/CBS poll published in February of 1990 revealed that 25% of people in the United States feel "generally unfriendly" toward Japan (Burress, 1990, p. A7). An earlier *Newsweek* poll showed that most Americans considered the economic strength of Japan to be more of a threat than the Soviet military (Burress, 1990, p. A7).

In the Silicon Valley, for example, Robert Noyce, the co-inventor of the semiconductor (the tiny chip that is the "oil of the Information Age"), has repeatedly warned of the "predatory nature" of the Japanese in the electronics industry. He has argued that the United States is under siege and must ward off the impending domination by Japan. The facts, he and others present, are that in 1984 United States computer manufacturers such as IBM and Apple controlled the world market with a 79% share, compared to Japan's 9%. In 1988, the margin was 62% to 22%. It was feared that this trend would mean that Japan would overtake the country's market share (as cited in Nesbitt, 1990, D-14).

The Japanese have also been accused of buying up the country through capital investments, real estate purchases, and business transactions. They have been cited for "unfair trade practices" and "unprincipled greed." The strong valuation of the yen has also brought disparaging remarks from many quarters. Glenn Bernbaum, a high-society restaurateur in Manhattan, is said to have been approached by some Japanese shoppers requesting directions to Bloomingdale's Department Store. His reported response was: "Look, if you could find Pearl Harbor, you can certainly find Bloomingdale's" (Burress, 1990, p. A7).

Charles Burress, the insightful San Francisco journalist, in an article entitled "Godzilla Takes America," accurately states the dangers of promoting such fear and loathing of Japan:

> The racial antagonism kindles resentment that not only threatens Japanese people but can extend to Japanese Americans and anyone of Asian descent. When influential Americans help create a pervasive anti-Japanese atmosphere, they furnish encouragement to others who would aim worse racial abuse—both verbal and physical. (1990, p. A7)

In the late afternoon of a summer day in 1982, Vincent Chin, a 27-year-old Chinese American, went to a Detroit bar with two friends to celebrate on the eve of his wedding. Two white autoworkers, Ronald Ebens and his stepson, Michael Nitz, called Chin a "Jap" and a "Nip" and yelled: "It's because of you motherfuckers that we're out of work." A fistfight erupted but Chin managed to leave. Ebens and Nitz, however, secured a baseball bat from the trunk of their car and chased Chin until he was cornered. While Nitz held Chin, Ebens struck him with numerous blows to the knees, chest, and head. Chin died from a shattered skull.

The two defendants were charged by the Wayne County District Attorney's office with second degree murder. In March of 1983, they both entered pleas to the charge of manslaughter. Circuit Court Judge Charles Kaufman sentenced both Ebens and Nitz to three years probation and a fine of $3,780 each (U.S. Commission on Civil Rights, 1986, p. 43).

Lily Chin, Vincent's mother, cried out at the injustice meted out. Her only son was killed, and his murderers would not spend a single day in prison. Her outrage and shock were shared by Asian Americans across the country. Chinese Americans especially were disturbed that the events of 1882, the year of the Chinese Exclusion Act, would reappear in almost the exact form one hundred years later. In San Francisco's Chinatown in 1882, an angry lynch mob had shouted, "Kill the foreigners to save our jobs! The Chinese must go!" (Takaki, 1989, p. 483).

Asian Americans and their supporters demanded an investigation of Chin's death by the U.S. Department of Justice. A Federal grand jury eventually returned indictments against both defendants for civil rights violations. On June 28, 1984, a U.S. district court jury convicted Ebens but acquitted Nitz. On September 18, Ebens was sentenced to 25 years in prison. But one year later, a U.S. Court of Appeals overturned the conviction, forcing a retrial. The trial ended in May of 1987, when a jury in Cincinnati, Ohio, acquitted Ebens (Attorney General's Asian and Pacific Islander Advisory Committee, 1988, p. 44).

The corporate executives of the automobile industry may also bear partial responsibility for the murder of Vincent Chin. Inflammatory campaigns against buying Japanese cars and bumper stickers that read "Unemployment—Made in Japan" and "Toyota–Datsun–Honda–and–Pearl Harbor" only serve to agitate and mislead threatened American workers. U.S. auto manufacturers in fact have themselves located major plants outside the country. One such plant at Ciudad Juarez is referred to as the "little Detroit" of Mexico. They have also invested in the very Japanese companies that they are lambasting. General Motors owns 34% of Isuzu, Ford 25% of Mazda, and Chrysler 15% of Mitsubishi. Many Japanese auto makers are moreover contracted to build "American" cars for their U.S. counterparts.

The other areas in which Japan is seen as capricious and unscrupulous also distort the facts. Japan, for example, gives more foreign aid than any other country, including the United States. Japanese firms, in addition, have been generous to U.S. charities, including being the third-largest donors to the United Way. After the October 1989 San Francisco earthquake, more than half of the donations given to the city for earthquake relief came from Japanese sources and the largest single amount was from San Francisco's sister city of Osaka (Burress, 1990).

Furthermore, there are more British investments in the United States than Japanese, and Canadians own 26% of the foreign-owned real estate, compared to 15% by the Japanese. The Japanese purchase of New York's famed Rockefeller Center did, of course, pique national interest. But the British buy-out of Holiday Inn, "America's Innkeepers," caused far less publicity or alarm. To many observers there is more than a hint of racism present in the difference. As Burress recommends:

> It is not a radical idea to suggest that the Japanese possess as much complexity and human decency as we do. Like people of every nation, they are more inclined to cooperate if we approach them with respect as equals, good will and a sincere desire to understand how they see the world. Why not focus on the riches we can exchange as friends? (1990, p. A7)

Hostilities toward Asian Americans based on attitudes toward Asian countries, however, are not restricted to Japanese Americans and Japan. Jim Loo and his friends, all Chinese American students, were in a Raleigh, North Carolina, billiards parlor on the night of July 29, 1989. As they were playing, Robert Piche and his brother Lloyd began cursing at them, calling them "gooks" from Vietnam. The Piches attempted to instigate a fight, but Loo and his friends refused. Robert Piche then retrieved a shotgun from his car and aimed it at Lanh Tang, one of Loo's friends; it misfired. Lloyd Piche immediately grabbed Tang and held him while his brother swung the shotgun at Tang's head, missing twice. Tang was able to free himself and fled.

Robert Piche went again to his car and obtained a handgun. He ran toward Loo and, swinging the gun, struck him in the head. Loo fell, smashing his face on a beer bottle. Splintered facial bones pierced his brain. Loo died shortly thereafter. As he was arrested and being transported to jail, Piche screamed: "I got enough of those gooks in Vietnam, and when I get out I'm going to kill them."

On March 19, 1990, a jury found Robert Piche guilty of second degree murder. As he sentenced Piche to 35 years in prison, Wake Forest Superior Court Judge Arnold Manning, Jr. admonished Piche: "Because your behavior was motivated by hatred for people from Vietnam, this case takes a leap into hyperspace." Lloyd Piche received a two-month sentence on misdemeanor charges. On May 11, 1990, a delegation of prominent Asian American community leaders and attorneys met with representatives of the Civil Rights Division of the U.S. Department of Justice. Because North Carolina lacked a relevant civil rights statute, the Piches were not prosecuted for any such violations. The delegation urged, therefore, that the Department of Justice initiate prosecution under federal laws.

Lloyd Piche was prosecuted by the North Carolina U.S. Attorney's Office under Federal Code 18-2 USC 24 ("interference with the federally protected right of activity") and convicted on July 15, 1991. In October of 1991, he was sentenced to four years in prison with five years supervision on release and ordered to pay $28,000 in restitution to the victim's family. Piche appealed, but his conviction was affirmed. He was resentenced to 70 months in prison but his restitution was reduced to $4,750 (S. Darnell, personal communication, 1997).

There have been numerous other instances of violence directed against Southeast Asian refugees across the United States. In May 1983, Thong Huynh, a Vietnamese high school student in Davis, California, was stabbed to death by a white student. The campus had been the scene of prior racial altercations, slurs, and tension. Several months after the killing, a memorial built near where Huynh died was spray-painted with swastikas and the words, "Death to Gooks." The defendant, however, was convicted of voluntary manslaughter with no reference to racial hatred as motivating the crime and sentenced to six years in the California Youth Offenders Program. The district attorney's omission of racism as an issue, the level of conviction, and the light sentence in the case caused Asian Americans to question the commitment of the criminal justice system to respond to such crimes (U.S. Commission on Civil Rights, n.d., pp. 44–45).

Physical violence, verbal harassment, and racial threats have moreover victimized Vietnamese fishermen in Bodega Bay and Monterey, California, Galveston Bay and the Gulf Coast of Texas, and the Florida coastline over a period of more than 10 years. The "illegal and unfair practices" of the Vietnamese, caused by them being unfamiliar with U.S. fishing and marine regulations, and the threat of them encroaching on waters claimed by competitors in the fishing industry have led local white and Hispanic fishermen to counter with vandalism, arson, and personal assaults.

In Seadrift, Texas, in 1979, the conflict resulted in the shooting death of a white fisherman after an argument over the placement of crab traps. Within three hours, three Vietnamese boats were burned, a home firebombed, and a bomb attempt reported at a packing house that employed Vietnamese people. The two Vietnamese who had been arrested for the shooting were later acquitted. In response, some of the white fishermen sought the assistance of the Ku Klux Klan (U.S. Commission on Civil Rights, n.d., pp. 51–52).

On April 22, 1990, two University of Wisconsin students from Japan were physically assaulted in La Crosse. Taro Imamura and Yasushi Kikuchi, both 21, were returning from a party given for another foreign student when a group of six white men, believing that the two were Hmong refugees, began making racial taunts and slurs. They commenced to punch and kick Imamura and Kikuchi. Two white women who witnessed the attack, one a probation officer and the other a county social worker, tried to intervene. The offenders laughed at them and justified what they were doing by saying they hated "gooks." After the assault, Imamura and Kikuchi were taken to the hospital for treatment. The two assailants, Thomas Forer and Steve Johnson, were apprehended. Forer had no charges filed against him. Johnson was found guilty of battery on April 15, 1991, and received thirty days in jail with work leave and two years probation (S. Darnell, personal communication, 1997).

Imamura had heard about the prejudice toward the Hmong. He had a Hmong roommate and he taught English to the Hmong through the Friendship Program of a local Episcopalian church. He called those who attacked him cowards and expressed sorrow for the Hmong people:

> In my country, no one could be proud of six against two in a fight.... All I want to do is learn and study here. I want no trouble.... I can always go back to Japan, but Hmong people can never leave. They are now Americans. ("Japanese Students," 1990, pp. 1, 5)

Cambodians in Revere, Massachusetts, Hmong in Philadelphia, and Laotians in Fort Dodge, Iowa, are just a few of the other Southeast Asian populations against whom acts of hate violence have occurred. The "yellow peril" may now be viewed differently than 50 or 100 years ago, and the "yellow hordes" may have diversified from only Chinese and Japanese to include Koreans and all Southeast Asians. But the sapping of the political, economic, and social strength of the United States does not emanate from the East. That is done by a more tenacious adversary called racism.

RACISM AND CRIME

Charles Stuart Is Not a Black Male

Charles Stuart and his pregnant wife Carol had just left a childbirth class at a Boston hospital on the night of October 23, 1989. While stopped at an intersection in the Mission Hill district, a racially-mixed neighborhood, a black man forced his way into the car armed with a gun. He demanded cash and jewelry. Shortly thereafter, Carol Stuart lay slumped on the front passenger seat dying from a gunshot to the head. Her husband, seriously wounded in the stomach, desperately summoned help over his mobile phone. What followed was an onslaught of racial tensions, media frenzy, and political and criminal justice pie-in-the-face (Alter & Starr, 1990, p. 21).

Carol Stuart was seven and one half months pregnant when she died. Her son Christopher was delivered by emergency Caesarean section and lived just 17 days. Charles Stuart was hospitalized and recovered from his wounds. His story of what happened the night of his wife's murder gripped Boston and the nation and emblazoned across TV screens one of the worst scenarios that much of our society fears—the brutal and senseless attack of a virtuous and innocent couple by a violent black male. Fear and outrage erupted. Quickly, Stuart was not only perceived as the victim of a grisly crime but also the tragic and grieving hero who represented good versus evil (Mann, 1990, p. C-4).

Stuart's story, however, began to unravel over time. His brother eventually came forth and confessed to his complicity in the chilling plot devised by Stuart to kill his wife. On January 4, 1990, Stuart, by then under suspicion as the villain in his wife's murder, leaped to his own death from the Tobin Bridge into the Mystic River 145 feet below. The consequences of his deceit did not end with his suicide. Based on Stuart's story, which included the idea that he and his wife were shot because their attacker saw his car phone and thought he was a police officer, the Boston police had embarked on a massive sweep of black neighborhoods. They stopped and questioned numerous young black males at random. One, William Bennett, an admitted career criminal, was arrested. Stuart identified him as looking "most like" the assailant. An indictment against him was being prepared at the time of Stuart's suicide (Martz, 1990, p. 18).

Reverberations were immediately felt. The police were suspected of fabricating evidence against Bennett under public pressure. Government officials, including Boston's mayor, were accused of too readily accepting Stuart's story and inflaming rather than controlling racial unrest. The press was laid bare for its "pack mentality" in printing stray rumors and abandoning journalistic standards to sell sensationalism to its predominantly white readership.

Stuart's story was primarily successful because it was concocted to exploit deep-seated fears about race and crime. Boston has a long history as a cauldron of race relations, periodically spilling over in violent anti-busing demonstrations and hate violence. Many felt that if Carol Stuart had been black, her murder would have received scant attention. Many also feel that if William Bennett had been mistakenly prosecuted, he would have been convicted for a murder he did not commit.

The too easy identification of violent crime with black males that Stuart used to deflect investigation away from himself is not, of course, restricted only to Boston. Many in urban areas of the United States know that black males commit a disproportionate amount of violent crimes. This is not denied by the black communities themselves. But what is vitally important is what one does with this fact. A 79-year-old white woman in Georgia, for example, commenting on Andrew Young's 1990 bid for state governor, offered, "He's probably one of the smartest black people around. But I don't know. He used to be mayor of Atlanta, and that downtown Atlanta, well, it's full of blacks. That downtown's scary" (Schmich, 1990, p. A-4). Susan Smith, convicted in Union, South Carolina, in 1994 for the drowning death of her two sons, 3-year-old Michael and 14-month-old Alexander, had first told police a black man forced her at gunpoint from her car and kidnapped her children.

Using a composite described by Smith, law enforcement officials launched a nationwide search. Racial tensions mounted as several black men were detained in the Union area. After Smith confessed, her family apologized to the black community (Vobejda, 1994, p. A8).

Charles Stuart and all those who heedlessly swallowed his story heat this climate of danger and widen divisions between the races. They also help to create a lack of sympathy for black and other minority victims by elevating the trauma and devastation felt by whites victimized by "crazed" blacks. As William Raspberry has stated, an accusation against a black man can seem an accusation against black *men* (1994, p. A19). The sensibility of Carol Stuart's family, the DiMaitis, is therefore significant and constructive. The Carol DiMaiti Foundation, Inc. was established and announced just three weeks after Charles Stuart's death. The Foundation, in an effort to "promote better race relations throughout the city and greater Boston," grants college scholarships to students from the Mission Hill area where Carol Stuart was killed and which had received so much notoriety.

Donations and letters arrived from all across the country expressing sadness and compassion for the DiMaiti family. Along with small and large donations came expressions of shared grief. One couple mailed a $10 check with the note: "My wife and I lost our 18-year-old son in December, 1984. He was shot to death, and his girlfriend was raped. They have never found his killer, and after five years, we still live with this every day" (Mehren, 1990, p. 19).

Certainly the DiMaiti family could have retreated into a private grief. Their world was horribly altered and cruelly manipulated by Charles Stuart. But the DiMaitis are an example of people who came together and worked for better understanding rather than deepening mistrust. As Carl DiMaiti, Carol's brother, explains, "I think there's an unspoken bond between us and the residents of Mission Hill. An unspoken bond as victims" (p. 19).

Killing Fields

It was 11:40 A.M., Tuesday, January 17, 1989, and the students at Cleveland Elementary School in Stockton, California, were absorbed in playground activities during primary recess. They were entirely unaware of the white 26-year-old drifter, Patrick Purdy, who approached them dressed in paramilitary clothing and armed with an AK-47 style assault rifle. From the corner of a cluster of portable classrooms, Purdy raised the rifle to his waist and sprayed 66 rounds into the crowd of 300 children on the playground at that time. Terrified and screaming, the children ran for safety. Many of them, nonetheless, were hit directly or by bullets madly ricocheting off the playground's asphalt. Purdy then dashed to another vantage point, expended the remaining nine rounds of his 75-round magazine, reloaded with a 30-round magazine, and began firing once more. Hearing the sound of police sirens, Purdy dropped the rifle and without hesitation fired a fatal shot from his 9mm pistol into his right temple.

In less than two minutes, five children were dead and 29 children and one teacher were wounded. No one was prepared for such an enormous tragedy. Disbelief and shock were felt throughout the city of Stockton, the state, and the nation. At the same time, explanations for what had occurred were quickly offered. Gun control proponents placed much of the blame on the easy availability of "deadly weapons of war." Purdy had suffered a history of mental illness, criminal offenses, and drug dependency, but in Oregon he was able to purchase the AK-47 assault rifle. In Connecticut, he bought the 75-round drum and 30-round magazines and 10 boxes of ammunition. In California, he secured the 9mm handgun. All of the purchases were legal and over-the-counter.

How could such a person, or in fact any private citizen, so easily possess a firearm that was designed to kill and maim persons? As the State Attorney General's official report on the Stockton shooting states: "Patrick Purdy's murderous rampage could not have happened as it did without the weaponry he was able to purchase quite legally" (as cited in Kempsky, 1989, p. 18). The force of such arguments and the undeniable horror of the shooting of the schoolchildren eventually helped lead to a ban on the sale of assault rifles in California (Hanaver, 1990, p. D-4).

Another explanation for the shooting was even more controversial and compelling. Four of the slain children were Cambodian; the other one was Vietnamese. Sixty-nine percent of Purdy's victims were Southeast Asian and 25% were Caucasian. A Native American child and a Hispanic child were also among the wounded. All of the children were between the ages of six and nine. Because the majority of Purdy's victims and 70% of the 970 children at Cleveland School were of Southeast Asian families, many citizens determined that Purdy was a deranged racist whose hatred was particularly aimed at Cambodians and Vietnamese. Was it a cruel coincidence or part of Purdy's plan that the preceding day had been a school holiday—the celebration of the birthday of Martin Luther King, Jr.? The State Attorney General's investigation concluded:

> He [Purdy] blamed all minorities for his failings, and selected Southeast Asians because they were the minority with whom he was most in contact. It appears probable that his planning finally centered on Cleveland School because it has a majority population of Southeast Asian children, because it was a school which he had once attended and because children were the most vulnerable target he could attack.... Patrick Purdy grew up in a disturbed family setting.... He became a young man with virtually no self-esteem and a high level of anger at the world around him.... There is no indication that Purdy acted in conjunction with any hate group.... He was essentially a loner. (As cited in Kempsky, 1989, p. 2)

Although school teachers initially tried to reassure their students that the shooting was a single, isolated incident committed by an individual who was now dead, many of the families of the victims felt differently. Most of the Cleveland schoolchildren are Cambodian. Their families had fled their country during the murderous reign of the Khmer Rouge. They settled in the San Joaquin Valley in the late 1970s because of the area's mild climate and delta landscape, not unlike their homeland. For the approximately 11,000 Cambodians living in Stockton, there were real and persistent fears that the threat to them was not buried with Purdy. The father of one of the murdered children expressed his worry that Purdy was part of some conspiracy to exterminate all Southeast Asians. Another father, whose daughter was killed, wept and said, "I feel like I try to escape the killing fields in Cambodia, but here is only more killing field for my family" (Fitzgerald, 1989, p. A-10).

The United States was no longer the safe haven for which these refugees had hoped. They had already experienced social and economic hardships and language barriers in the United States. They did not expect the slaughter of their loved ones to continue. But the Cleveland School shooting not only alarmed the Southeast Asian community, it also thrust them into a media blitz, an outpouring of support, and a deluge of attention from political dignitaries, government agencies, social workers, and therapists (D. Batres, personal communication, January 30, 1990).

The Cambodians, who had lived "hidden" in housing projects and who worked in unglamorous jobs, suddenly saw their faces and names printed in newspapers and magazines and aired on radio and television. Even music superstar Michael Jackson made a whirlwind tour of the school and the hospital where some of the children were still being treated. The children were generally in awe of his presence. Jackson's appearance, however, elicited both excitement and bewilderment (Feist & Hedgecock, 1989, p. A-1). The Cambodian families were appreciative of such gestures but were somewhat timid. Receiving so much attention was new to their experience in the United States and a departure from the norms of their culture. Asians are usually humble and uncomfortable with any public demonstration that conveys that their own suffering is greater or more serious than that of others.

The support offered to the Southeast Asians, moreover, included both fumbling attempts to provide mental health services and a heightened awareness of how Southeast Asians cope with crisis and suffering. For months after the shooting, parents of white children at Cleveland School demanded services and expressed unhappiness about the lack of counseling resources or school security measures. The Southeast Asians, of course, cared equally for the well-being of their children but they rarely asked for anything or complained (D. Batres, personal communication, 1990).

This did not mean that they suffered in complete silence. The Western concept of telling a stranger—albeit a mental health professional, social worker, or psychiatrist—how you are feeling would be peculiar for any Southeast Asian. It is instead customary to rely on a trusted friend, relative, or monk. It was necessary, therefore, to establish a relationship of trust with the Southeast Asian families in Stockton before any true services could be provided. The nature of these services was also determined by the needs of the families and not derived from one concept of *mental* health. In many ways, it was the respect shown by others for their religious rituals and their new-found notice and acceptance by the larger community that made the critical difference for these families.

The parents of the murdered children, for example, wanted a joint Buddhist service. Patricia Busher, the principal at Cleveland School, and Diane Batres, director of the San Joaquin District Attorney's Victim Assistance Program, were both instrumental in assuring that the funeral arrangements were appropriate. They gave instructions to the victim advocates such as not to hug the grieving parents because physical contact from strangers is only slowly accepted, never walk in front of a monk or try to shake his hand, and remove one's shoes before entering a Southeast Asian home.

Approximately 4,000 people attended the funeral, including then California Governor George Deukmejian. The funeral proved that caring and dedicated service providers, by making necessary adjustments, could reach a previously isolated and unfamiliar group of people. An additional misunderstanding arose when an item of jewelry was mislaid prior to burial rather than placed in a casket of one of the children, according to Cambodian custom and the parents' wishes. Once the casket was closed and buried, it could not be exhumed according to state law. Apologies were made and, equally important, victim advocates understood their wishes and were committed not to make the same mistake again.

Several weeks after the shooting, the Venerable Dharmawara Mahathera, a 100-year-old Buddhist monk, came to the school to chant scripture and sprinkle holy water on the playground where the children were shot (Roark, 1990, p. A-28). A Cambodian boy had reported seeing the ghosts of his slain classmates. This was not a hallucination. Many Asians, as well as people of other cultures, accept the existence of the realm of spirits and often experience seeing or sensing the spirits of deceased loved ones. The spirits of the dead children, because they had died unnaturally and violently, were not at rest. The purification of the playground and later the religious ceremony held the traditional 100 days after the deaths were meant to release the children's spirits from the "intermediate state" between life and death. They thereafter would be free for reincarnation. To some outsiders, these may appear to be primitive rituals. But to the Southeast Asians they provided the major sources of comfort in their painful loss, knowing that their children could now pass into another life.

The Southeast Asians have also been helped by the change of attitude toward them by the larger community. There are some who resent the attention the Southeast Asians received, and they have criticized Patricia Busher, for example, of "bending over backwards" for them. Many others, nonetheless, felt that "walls have been broken down" to give a better understanding of the Cambodian people and more of a willingness to learn about their culture (Gross, 1989, p. 11).

Perhaps the most important long-term service that can be made to the Cambodian people themselves, however, is to guarantee that the "killing fields" of Cambodia, which re-emerged in Stockton on January 17, 1989, do not continue to destroy them through any form of assimilation that eliminates their culture. This can be accomplished by providing equal opportunities for their children to find a secure place in life in the United States *and* some means for the Cambodians to preserve pride in their customs and lifeways. Anne Roark, a journalist, has captured the essence of their cultural struggle in her account of a 13-year-old Cambodian girl whose best friend's sister was killed by Purdy:

> Early every morning, she races off to the kindergarten class where she helps the American teacher translate into English what the children are saying in Cambodian. She likes it, she said, because the children tell her their fears and

she can tell them her dreams. "I dream we play and no one will come and shoot. I dream there is no mean men to do no good. I dream it's going to get better." And when she grows up, does she want to become a teacher too? With a grin big enough to span two cultures on one little face, she replied, "That, or a counselor." (Roark, 1990, A-29)

Hooty Croy

The prosecutor called it a smoke screen. The defense attorney called it a smoke signal. Was the murder trial of Patrick "Hooty" Croy a simple case of a "drunken Indian" killing a Northern California lawman? Or was it a historic moment in which the United States criminal justice system itself was summoned to deliberate on the fierce racism that had decimated Native American culture for 150 years? According to the prosecutor, Gary Rossi, any diversion from the actual events that occurred on the night of July 16, 1978, in Siskiyou County that ended in the death of deputy sheriff Jesse Joe "Bo" Hittson would be a travesty of justice. According to Croy's attorney, J. Tony Serra, injustice would have been perpetuated had the events of that night not been viewed in the light of the Native American struggle— as the culmination of a history of extermination and mistreatment of Native Americans in Northern California since the Gold Rush.

The prosecution's version was that Hooty Croy, a Karuk-Shasta, and four relatives spent a weekend of smoking marijuana, drinking whiskey, and whooping it up late at night. They then went on a warpath, robbing the Sports and Spirits Liquor Store in Yreka and fleeing in their aging Pontiac sedan. They were soon chased, with the sirens of the town police screaming, down Route 263 and onto a dirt road called Rocky Gulch. They were headed for Croy's grandmother's house, an old cabin in the foothills of Badger Mountain. There Croy and his sister Norma Jean and his cousin Darell Jones jumped out of the car and scrambled up a chaparral-covered ridge with the intent to bushwhack their pursuers, a contingent of Yreka town police, county sheriffs, and California Highway Patrol officers. During a lull, Croy stripped to his waist like a half-naked warrior, then crept to the rear of the cabin with a .22 caliber rifle in hand. Deputy Sheriff Hittson confronted him, and Croy shot him fatally in the heart. After Croy himself was wounded, he and his relatives finally surrendered.

The prosecution's version was believed by an all-white Yreka jury in 1979. Croy was convicted of first-degree murder and sent to San Quentin's death row. His co-defendants were convicted of lesser homicide charges. His sister was sentenced to a life term and transported to the California Institution for Women in San Bernardino County whereas the others (Jones, Carol Thom, and Jasper Alford) received lesser terms. In 1985, however, the state Supreme Court overturned Croy's conviction and ordered a new trial on the grounds that Placer County Superior Court Judge Keith Sparks had given incorrect instructions to the jury. Croy's attorney later successfully changed the venue to San Francisco for the second trial, which began in September of 1989. The precedent was thereby established for a "cultural defense" argument.

During the first trial, Croy was defended by a former prosecutor, whom Croy claimed he did not trust because he was racist and was known for prosecuting Native Americans. But his new attorney was Tony Serra, a long-haired, silver-tongued crusader reputed as an impassioned and legendary champion of sixties' idealism. Serra could charm and sway juries with his peculiar courtroom style of forging together drama, logic, and moral outrage. He eschewed what he termed the "dry, technical linguistics of the law" and abhorred what he perceived as the way the legal profession capitulated to the wealthy, business pragmatists who governed in U.S. society. The true calling and "metaphysical appointment" of a lawyer, according to Serra, is the "romance of the law," to argue boldly in the defense of freedoms (Talbot, 1990, p. 9).

Serra's (in)famous murder cases have included the trial of Huey Newton of the Black Panther Party for the killing of a prostitute, Russell Little of the Symbionese Liberation Army for the assassination of Oakland school superintendent Marcus Foster, Jacques Rogiers of the New World Liberation Front for his mad bombing escapades, and Chol Soo Lee for a Chinatown homicide. This last trial inspired the 1988 movie, *True Believer,* starring James Wood.

Needless to say, Serra's account of what happened 11 years previously was vastly different from the prosecution's. The story began not when that first puff of weed or initial swig of alcohol was taken by Croy or his relatives. The story traced back to the Gold Rush days when thousands of greedy miners converged on the peaceful valleys of Northwest California, rampaging across Native American territories. Vigilante groups marched out from towns such as Yreka to slaughter the Natives who impeded them; local governments paid 50-cent bounties for Native American scalps and heads; Native Americans were invited to celebrate a treaty and then fed poisoned meat; Native American children were kidnapped and sold as sexual slaves and beasts of burden; Native American babies were killed by having their brains bashed out against tree trunks.

These horrors did not end with the bloody Modoc war of the 1870s, which culminated in the near-extinction of the tribe and the heads of executed Native American leaders being shipped to the Smithsonian for study. According to Serra and his witnesses, including Native American scholars and residents of Siskiyou County, intense and unmitigated hatred for them has continued to this day. Racist articles and cartoons have been printed in local newspapers; Native American schoolchildren have been beaten by white students and teachers; the police have harassed the Native American population.

That night in July, Serra argued, there was no robbery or murder. Croy, just 23 at that time, should never have been charged. Croy had stopped for beer before going night-hunting for deer. There had been a minor altercation at the store between Croy and the white clerk over the proper change owed. The clerk had fabricated the robbery to collect insurance money to cover damages incurred during the dispute and because he disliked Native Americans. The ensuing chase by the police frightened Croy, who from childhood had suffered beatings at the hands of abusive grade school teachers and police officers. He had also been haunted by the stories his grandmother told him of the tragedies that the Shastas and Karuks had endured and the Humbug massacres that took place not far from her cabin, a time when the rivers ran red with the blood of their people.

Croy therefore knew that the law did not exist to safeguard Native populations. Mining and timber companies were instead protected though they obliterated Native American sources of food, the forests, and water ways. White townspeople were protected through harsh and swift means used against Native American trouble-makers. As Serra explained:

> Hooty never cooperated with authority because he never trusted authority, because authority was always the symbol of oppressor…the symbol of those who had killed his forebears and taken a culture and stripped it of all meaning and value. (As cited in Chin, 1990c, p. A-11)

Croy and his relatives, Serra continued, fled literally for their lives. He described the scene as a wild and ragtag cavalry of 27 law enforcement officers charging after three young Natives racing up a hill to safety:

> There is complete chaos in the quarters of the police, no chain of command, just unbridled, random destruction—a mob scene. All of them shooting, shooting at anything that moved, AR-15's, handguns, shotguns, M-16's, semi-automatic weapons. They [Croy and his relatives] were like animals under fire! In their minds they knew they were going to die. Because what was in their minds was the history of relations with the white settlers, the genocide, 95 percent of the Indians *wiped out* in that area. (As cited in Talbot, 1990, p. 8)

Serra dramatizes the scene as follows to bring the jury into the mind of Croy that night: Jones is wounded in the groin. Croy believes that his sister, who had been shot in the back, is dead. He fears for his grandmother and elderly aunt inside the cabin, which may be engulfed in flying bullets. He retrieves the hunting rifle thrown to the side by Jones—the single weapon in their possession. He removes his T-shirt and shoes to move undetected along the ridge to rescue his elders. He knows the area well because he would often wander there at night like an owl—the reason for his nickname. When he reaches the rear of the cabin and is preparing to enter a window, deputy sheriff Hittson surprises him from behind. Hittson immediately shoots Croy twice—in the back, the buttocks, and forearm—with his .357 magnum. Croy turns and fires one shot, killing the deputy.

Serra urged the jury to judge Croy's actions as self-defense and therefore the right of any citizen when excessive force is used against him or her by law enforcement officials. Croy symbolizes an "aggrieved Indian," who illuminates generations of treachery, discrimination, and violence against his people. Although presiding Judge Edward Stern reminded Serra that the court was not a classroom for history lessons, he allowed Serra's indictment of racism to span three weeks because, he told the jury, it was relevant to the extent it "seeped into the consciousness" of the defendant and affected his state of mind that night.

Prosecutor Rossi subsequently attempted to discredit Croy by portraying him as the stereotypic drunken Native American with long-braided hair and cold, empty eyes. He led Croy to recount at length the large amounts of marijuana and alcohol consumed the weekend of the shooting. Croy's most telling response to cross-examination, however, was perhaps this emotional statement: "I realized that all the things my grandmother and father had told us was coming true, that they were going to kill us all" (as cited in Talbot, 1990, p. 11).

In the rebuttal phase of the trial, the prosecution offered the testimony of Siskiyou County Sheriff Charlie Byrd, the first elected black sheriff in California. In order to cast doubt on Serra's rendering of Yreka and its environs as a seething and dangerous kettle of racial unrest, Rossi guided Byrd to say that he had never himself experienced any prejudice. He was born and raised in Weed and was that town's police chief before being elected sheriff.

Serra's cross-examination of Byrd aimed at having him admit to his unique status in the predominantly white county:

QUESTION: How many black families lived in Yreka before 1978?

ANSWER: One family.

QUESTION: How many blacks were there on the Weed police force when you first joined up?

ANSWER: None.

QUESTION: When you became chief of police, how many blacks were on the force?

ANSWER: None.

QUESTION: And you don't regard yourself as unique?

ANSWER: No.

Serra next drew the attention of Byrd to an incident when the sheriff was just 19 years old and had been charged by a white police officer in Weed with resisting arrest.

QUESTION: But you didn't resist arrest, did you?

ANSWER: No.

QUESTION: And you went to court and won, you were found not guilty, isn't that right?

ANSWER: Yes. (As cited in Talbot, 1990, p. 12)

To Sheriff Byrd's credit, he answered Serra's questions forthrightly and without wavering. His honesty could not be manipulated by the prosecution or assailed by the defense.

In his closing argument, Serra brought out a long-stemmed white flower and began plucking it one petal at a time. The flower represented the once-blossoming

Native American civilization that had been made barren by the white man. The flower was not dead, he said, but it needed the opportunity to flourish once again. They, the jurors, were critical to restoring some measure of fairness not only for the sake of Hooty Croy but also for all Native Americans. Native Americans had learned disdain for the legal system of the United States but in this trial they would wait "with open hearts and open hands," laying their faith in the white man's law (Chin, 1990c, p. A-11). By setting Croy free, Serra exhorted:

> ...like a smoke signal, the word will spread to Indians all over the country that the courts can be trusted, that they will be treated with dignity, that the white man has not continued to break his word, that justice will be done. (As cited in Talbot, 1990, p. 12)

On April 20, 1990, a jury of several whites, blacks, and Hispanics, one Asian, and one Guamanian began deliberations on the eight months of testimony and evidence presented to them during the trial. In the days that followed, speculation ran high whether or not Serra had been successful in his cultural defense strategy. Was the issue of racism foremost in the minds of the jurors, or would that be negated by the grim reality that a law enforcement officer had been killed?

On May 1, the verdict was announced: "Not guilty on all counts." Serra termed the decision "a strike against racism," albeit 12 years too late (Chin, 1990d, p. A-4). He was grateful that the jurors understood the enormous meaning of their task. Croy himself beamed at the conclusion of his long ordeal. He vowed to help other Native Americans and minorities facing trials in which cultural defense is appropriate. The owl wing, crystals, tree bark, and a wreath of herbs that were on the defendant's courtroom table each day of the trial to give Croy strength, would now be passed on as the spiritual items of his new freedom and reminders that Native American culture had found a place within this nation's halls of justice (Chin, 1990a, p. A-10).

The outcome of the Croy trial is, of course, not without controversy. Should the issue have been decided by the jury as one of racism and past prejudices or simply a shooting stemming from Indians and alcohol? Earl Gray, one of the jurors, however, is quoted as saying,

> We found definite evidence that there was racism there that could have led to that kind of thing happening. I'm glad that Serra was thorough enough to bring that up. Some people may not have understood this. (As cited in Chin, 1990, p. A-4)

The cultural defense strategy would likely not have succeeded without Serra's persuasive theatrics. But this does not mean that racism toward Native Americans was not the central issue. The Hooty Croy trial is perceived by many Native Americans as a landmark case for their legal and cultural rights. Its historic importance should not be diminished by the attention directed at Serra. What occurred in 1978 was unsettling and tragic, no matter how one explains and judges the events that took place near Badger Mountain.

5

IMPROVING THE CRIMINAL JUSTICE SYSTEM

Tecoatlaxopeuh
Madonna of the Americas

Latino culture has been strongly influenced by Catholicism. The Aztec and Spanish heritages, however, are both honored and reflected in the story of Our Lady of Guadalupe, the patroness of Mexico and the Americas. *Tecoatlaxopeuh* ("the one who crushed the serpent") is the Aztec name chosen by the Virgin herself and transliterated into the Spanish *de Guadalupe.*

According to tradition, in the early morning of December 9, 1531, only a decade after the overthrow of the Aztec civilization, the Virgin Mary appeared to a poor Aztec peasant named Juan Diego, who had recently converted to the faith. The appearance was on the outskirts of Mexico City at a hill sacred to the Aztecs. The Virgin, surrounded by dazzling rainbows of colors, expressed to Diego her wish to have a church built on the hill. She instructed him to give this message to the bishop. Diego did so but encountered suspicion and disbelief.

Discouraged, Diego returned to the hill and beseeched the Virgin to send a more respectable and acceptable person as a messenger. Instead, he was instructed to gather in his *tilma* (cape) the fresh Castilian roses from the hill, which was usually cold and barren during the winter. He was then to unfurl his tilma with the roses in the presence of the bishop. Once again before the bishop, Diego unfolded his tilma and the roses tumbled to the floor, revealing the Virgin Mary's image imprinted on the cape's rough inner surface! Today this likeness adorns countless homes and churches.

Chapter Overview

- Communication and Outreach
- Prerequisites for Service
- Minority Perceptions of the Criminal Justice System
- Restorative Justice

Can the criminal justice system in the United States meet its formidable and inescapable responsibility of meting out equal justice in a racially diverse society? This chapter discusses how the criminal justice system must develop appropriate language, interactive skills, and comprehensive outreach programs to serve multicultural populations. It emphasizes the recruitment of minority police officers, prerequisites for serving diverse communities, and the effectiveness of various attempts to assist minority crime victims. The chapter concludes with examples of how minority victims have interpreted their treatment by the criminal justice system and presents issues of restorative justice as they apply to minorities.

COMMUNICATION AND OUTREACH

Stephen Hennessey, training advisor for the Phoenix Police Department, Arizona, observes that "Every law enforcement agency is struggling with the issues of cultural awareness and the changing populations of our communities" (1993, p. 46). He adds that becoming a culturally competent professional is "much more complex" than just learning differences between various cultures. Bickham and Rossett (1993) concur that simply knowing about the history and values of different groups is insufficient, because many citizens have come to perceive police officers as unable to effectively serve diverse communities. A change in basic attitude and instituting clearly defined behaviors must occur.

The National Institute of Justice conducted a survey of 319 full-service victim assistance programs in law enforcement agencies and prosecutors' offices in 1995. The most pressing need identified in this survey was the need to reach out to special populations, especially minorities. Respondents noted that additional training in cultural sensitivity, recruiting and maintaining bilingual staff members, and effective outreach programs would enable victim assistance programs to improve service delivery to these groups of people (as cited in McEwen, 1995).

Why Not English Only?

One of the most interactive workshops I have conducted on minority crime victims occurred in Southern California in 1990. At the workshop, I played the fictitious director of a major criminal justice planning office that administered funds for public safety and victim assistance programs. The setting for the role-playing exercise was an important meeting of division supervisors to discuss pending budget cuts. The workshop participants were divided into staff members who either supported or opposed allocations for agencies with bilingual and bicultural services. I asked for candor and sound arguments.

Those that resisted the need to give these agencies high priority expressed annoyance at the demands made by minorities. Why should they be allotted special treatment? If they do not understand English, they should learn it before coming to America. If they are having such a difficult time here, they should return to their native countries. It is impossible to accommodate all different kinds of languages and customs. Having one standard language (English) and one standard approach (the "American" way) would simplify matters and be more fiscally manageable. By tampering with allocations just to appease minorities, they would be encouraging them to remain culturally deprived and disadvantaged.

Those who supported bilingual and bicultural services characterized all people from other cultures as "immigrants." If Native Americans and the first Spanish settlers had imposed a standard language requirement, English itself would not have been recognized. Minorities, in fact, have been relatively restrained in their requests. There is no shortage of funds, they contended, only a pattern of appropriations wherein minority programs are funded least and eliminated first. Many of today's immigrants are also refugees that the U.S. government promised to welcome here if they were defeated in the wars that ravaged their countries. They were our allies. Isn't the essence and strength of U.S. democracy its pluralism?

Each group became livid at the arguments being made by the other group. There was no resolution of differences. What could be reasonably distilled from the discussion, however, was that a policy of "English only" seemed too inflexible, whereas unlimited approaches within the cat's cradle of minority languages seemed highly impractical. The group seemed to prefer the solution of a beneficial compromise— for all persons in the U.S. to have at least some command of the English language *and,* if possible, to retain the language of their heritage.

Fonua Kotobalavu probably wishes that his fluency in English had been better in late December of 1989. Kotobalavu, a young Fijian, was waiting for a friend outside the Fun Factory arcade in Kahului, Maui. A police officer, patrolling for suspicious loitering, ordered him to leave the area. An argument ensued and Kotobalavu threatened to (what sounded like) "shoot" the officer. He was immediately arrested for first-degree terroristic threatening, a felony, because the recipient of the threat was a law enforcement official. The charge, however, was later reduced to disorderly conduct, a petty misdemeanor. According to the deputy prosecutor handling the case, the police officer had misunderstood Kotobalavu. Kotobalavu had said that he was going to "suit" the police officer not shoot him, meaning that he wanted to take legal action against him. In these circumstances it would have been untenable for the officer to ask for a slower pronunciation of Kotobalavu's threat. The safety of the officer was paramount in this situation.

How the balance of languages occurs within immigrant families is instructive. Those who are raised by immigrant parents with limited English-speaking ability know the meaning of intentional and patient listening. They are not easily deterred by jumbled English grammar or mangled vocabulary. Their context of listening is caring. When the offspring, moreover, learn the native language of their parents *as well as* assist their parents with English, a new model of family communication emerges. As Rodriquez and Casaus emphasize:

> Many Latino professionals and community members believe that a positive relationship exists between an individual's level of bilingualism and his or her feelings of ethnic identity and self-worth. Thus, the degree to which family members can support and assist each other not only in learning English, but also in communicating effectively in Spanish is a source of internal strength for the Latino family. This internal support can be magnified by using the language of origin to recount to the youth the Latino group's heritage, cultural traditions, and an overall sense of identification with the group's norms and values. (1983, pp. 43–44)

For a widowed Vietnamese woman suffering from depression, the family counselor's respect for her native language proved critical. The counselor had been using the woman's children to assist with translation. This practice, however, only served to heighten the mother's sense of worthlessness. The counselor wisely reversed the process by having the mother teach him and the children the

Vietnamese language as she spoke about her difficulties. This instilled pride in the family members for their heritage and allowed the mother to develop increased confidence in her struggles to make the transition into American life (Lefley, 1989, p. 258).

For other families, unfortunately, differences in language ability exacerbate other differences. Many children of immigrant and refugee families experience the painful ambivalence of not being fully a part of their parents' culture and not being completely accepted as American. Parents, in turn, are anxious that their children not disconnect from their cultural ties or reject their ancestry by not maintaining their native language. In the Korean community, for example, many young people are in what has been called the "obscure zone" between being Korean and American. In the mainstream community they remain "foreigners" while to their immigrant parents they are developing an unacceptable, or non-Korean, value system from their contact with Westerners (Kim, Lee, & Kim, 1981, p. 58).

Kenneth Kim and other social workers have attempted to halt the widening gap and deepening alienation between Korean immigrant parents and their children. They argue that the Korean culture must be preserved as a "point of reference" for learning U.S. culture so that an "overdose" of unfamiliar values will not have detrimental psychological and emotional effects on either. They maintain that because the melting pot theory of assimilation into life in the United States is unrealistic, it is imperative that a person's primary identification be "ethnic." Their octogenarian colleague writes: "A person is really prepared to be American…only when he [she] understands his [her] heritage and can relate as an equal to persons of other cultures" (Kim et al., 1981, p. 59). In other words, a feast of multicultural stew provides more sustenance than a ladle of unseasoned broth.

Language is a primary purveyor of culture, and the degree of respect one has for other ethnic groups is mirrored in one's attitude toward proficiency in English. As Tony Leong, of Asians for Job Opportunities, which assists immigrants in Berkeley, California, states: "Thinking that your English is not vanilla enough, your self-esteem is challenged. We're a nation of different people. People have to learn to be more tolerant" (as cited in Gust, 1990, p. D-4). Leong is addressing the abhorrence that some persons feel toward the native accents of many Asians. He believes that it is a form of discrimination to expect Asians to conform to a "California brand" of English. Kenneth Cushner of Kent State University's Education Department adds, "While immigrants from European backgrounds who retain an accent are often viewed as sophisticated and continental, Asians with an accent tend to become the subject of ridicule and satire ('rots of ruck')" (1996, p. 233).

A Vietnamese high school student in Santa Clara County, California, for example, was often mocked by a white student of another school. Humiliated in front of his classmates, the Vietnamese youth shot and killed the white student. According to an investigator assigned to the incident, which occurred in the spring of 1990 at Mt. Pleasant High School, Vietnamese youth may see a gun as an equalizer for countering the threats and intimidation of others. This may be an extreme form of retaliation but one brewed by intolerance.

Self-Translation

In relating to minority crime victims, law enforcement and other criminal justice professionals should see themselves as "self-translators." To "translate" means to convert or change to a parallel form. Self-translation is the accepting of primary responsibility for finding appropriate means to communicate one's role and service to minority victims. Too often that burden has been levied upon minority victims themselves in the requirement to follow procedures that were established without their needs being addressed.

An example of self-translation is the Los Angeles County Bar Association and Barristers Domestic Violence Project. In the Family Court of that jurisdiction, private attorneys volunteer their time to assist mostly minority women obtain restraining orders by helping them to complete the necessary forms. The Court has assigned a glass-partitioned office in the back of the courtroom for the use of the project. The convenience of having the office actually a part of the courtroom helps the court staff handle cases and conveys to the victims that legal proceedings are meant to support and not discourage their efforts to escape violence.

The afternoon that I observed the project, the courtroom was filled with approximately 30–40 women, primarily Hispanic, waiting for their cases to be heard. Volunteering that day were two female attorneys, one white and one Chinese American, and one white male attorney. I sat with Madeleine Bryant-Kambe during several of her interviews in the project office. Bryant-Kambe forewarned me that her Spanish was limited but added that she had never used that as an excuse to avoid relating to Latinas.

A reserved and apprehensive Latina, perhaps in her 50s, was the first to enter the office. Bryant-Kambe greeted her warmly in Spanish, invited her to take a seat, and requested the intake sheet, written in both English and Spanish, that the woman had been given earlier to complete. During the interview, Bryant-Kambe explained to the woman, again in Spanish, the precise role she had in assisting her, and then asked the woman her circumstances for seeking a restraining order. The woman replied that her husband had come home at 4:00 A.M. after drinking all night. He demanded to have sexual relations. She refused because the loud noises he made had awakened and frightened their six-year-old son. Her husband thereupon beat her and threatened to take the child back to Mexico unless she gave him $1,000.

When the woman began to cry during the interview with Bryant-Kambe, she requested the presence of her teenage daughter, who had been waiting outside the room. The daughter assisted her mother in completing her story. They were then given written instructions in Spanish on how to secure the actual restraining order, suggestions for appearing in court, and how to notify the police of any violation. At the bottom of the instruction form were these words of encouragement:

> Buena Suerte. Sobre todo, protéjase. Esta Orden no es una protección mágica. Manténgase lejos del demandado si sea necesario aunque Ud. esté en su derecho. Protega su seguridad y la seguridad de los hijos.

(Good Luck. Above all, protect yourself. This order is no magic shield. If it is necessary to get away from the other person, even if you are right, stay away. Protect the safety of yourself and your children.) (Los Angeles County Bar Association and Barristers Domestic Violence Project, 1990, Client Information Intake Sheet, p. 1)

Bryant-Kambe and the other attorneys in the project "translate" and demystify the procedures for obtaining restraining orders by physically being where they are most needed, having the willingness to communicate through learning key words of other languages, and being sincerely concerned with what these minority women are facing. Their presence and friendliness in the often intimidating environment of the courtroom tell abused women that they deserve the help that is being offered to them.

The criminal justice system has attempted to become accessible to non-English-speaking minorities by using interpreters and distributing written materials in different languages. The California Penal Code mandates, for example, that translation services be made available for the non-English-speaking populace in comprehensive victim service centers and at certain court proceedings. Not all interpreters, however, understand the criminal justice system or are tested and monitored carefully.

At one particular criminal trial, an interpreter was called upon to facilitate court proceedings. It was reasonable to trust that he was unbiased. On the first day of the trial, an elderly Filipino man, who had been the victim of a brutal assault by a machete-bearing neighbor, testified. The court-certified interpreter, fluent in the Ilocano dialect, stood next to the victim. Also present at the trial was a victim advocate, who was herself an immigrant from Manila. During the prosecutor's questioning, it became apparent to the advocate that the interpreter was substantially altering the victim's answers. He would either embellish or disregard certain responses in the direction that he, the interpreter, felt was needed to win the case. The advocate managed to interrupt the prosecutor and explained what was occurring. A recess was ordered and the interpreter was admonished by the court.

All criminal justice professionals who rely on translators must be properly trained in the optimum use of their services. Outside the courtroom, interpreters should not be regarded as merely the mouthpiece of the peace officer, prosecutor, or advocate. Interpreters can also be used as important sources of information about the cultural heritage of victims. They may thus be as helpful in *preparing* for interviews as in assisting during the interviews. Knowing the individual backgrounds of the interpreters also aids in matching victims with appropriate interpreters. Trust and confidentiality, for example, may be jeopardized if the interpreter is either too far removed from or too familiar with the victim's personal history and situation.

Accessibility to the criminal justice system moreover includes multilingual written materials. The Survivor series prepared by the Los Angeles Commission on Assaults Against Women (LACAAW) and other agencies, in cooperation with the Victim/Witness Assistance Program of the City Attorney's Office, excels in its treatment of minority concerns. Supportive counsel, practical suggestions, and pertinent information concerning sexual assault are provided in Spanish, Chinese, Vietnamese, Korean, Japanese, and French as well as English. The best of such resources, however, go beyond simply using equivalents to the previously written English text. As Jerry Tello argues:

> Agencies typically offer Spanish translations of materials, information and articles that are based on conventional theory. The idea being promoted is that a linguistic translation alone makes information culturally appropriate. Clearly, this is a false assumption. All it does is make the information readable to those literate in Spanish. Frequently, mere translations have done more harm than good. (n.d., p. 6)

Written materials for minorities must reflect their individual cultural symbols and practices, concerns, and needs. Ideally, these materials should be written first in the languages of the various minorities to help ensure their cultural relevance. They should then be translated into English so that English-speaking criminal justice professionals can better understand minority perspectives. In designing strictly-worded technical forms and brochures, such as legal phrases or courtroom protocol, English terms should be included whenever feasible within the multilingual translations to help users recognize and become familiar with customary legal terms.

The criminal justice system, in effect, translates itself to minority groups by committing its resources and directing its staff to fit their distinctiveness. Some may resent this mandate. The requirement to learn new methods to supplement what is already standard practice is often resisted. There is, for example, almost a total absence of any comprehensive training for prosecutors on minority crime victims. They have, in large part, overlooked the needs of victims in favor of trial techniques, legal issues, and evidentiary concerns. Even though they agree that the rigors of prosecution compel them to constantly update their knowledge in these typical areas of training, when a rape crisis center director suggested to a group of prosecutors that they would benefit by learning the needs of minority sexual assault victims, they responded that such a workshop was "irrelevant" to the duties of the prosecutor. They added that they refused in part because they did not want to endorse the notion that minority rape victims suffered more than white victims and therefore deserved "extra attention." Prosecutors, they said, are required to evaluate cases objectively and with unswaying adherence to law.

Only, however, if prosecutors are able to examine and set aside their personal ethnic prejudices, become educated on the dynamics of minority victimization, and learn to elicit the confidence of their racially diverse witnesses will they truly have the acuity to gather and present the elements of minority cases. How many prosecutors have hidden behind a cloak of "impartiality" to mask their discomfort and inexperience in working with minority victims? Cloey Hewlett, a highly regarded black San Francisco deputy district attorney, indeed argues for a specific prosecution unit to relate to minority victims in jurisdictions with large minority populations.

Prosecutors, she believes, have the obligation to understand *all* the issues affecting a case and to gain the trust of the communities they seek to serve. (C. Hewlett, personal communication, 1990).

The Garden Grove, California Police Department, recognizing that its jurisdiction has large populations of Hispanics and Asians, has attempted various strategies to meet the problem of language and cultural differences between its officers and minority members of the community. In the early 1980s, its approach involved using bilingual police officers and community service professionals to act as liaisons to their own ethnic groups. This approach has been marginally successful because it lacked qualified or interested minority persons to fill these positions. The department also discovered that 92 different dialects are spoken within the city boundaries, making it impossible to implement the liaison approach (Chief of Police Robertson, personal communication, April 23, 1990).

The department has retained the original emphasis on minority recruitment, but it realizes as well that liaison work will never fully meet the needs of the community nor adequately translate the mission of the department to all segments of the minority population. In 1990, there were 172 sworn officers on the Garden Grove force: 15–20% were Hispanic, 8% were black, and 2.3% were Vietnamese. The goal at that time was that every other newly hired officer would be a minority person. This goal proved to be unrealistic, and the majority of police officers continued to be white males. Therefore emphasis was placed instead on cultural awareness training for all officers.

The department instructed its officers of the need to treat all citizens with "dignity and respect, guided by common sense" (Chief of Police Robertson, personal communication, April 23, 1990). This type of directive merits closer examination because it was promoted by the highest in command, the police chief, and this set a clear level for desired performance. The challenge was to discern what was in fact regarded as dignified and respectful for each culture. Common sense, which is based solely on understanding what is common to one's own group, precludes rather than achieves culturally sensitive treatment.

The Laotian people, for example, are traditionally less expressive in body language than most Americans. Waving one's hand to call someone, a common gesture for many Americans, is regarded by Laotians as a sign of contempt. It is only used to summon small children or servants. If waving must occur, the palms are pointed downward and the fingers fluttered inward. Placing one's hand on someone's shoulder to show friendship or concern is also rude to a Laotian because those areas of the body closer to the head are inhabited by "souls" believed to be superior to those nearer the feet. To point one's finger at a person, especially directly at the face or upper body, is thus a particularly offensive gesture.

Laotians, in their attitudes toward nonverbal communication through bodily movements and positioning, have much in common with other Asians. Most Asians avoid outward displays of emotions and conduct that may appear too aggressive, critical, or confrontational. Dignity and respect are preserved by an ethic of modesty, an economy of physical intrusions into the space of another person, and sensitivity toward disturbing others by one's words and behavior. To thrust one's hand forward to render a handshake, for example, is considered by most Asians to be bold and presumptuous. To offer a slight bow is preferred because it does not demand a response by the other person. Naturally, if a handshake is offered, it will not be refused. The bow, nonetheless, will likely also occur simultaneously.

Some years ago, I met a Filipino immigrant, Romel, who at that time was attending group sessions for parents of sexually abused children in the Salinas area of California. He felt discouraged by the group process. The rest of the members were Anglos and Latinos. Language, however, was not the problem because Romel spoke English moderately well. In one of the sessions, the group vented their frustration at Romel for not participating more. They accused him of being discourteous because he seldom looked at them when they were speaking to him. They did not understand that Filipinos are taught that prolonged eye contact is a sign of disrespect. Romel's intent was the same as that of the others—to courteously give and receive support—but it was manifested differently. Fortunately, the group was motivated to continue to work on improving communication by recognizing cultural differences without necessarily eliminating them. To treat everyone with dignity and respect, in other words, is to honor how these are defined in various cultures.

First Contact

Maranne Stebbins is a victim advocate with the Alameda County District Attorney's office in California. She is a serious, personable white female, married to a Chinese American deputy prosecutor. When I asked whether or not her racial background had ever constituted a hindrance in relating to her area's large minority population, Maranne candidly could not recall any specific instance in which this might have been a problem. Only several days later, however, she was making her first visit to the home of a black girl who had been sexually assaulted. The girl's father, a man in his forties, was quick to make his feelings known about Maranne's presence. With his eyes fixed upon her, he brusquely announced, "I hate police officers. I hate the system. I don't trust anything that has to do with color lines."

The man's honesty caught Maranne off-guard and tested her composure. The only response she could muster initially was to cautiously nod her head in agreement. But Maranne also wisely chose not to become overly defensive. She could not ignore his remarks but also would not allow them to discourage her from helping his wife and daughter, who both welcomed her visit. Maranne understood that at some time the legal system had demonstrated to this father that it was a system for whites and against blacks. She hoped that her actions and words would not reinforce his opinion but would at least demonstrate that she was there to offer her best.

For minorities, the nature of their first contact as victims with the criminal justice system may either confirm or dispel suspicion regarding how they will be treated. Home visits by advocates thus communicate not only a desire to accommodate the convenience of the victims but also a willingness to take the first step toward bridging any barriers, racial or otherwise. There is also a worthwhile difference in seeing minority victims in their homes rather than conversing with them across a cluttered office desk. The culture, lifestyle, and values of people are reflected in the items displayed on the walls and shelves of their homes, witnessed in the unrehearsed interactions of family members, and appreciated in the social setting of their neighborhood.

There are, of course, situations when service providers would not want to arrive at a home with an agency or government insignia emblazoned on the door panel of their car. Such "official" visits could easily arouse curiosity among neighbors or place the victim's family under embarrassment or stigma. Elaine Lopes, a supervisor of victim services, who is racially black and ethnically Portuguese, also points out the importance of being dressed appropriately. She and a deputy prosecutor had made a home visit to a Cambodian family to interview a 12-year-old boy who had been sexually molested. The prosecutor was naturally accustomed to making a favorable impression in court by wearing a three-piece wool suit. The Cambodians, however, were intimidated by the overly formal attire of this tall, husky white male in a suit. In fact, both the family and the prosecutor already felt stiff and uncomfortable in anticipation of the visit due to the cultural and language differences.

By chance, it was an oppressively hot day and the prosecutor was eventually forced to take off his coat. Almost instantly, Elaine remembers, the facial expressions of the boy and his parents became noticeably more relaxed, which in turn helped the prosecutor to become less tense. In this case, a deceptively small gesture created the mood for a successful interview because the Cambodians, like most Asians, were sensitive to cues of body language. Removing his coat was an overture by the prosecutor, though not an intended one, to relate to the family's interests in a more friendly manner. It was a lesson that maintaining one's office uniform and demeanor in someone's home defeats the very purpose and benefit for such a visit.

Another means for establishing positive first contact with victims are mobile crisis units. Making supportive and practical services available immediately following a crime has extended the image of law enforcement beyond the traditional role of safety and protection of the public. Especially in minority communities, this practice has introduced the idea that the criminal justice system is concerned about the lives of people and not merely their status as case evidence.

In 1984, San Joaquin County became the first jurisdiction in California to organize a mobile crisis unit. Since then, other counties have instituted some form of crisis response modeled after a pioneering program in Tucson, Arizona. These units are ready 24 hours a day to counsel victims at crime scenes, transport abused women and children to shelters, console families at hospital emergency rooms, make referrals to social service agencies, and provide instant information on the criminal justice process. Victim/witness assistance program staff in San Joaquin County rotate night shift and on-call duties and, from their office, monitor law enforcement dispatch radios for requests.

In Alameda County a separate unit of the assistance program continuously cruises the streets of Oakland nightly. I rode with the Alameda unit on two occasions. All three of the crisis workers had considerable experience in working with people in stressful circumstances. One, Becky Wiltrout, had previously been a police dispatcher. Brian Connolly had worked with troubled youth. Laura Haight had been a social worker for battered children. They were not naive about the personal risks of traveling into what is known as a "war zone" late at night and admitted a healthy respect for the dangers. Most of the victims that they had assisted were either black or Hispanic. Becky and Brian are white and Laura is part Hispanic in ancestry. Because there is the potential for misunderstanding, it is important, as Becky articulated, to "keep your eyes, ears open and your mouth shut." There is little room, she added, to be judgmental, even though the white middle-class perspective is to ask "How can a woman get into that situation?" or "How can people live like that?" There is only room for empathy, seeing to the victim's needs, and acting decisively.

On one call we arrived at the home of a black woman who had reported that her daughter had been raped. She was being interviewed by a police officer in her apartment when we knocked at the door. The woman was upset by what had occurred to her daughter so on opening the door, she looked at us and snapped "What do you want?" Becky, without taking offense, quickly identified herself and briefly explained that she was there to offer help. The woman's hostility toward us melted. Becky then handed her some written information before we left, assuring the woman that she could telephone the numbers provided for assistance.

From there, we drove to a housing project where an elderly woman had suffered a heart attack after being beaten by her son. The woman was being treated by paramedics and no real assistance was needed. Next, we hurried to another part of town where police were sweeping the area searching for three heavily-armed drug dealers. We stood by for the eventuality that innocent people might be shot. We then traveled to the location where a man had gone berserk in a bus and threatened passengers. The police were establishing a perimeter around the area in which the man had hidden.

Later, we went to Highland Hospital, the busiest trauma center in the East Bay. Speaking with the emergency room staff, we came to understand how they appreciated the presence of the crisis workers. They knew the crisis workers were there to help shoulder the immense responsibility of caring for victims of gunshot wounds and stabbings as well as their distraught family members. For many people a hospital visit is a bewildering and foreboding experience. In an emergency situation these emotions are greatly intensified. But by patiently sitting and talking with traumatized persons, the crisis workers take part in binding the psychological wounds of victimization and the injuries of racial mistrust.

Community Oriented Policing

The relationship of law enforcement agencies to the communities they serve has been changing. Efforts have been made to bring policing closer to citizens and non-criminal justice resources to achieve crime reduction and prevention. As Joseph Brann, director of the Office of Community Policing Services (COPS), U.S. Department of Justice states, community policing is a "philosophy that promotes and supports organizational strategies to address the causes and reduce the fear of crime and social disorder through problem-solving tactics and community-police partnerships" (1997, p. 1). Participation and cooperation are considered key to this approach in order to gain trust and improved communication between law enforcement and community members.

Community oriented policing has been successful in a number of cities with large minority populations (COPS, 1997):

1. On the east side of Amsterdam, New York, for example, police have established a substation at Central Civico, a Hispanic community center that donated space. Officers attend Central Civico staff meetings and work with its after-school program, tutoring children and organizing field trips. Officers also teach bicycle safety at the city schools. One officer related how a 13-year-old boy would not talk to officers except to swear at them on the street. Now he brings his bicycle to Central Civico for the officer to teach him fancy bicycle maneuvers.

2. In El Paso, Texas, a city with a majority Mexican American population, the police department opened full-service, regional command centers. Citizen Advisory Boards that are made up of a diverse cross-section of residents work together with police commanders to help set priorities and solve problems. The police and advisory boards also sponsored an El Paso Pride Day, rallying 5,000 volunteers to repair damage caused by vandalism, paint over graffiti, and clear parks of litter. A Citizens on Patrol team was formed to pair citizen volunteers with police to walk neighborhood beats together. Residents learn about police procedures and limitations, and officers gain information from people who know their community best.

3. In Lowell, Massachusetts, neighborhood storefront substations were established from which community police officers walked beats and rode bicycle patrols. A mobile precinct was also equipped for public events, contributing to community outreach through decentralization and preventive policing. Increased reports of domestic violence have been credited to women feeling more comfortable with the police.

One of the most concerted efforts to link the police department with its surrounding community has been in Gainesville, Florida. This small city in north-central Florida—and the home of the University of Florida—has a sizable African American community of approximately 22%. In 1985, former Police Chief Wayland Clifton, Jr. created the Citizen Advisory Commission to assist in the review of police policies, training, hiring practices, and crime prevention programs. The commission meets regularly with the police department's command staff in open, candid discussion on the community's crime concerns.

Chief Clifton also established the Black on Black Crime Task Force, demonstrating the commitment of law enforcement to work in partnership with the African American community. Forty-two members (attorneys, judges, police officials, community agency representatives, and ordinary citizens) meet monthly. Sponsored programs reflect a variety of needs and services:

- **Partners Against Crime**—one-to-one mentoring of at-risk youth
- **Mi Boy (Men Involved in Building Our Youth)**—tutoring and mentoring
- **Reichert House**—high risk youth counseling and academic assistance
- **Youth Leadership**—positive modeling of educational and career opportunities
- **Neighborhood Crime Watch**—crime prevention and deterrence
- **Rites of Passage**—enhancing self-esteem for public housing youth
- **Summer employment**—jobs for high-risk youth
- **Community-Oriented Police Teams**—officers on neighborhood beats
- **Ministerial Alliance**—participation by 11 churches

The Gainesville Police Department, in other words, realizes that public safety, especially in minority communities, requires proactive involvement in a host of nontraditional law enforcement activities. Police intercession is assisted by community ownership for reducing crime, and crime victims are better served when criminal justice and social, educational, and religious groups join to address both the causes and impact of violence. As Captain Sadie Darnell, a 20-year veteran and commander of the Gainesville Police Department's criminal investigation division and narcotics unit emphasizes,

> Community oriented policing in order to be successful must be an agency-wide mission rather than contained within specific units. Every officer within the agency must believe in and feel a part of the community in which we serve. Citizens must be able to trust and depend upon police officers. Community oriented policing concepts, properly applied and managed, are able to provide these opportunities for officers and citizens not only to learn about each other but also to work together to develop a plan which will permit their communities to not just survive, but to strive. The Black on Black Crime Task Force began due to a need to understand and have dialogue with African American citizens about our (Gainesville Police Department's) growing concern about violence between black citizens. Any solution to this problem could best be achieved through citizen input coupled with progressive law enforcement practices. The task force is the longest standing committee ever established at the police department (12 years and counting). Over the years, it has evolved into a committee which has learned a great deal about law enforcement in our community; and we in turn have an honest and genuine rapport with community leaders concerned about issues within the black community. (personal communication, September 28, 1997)

This coordinated effort is further exemplified by the start-up in September, 1997, of the Florida Regional Community Policing Institute, funded by the U.S. Department of Justice. The Institute is a partnership between the City of Gainesville and the Gainesville Police Department, the Alachua County Sheriff's Office, the University of Florida, Santa Fe Community College, State Attorney Eighth Judicial Circuit, and the Black on Black Crime Task Force. Its goal is to provide innovative and comprehensive community oriented policing education, training, and technical assistance to law enforcement agencies, civilians, and community groups in the State of Florida and throughout the nation. The Institute's curriculum plans include core courses in community policing and problem solving through partnerships.

Partnerships with Refugee and Immigrant Communities

It is widely recognized that underreporting of crimes is a serious problem in immigrant and refugee communities. According to findings released in 1988 by the Attorney General of California, most of the police and sheriff's departments surveyed within the state estimated that only 40–50% of the crimes committed against Asians are reported. Four jurisdictions—law enforcement agencies in Oakland, Long Beach, Modesto, and San Diego—believed the rate to be just 10% (Attorney General's Asian and Pacific Islander Advisory Committee, 1988).

Since one of the reasons for underreporting may be community members' lack of knowledge of how and to whom to report, the agencies have produced videotapes and information printed in Laotian, Cambodian, Vietnamese, Chinese, and Spanish to acquaint these communities with the U.S. legal system. The Oakland, California Police Department, for example, has produced a video entitled *Justice for All*. It has also subscribed to a multilingual telephone service where 911 calls are received. Videotape resources and installing telephonic channels of communication, however, do not in themselves lead to their use by immigrants and refugees. Law enforcement programs such as Neighborhood Watch have traditionally been a means to educate the community about crime prevention and police services. These, however, have had only a limited effect in immigrant and refugee communities. What has succeeded is a comprehensive approach:

- telephone hot lines
- meetings between criminal justice officials and immigrant and refugee community leaders
- innovative approaches that make possible personal contact
- emphasis on criminal activity specifically affecting these communities

Thien Cao, a community service officer with the Garden Grove, California Police Department, attempted to start a Neighborhood Watch Program for the Vietnamese that was unsuccessful. He printed and distributed hundreds of flyers in Vietnamese announcing the first meeting. Only five people came—all of them crime victims that Thien had previously assisted. Thien made a subsequent effort by sending dozens of letters to Vietnamese businesses. Only two people came. Thien decided therefore to disseminate flyers describing the existence of a telephone hotline for callers who wanted to remain anonymous. He realized that attendance at open meetings for many Vietnamese could be uncomfortable. But by dialing a telephone number in the privacy of their home, they could safely make inquiries and test the helpfulness and trustworthiness of those in the criminal justice system before they exposed themselves to any risks.

In New York on December 26, 1989, five Asian American teenagers playing video games at an arcade were attacked by 30 to 40 white youths with broken beer bottles and crowbars. After the melee, which lasted 15 minutes, the police arrived in response to the 911 emergency call made by the victims. Two of the wounded were Chinese youth who were taken by ambulance to the hospital, but the most seriously injured boy—a Korean who later required 85 stitches—was somehow not transported. He and another Korean youth claimed that the police refused to summon an ambulance for them. Police denied this account and insisted that the Korean youth had denied medical assistance when it was offered.

The follow-up investigation proceeded slowly. The police blamed the Asian teenagers of being reluctant to cooperate with them. The youth countered that their attack was not taken seriously by the police because it was not classified as a racial incident. Local Asian leaders contended that the police tried to close the case without delving further into it, and that the task force was unresponsive to the concerns of the community. Tension and misunderstandings were eventually reduced through a series of meetings between representatives from the mayor's office, the district attorney's office, and the police; intervention by a state senator; and the assistance of the local Asian community. Differences were aired and accusations answered, and eventually the youth agreed to cooperate with the police. The police, in turn, began looking for four suspects, all members of The Master Race youth gang in Queens. Participation of the Chinese Parents Association, the Organization of Chinese Americans, and the Korean American Association helped to both guarantee advocacy for the five victims and assure the police that the nature and conduct of their investigation would be supported.

Formal groups of criminal justice officials and community leaders have been organized in several California cities. In 1986, the Oakland Police Department and the Oakland City Council Public Safety Committee established the Asian Advisory Committee on Crime (AACC). The goal of the AACC is to build "a strong working relationship by sharing information and building mutual trust" between the Asian and law enforcement communities (H. Boscovich, Jr., personal communication, 1990). Member agencies include all of the following: Asian Community Mental Health Services, Center for Southeast Asian Resettlement, Buddhist Church of Oakland, Chinatown Chamber of Commerce, Lao Iu Mien Culture Association, Alameda County District Attorney's Office, Probation Department, Oakland Unified School District, Community Relations Service of the U.S. Department of Justice, and a number of other specific agencies related to victim's concerns. The group has monthly meetings and has sponsored conferences on crime affecting the Asian community.

The Coalition of Asian Americans for Public Safety (CAAPS) is similar in its support of the community to the AACC. When I was a guest at one of their meetings at the San Jose, California Police Department, the agenda included writing informational brochures and using Asian-language newspapers for news releases and advertising. The owner of one of the newspapers offered free space on an interim basis. It was pointed out by other members, however, that he would then invite pressure and threats from the criminal elements for cooperating with the police. Thereafter, it was decided, all advertisements should be on a paid basis to avoid appearing as favoritism.

The primary concern of this CAAPS meeting, however, was to discuss the shooting death of the white student at Mt. Pleasant High School by the Vietnamese student (as described earlier in this chapter). The Vietnamese representatives expressed concern about the number of Vietnamese youth that had been brought in for questioning by the police as possible suspects. They were also wary of the repercussions against their people by the larger community. Although two teenagers, one 14 and the other 16, had been arrested, the CAAPS leaders were concerned that all Vietnamese youth would be seen as troublemakers and gang members and that Vietnamese and other Southeast Asians would encounter a backlash of racial hostilities.

Leaders from the Southeast Asian community therefore went to Mt. Pleasant High School to meet with the principal and counselor about the nervousness felt by the Vietnamese students at the school. They also attended the funeral of the slain boy to express condolences. The boy's family fortunately showed no animosity toward the Vietnamese people in general. CAAPS continued to monitor the criminal proceedings of the case and communicated their perspective on how police and prosecutors were portraying the Vietnamese community when they provided releases to the English media.

Personal contact between law enforcement and Asian immigrants and refugees has also been strengthened through storefront outreach offices. The Los Angeles Police Department, for example, has storefronts in Koreatown and in Chinatown. A group of sworn officers, bilingual staff members, and volunteers serves in these outreach centers. These centers have not merely been grafted onto these communities from the outside. Rather, they are formed in response to concerns brought to the attention of law enforcement within the communities themselves. The continued viability of such centers therefore depends on their popular image of being more than a command post for the sole protection of certain businesses and stores or simply a tactic by police to monitor Asian gangs. Their role, which is to provide information and referral services and to be more directly and immediately available to the public, identifies them as an integral and contributing part of the entire Asian community.

Other avenues of more personal contact with immigrant and refugee communities include the greater use of broadcast media. Roberto Arguello was a well-known Spanish radio talk show host in Los Angeles. He also served as a police officer for over 22 years. He criticized the limited amount of information available to the Latino community from the criminal justice system. He believed more than public service announcements should be submitted to radio and television stations that serve ethnic populations. Through his efforts a week-long series on Latino victims of violent crime was aired. It offered interviews with Latino service providers and discussions of timely topics such as criminal injuries compensation. Arguello offered to air other such programs if members of the criminal justice system would develop a well-organized format. As a busy media producer, he required more than vague ideas—he wanted solid content.

In Santa Clara County, two Vietnamese members of the District Attorney's staff, deputy prosecutor Thang Nguyen Barrett and investigator Cal Nguyen, with Detective Luu Pham of the San Jose Police Department, appeared on the local Vietnamese language television station, Channel 26, to present crime prevention tips and other basic information. Their broadcast was successful in reaching a number of homes and introducing themselves as Vietnamese professionals in both the police department and prosecutor's office who could assist their community. Unfortunately, the program was discontinued after only four segments were aired because of financial constraints of the television station. Sponsorship by major businesses for these types of programs is perhaps the only way to have them be a regular feature.

Closer relations between criminal justice professionals and immigrant and refugee communities depend on both simple and major adjustments to outreach methods. In the Latino community of Garden Grove, for example, it was two years after a neighborhood center was started before trust for the police began truly developing. The turnabout was the result of the police realizing the need for childcare during its scheduled neighborhood meetings and helping to organize such a service. This communicated to the Latino families that the police were sensitive to their personal situations and were willing to adapt.

A more dramatic shift in neighborhood meetings occurred in San Jose. Despite trying to generate interest among the Vietnamese community to attend educational meetings on general crime prevention methods, police and prosecutors were stymied by the low turnouts. Then during the three month span between November 1989 and February 1990, there were 36 robberies in Vietnamese homes. Many of the victims were terrorized, beaten, and bound. These home invasions were perpetrated by Vietnamese gangs who knew that the Vietnamese often hid money and valuables in their houses rather than rely on banks. When a meeting was called following this wave of violence, 150 persons attended to learn how to protect themselves, secure their homes, and alert the police to any leads that surfaced. With increased cooperation between the Vietnamese community and the police, a number of suspects were arrested, and over the next several months only three home invasions were committed.

PREREQUISITES FOR SERVICE

We Are One Color—Blue

There is a "ray of hope," stated Gaddi Vasquez of the Orange County, California Board of Supervisors, to correct the violence and crime in the barrios. Vasquez was recounting to a large audience of criminal justice professionals his experience being in a classroom full of predominantly Hispanic intermediate school students. He had been accompanied by a judge and a journalist to make presentations at the school on leadership and careers. When Vasquez, a former police officer, asked the young students what occupation they would like to pursue, he was encouraged to see an overwhelming number raise their hands to say the law enforcement field (Vasquez, 1990).

Active recruitment by law enforcement agencies in minority communities does show some promise. Most large cities in the United States, for example, have a sizable proportion of black law enforcement officers. In 1992 in Washington, D.C., the police force was 67.8% black; in Detroit, 53.3%; and in Atlanta, 54.6% (Marshall, 1997, p. 13). Innovative approaches have also been employed. The Los Angeles Police Department adopted the clever minority recruitment slogan: "We are all one color—blue." Identification with uniform color, in other words, could transcend differences in racial backgrounds. Job fairs in minority communities, employment announcements on ethnic radio stations, and newspaper advertisements with photographs depicting Latino, African, and Asian American individuals in police uniforms highlighted the department's recruitment drive. Los Angeles is now one of the few large cities that has a representation of black officers in proportion to the general population.

Most jurisdictions, however, must greatly intensify their efforts if peace officers are ever to reflect the composition of the neighborhoods they serve. The Monterey Park, California Police Department has been recognized as a noteworthy example of racial inclusion. In 1990, for example, 18% of its officers were Asian American. Monterey Park, nonetheless, at that time, had a population that was 50% Chinese alone. In 1960 the city was 85% white, 12% Hispanic, and only 3% Asian, mostly Japanese. Now the city is known as "Little Taipei" and the "Chinese Beverly Hills" because of its large influx of affluent Chinese from Hong Kong and Taipei.

The Asian Task Force of the Los Angeles Police Department was formed in 1975 to provide language and cultural expertise in investigations and community relations. It was properly considered an insightful and visionary approach to the growing numbers of Asians in the city. But according to a State Attorney General's report, in December of 1988 the Task Force had just ten sworn officers. These officers spoke Korean, Japanese, Chinese, Thai, and Tagalog, but none of the other languages spoken by refugees.

Still, in San Jose in 1990, 10% of the population was Vietnamese. To serve the more than 60,000 people that this represented, there were only six Vietnamese police officers. One of the more experienced was investigator Luu Pham, who arrived in the United States in 1975. His father was a Vietnamese Air Force lieutenant and his mother worked in the U.S. Consulate. They first settled in Illinois but later moved to California. Luu went to college in Hayward and had been a police officer for just three years. Because of his heritage, he was expected to be an expert on Vietnamese gangs and drug activities and to be highly visible and responsive to the Vietnamese community.

Even more glaring was that there was only one Vietnamese deputy district attorney to serve all of Santa Clara County at that time. Thang Nguyen Barrett was, in fact, the only Vietnamese prosecutor in California. Thang was born in Vietnam, lived in Laos, and moved to Belgium in 1971. In 1977, his family moved to Washington, D.C. Thang subsequently graduated from Hastings Law School in San

Francisco and relocated to San Jose. Both Luu and Thang were committed to serving the Vietnamese community as well as carrying out their other duties. They know, however, that there must be active recruitment of other Vietnamese and regular training of all officers and prosecutors on Vietnamese culture.

Serving minority communities, in other words, can never solely be the responsibility of minority staff members in criminal justice agencies. Their few numbers make this unfeasible. All staff should be expected to—and prepared to—relate to different minority victims in a professional and sensitive manner. In this regard, the experience and knowledge of minority staff members as resources in the departments are available and can then be incorporated into training. Two detectives of Mexican descent, Jorge Azpeitia and Chuck Salazar, for example, in the Rampart Division of the Los Angeles Police Department, have more than 33 years combined in law enforcement. The Rampart Division serves a large population of Hispanic persons, especially Central Americans. Azpeitia and Salazar have shared with their counterparts valuable insights into culturally sensitive police responses to domestic violence in that community.

Azpeitia and Salazar note that the police, as they arrive at the scene of a report of family violence, must realize that they will be viewed as intruders rather than peacekeepers. An abusive Hispanic male guards his home as his domain. When the police are summoned, it is a "slap in the face" to him and this makes him "difficult to control." The situation may indeed be volatile because the abuse likely has escalated over a long period. This partially results from the traditional Hispanic value of solving problems within the family. This value may persist even when it is apparent that the resources within the family have been exhausted. The Hispanic woman is raised to believe she must maintain pride in her family life. Discord with her husband may very well be seen by her parental family and relatives as *her* failure. It is her "obligation" therefore to learn how to cope with her husband's "moods," to discover ways to lessen his "stresses," and to stop shaming the family by involving the police and others.

Azpeitia and Salazar, knowing the dilemma and pressures the Hispanic woman faces, and the resentment that the Hispanic man feels toward the presence of outside authorities, advise patrol officers that they must try to preserve the dignity of both spouses. If urgent medical assistance or forcible arrest is not required, the responding officers should speak and act in a nonaggressive and noninvasive manner. The emphasis is for the officers to show that they are not there to interfere in the family but to help ensure that no one is injured. The call to a home where domestic violence is occurring can be extremely dangerous for a police officer. Knowing the cultural values and the family dynamics of minorities can contribute to mitigating that danger as well as providing the basis for more effective and sensitive outreach to victims. Veteran officers like Azpeitia and Salazar are a ready source of instruction toward this end. They wear the color blue in a way that does not mute their minority heritage.

"We are one color—blue" can, in fact, be a means to elicit a more positive approach by law enforcement to diverse communities. As Bickham and Rossett argue,

If officers are to begin to care, to have a positive attitude regarding diverse peoples, they must recognize themselves as participants in at least one culture, law enforcement. Thus sensitized to the law enforcement culture (and perhaps to other groups to which they belong), as well as to the associated stereotypes and prejudices, they are more likely to empathize with the experiences of [other peoples]. (1993, p. 43)

Prejudicial Attitudes and Behavior

The improvement of minority representation in law enforcement and other criminal justice related professions, while contributing to better racial relations, will not itself resolve racial misunderstanding. Minorities also have prejudicial and negative stereotypes about the dominant culture and between themselves. The increased presence of minority staff only provides the possibility of interracial dialogue and cooperation both within an organization and with those whom that organization serves. The attitudes and collateral behaviors of all recruits and existing staff toward those of another race, in other words, also need formal attention. Racial bigotry that directly affects the integrity and functioning of an organization should, for example, be exposed in the hiring process or during periodic review and be corrected though retraining or dismissal.

It is distressing and avoidable that a Vietnamese police recruit during training was approached by a non-Vietnamese recruit who snidely asked: "What side were *you* on?" The Vietnamese recruit had been called a "slant-eyed gook" and harangued from an early age since his arrival as a child to this country. But that he would be rudely treated by someone who was his professional peer and who was preparing to guard the public safety in a city that had a very large Vietnamese population was far more upsetting and serious.

A black lieutenant in a California sheriff's department faced a similar affront at the time for a written test for promotion to the rank of captain. On entering the room and taking his seat, the other candidates already present, all white officers, rose and walked out. They were disgusted that a black officer would even be considered qualified to take the examination for a leadership position. Their anger was a backlash at what they deemed preferential hiring and promotion practices (see also Marshall, 1997, p. 13). Again, this occurred in a jurisdiction that included a high percentage of the lieutenant's own minority heritage of African Americans. How, it should have been asked, can these high ranking sheriff's personnel who exited the room supervise their deputies to enforce laws fairly and equally when they themselves cannot relate appropriately to one of their own colleagues? It is a tribute to this lieutenant that he endured such discrimination over a long career, and since the time of the exam room incident, has earned promotion to an even higher rank than that of captain.

There are of course minimum qualifications attached to any service-oriented occupation. Physical strength and agility, emotional maturity and psychological health, relevant education and work experience are just some of the requirements that could be included in searching for prospective staff. Peruse various advertisements and announcements in any number of large city newspapers for counseling, social work, public safety, managerial and other positions, and there would likely be few that stress "sensitivity to racial/ethnic minorities" as a prerequisite.

A respected management consultant firm, moreover, conducted a comprehensive and ambitious study of victim/witness training standards (Warner Group, 1989). Their preliminary report listed 25 core tasks for victim advocates. Of these, however, only three tasks, ("crisis intervention," "notify friends and relatives," and "funeral arrangements") included "knowledge of cultural/ethnic/religious response to victimization" as prerequisites. In the 22 other core tasks, including resource and referral, follow-up counseling, crime prevention, victim impact statement, and emergency assistance, the requirement for such knowledge was omitted (pp. iv, 5–15). As a corollary to the study, an outline of entry level training subject areas and selection standards for new hires was given. The subject areas for training listed awareness of "cultural/ethnic differences" but the selection criteria did not (Warner Group, 1990, pp. 2, 3). Attempts, in other words, to summarize the essentials of either staff selection or training have traditionally and continually ignored appropriate reference to minorities. Any applicant for a position and any program that seeks funding and validation should be alerted to the need to address minority issues. Minority perspectives are not peripheral but span the breadth of services rendered to victims.

There must, moreover, be a clear and consistent method in personnel interviews and merit evaluations by which to identify prejudicial attitudes and behavior. How has the person demonstrated respect for different races and cultures? What is the person's commitment to learn how minorities cope with victimization? Are agencies motivated to discover persons who possess the talents and qualities necessary to be accepting of and acceptable to a variety of victims?

Perhaps the ideal candidate for professional employment today and for the future is a multilingual generalist who is computer literate, flexible and creative, and who has good communication and people skills (Perry, 1990). These attributes allow such an individual to gain practice in and assist in facilitating one element common to all successful interaction between individuals and among organizations— collaboration. Collaboration can only occur in an increasingly pluralistic society as all segments of that society move to interact in culturally appropriate and unbiased ways.

Shoes at the Door

Lieutenant Ray Howard of the Richmond, California Police Department arrived at a Laotian community meeting to find "a whole pile of shoes outside the door." A little surprised, but without undue hesitation, he removed his own shoes before entering. The purpose of the meeting was to discuss the recent surge in vandalism and terrorism directed at the Laotian residents of a federally-subsidized housing project. Tensions between Laotians and blacks in the complex and surrounding neighborhood had been rising. The cultural differences between the two groups and the shared frustrations of belonging to a crowded minority underclass were considered two of the underlying factors. Lieutenant Howard's removal of his shoes was an important gesture of courtesy to the Laotians. It was a sign that he came respecting their customs and feelings—the first step toward working together to find solutions. Improvements in relations between law enforcement and minorities have come in large part because of the efforts of certain police departments to make basic changes in hiring and training, forming policies and procedures, and conducting community relations to match the reality that racial minorities are not going to disappear or cower quietly. Victims, in general, are no longer just living in fear. They are becoming defiant and outspoken—for good reason.

Law enforcement has not always left behind its prejudices at the "doorsteps" of those who are being victimized. Fred Persily, a human relations consultant, warns that when police, prosecutors, and judges do not vigorously respond to hate violence, for example, accusations toward the criminal justice system of insensitivity are now more likely to be quickly lodged. He cites the example of one California city where a number of cases of racial violence against blacks were routinely designated merely as "malicious mischief." Because of the unwieldy felony case load, it was understandable that malicious mischief misdemeanors settled easily to the bottom of files ready to be screened for follow-up investigation or forwarding to prosecutors. The victims were also understandably upset that the police were "ignoring" what happened to them. Inevitably, the newspapers publicized the situation as one of police apathy. Persily has since assisted the city's police department in devising a protocol for handling such cases. (F. Persily, personal communication, 1990).

In Orange County, California, the case of Amber Jefferson, a 15-year-old black girl, also generated questions as to the sufficiency of the criminal justice response to racial violence. Amber was among a racially mixed group of adolescents who were attacked in August of 1990 by white males swinging baseball bats and shouting racial slurs. Her head was severely battered and her face ripped apart. Her near death and the way in which the case was handled spurred Mark Ridley-Thomas, then executive director of the Southern Christian Leadership Conference of Greater Los Angeles, to publicly decry the actions of both sheriffs and prosecutors. Their calling what occurred to Amber an "isolated incident" and ruling out race as a factor, according to Ridley-Thomas, are "tantamount to tolerating racial violence" and a denial of the "pernicious manner in which racism is manifested" (1990, p. B7).

Systematic ways of responding to hate violence have been developed in a number of states. In Montgomery County, Maryland, for example, the Human Relations Commission has a "memorandum of understanding" with the police. When an incident of ethnoviolence occurs, the police department directly notifies the Commission, which in turn contacts one volunteer of the Network of Neighbors team who lives closest to the victim. The Network member visits the victim immediately to assure the person of community support and to assist with other needs. As in Maryland, the police departments in New York and in Boston have created special "bias crimes units" whose officers are trained to respond exclusively to hate violence. As a result, racial minorities have been more willing to work cooperatively with police departments rather than just cast blame. Victims are being encouraged to report hate crimes committed against them at the same time police are learning to respond more appropriately to the needs of different groups.

In Contra Costa County, California, the Hate Violence Reduction Task Force meets regularly and includes representatives from the police, the Sheriff's Department, the District Attorney's office, other branches of the criminal justice system, the schools, religious groups, community-based organizations, and public agencies. The task force has accomplished the implementation of standardized incident response and uniform statistical reporting by law enforcement offices. The District Attorney is personally and promptly apprised of all crimes associated with race, religion, ethnicity, or sexual orientation. These cases are then assigned for vertical prosecution to ensure continuity and consistency, especially in contact with the victim.

In San Francisco, the police department initiated a model program to prepare officers to handle ethnoviolence. Mandatory training is given in identifying hate crimes, understanding penal codes, and writing reports. They have also formed strong ties with organizations such as the gay group called Community United Against Violence and the Asian group called Break the Silence Coalition. A complement to this initiative by the police is the recently-formed civil rights unit within the San Francisco District Attorney's office. The criminal justice system must, it has learned, work closely with the communities most affected by hate and violence, contribute to a network of organizations committed to hate reduction, and place high priority on the enforcement, prosecution, and adjudication of ethnoviolence.

MINORITY PERCEPTIONS OF THE CRIMINAL JUSTICE SYSTEM

Experiences from Native Countries

How immigrant and refugee communities generally perceive the criminal justice system is a principal factor in determining how best to serve those communities. These perceptions are often based on the experiences of these groups with the criminal justice systems in their native lands. In many Asian countries, for example, there is a history of police corruption. The reporting of a crime may not only be futile but could invite unwanted and costly attention. The turmoil of war and the instability of political leadership have also dissuaded many from depending on government institutions.

In Mexico, there is "pattern of excessive violence and abuse" by police according to the U.S. human rights group, Americas Watch, in a report released in June of 1990 (Brown, 1990, p. A-15). The anti-narcotics division is said to routinely commit crimes worse than they are trying to stop. Officers, without search warrants, raid small towns in rural areas, carry out mass arrests, loot shops and homes, and torture and kill. In one incident a six-year old boy was alleged to have been kicked to death for refusing to tell where his father was hiding. The Mexican government, the report concludes, has either tolerated such behavior or has lost control of its police, prosecutorial, and judicial agencies (Brown, 1990, p. A-15). In 1997, in fact, General Jesus Guttierrez Rebollo, Mexico's top drug enforcement czar, went on trial for narcotics, abuse of authority, and weapons charges. Rebollo himself has retorted that he is being prosecuted in order to protect other corrupt generals and senior politicians tied to the drug trade (Dillon, 1997a, p. 4A).

In Juarez, Mexico, the warfare between drug traffickers has literally spilled into the streets. In the first seven months of 1997, more than two dozen people have died in drug-related killings, including innocent bystanders. The uncle of one of the victims, while at the chapel for her funeral, exclaimed in a voice strained with emotion, "Why can't they eradicate the violence that took away my niece? It is intolerable violence. There is no control of the violence." Another Juarez resident adds, "It's getting bad. They are killing people in broad daylight. A poor person like myself can't buy a machine gun" (Schiller, 1997a, p. 20A).

Many Mexican immigrants to the United States, therefore, bring with them a mistrust of criminal justice authorities and do not readily seek their assistance. But there are also incidences in the United States that reinforce the ineffectiveness of justice systems. Roberto Franco's daughter, Irene, was living in Los Angeles and working until she would be able to return to Mexico to begin her university studies. Roberto had planned to visit her on her 21st birthday, traveling from their home in Tepatitlan near Guadalajara. On December 15, 1989, however, Irene was murdered. She and her friend, Jesus Martinez, were sitting watching a movie at a drive-in theater near the interchange of the San Diego and Harbor freeways. Three armed men forced their way into Martinez's car and abducted the couple, driving to a junkyard in an industrial area north of Carson. There they severely beat Martinez and repeatedly raped Irene. They then released Martinez but drove off with Irene. She was found the next morning in a vacant lot in Wilmington, shot in the head.

Roberto was shattered by his daughter's death. "In Tepatitlan," he stated, "the whole town is talking about the murder." Approximately 30,000 of Tepatitlan's 130,000 residents had settled in Southern California over the previous 40 years. But the ones remaining in Mexico are now afraid to visit relatives here. As Roberto commented, knowing that none of the killers was in custody, "People are able to do terrible things here." He also notes that one particular convict, Charles David Rothenberg, was paroled after serving only six and one half years for setting his son afire in a Buena Park motel room. "How can he do that and be freed?" he observes. Apparently, not only in Mexico are there reasons to doubt the integrity of the justice system (Boyer, 1990, p. B3).

Whites Enslaved the Blacks

Melinda was 10 years old when her stepfather's friend raped her. Sandra, her mother, was away at work and her stepfather, Louis, had gone on an errand. James, her attacker, was visiting that afternoon and was left alone with Melinda. He was known in the neighborhood as a drug addict and violent individual, but Melinda's family had little idea of the danger in which they had placed her.

James roughly fondled Melinda, attempted intercourse, and forced oral copulation. He was a large man, over six feet in height and weighing well over 200 pounds. Melinda was too frightened to tell anyone what had happened. It was not until nearly two weeks later, when she complained about stomach pains and her mother was preparing to take her to the hospital emergency room, that Melinda was finally able to say what James had done. Upset and angry, Sandra immediately called the police. She was assured that a patrol officer would arrive soon to take a report.

After several hours, Sandra decided that she could wait no longer. She and Melinda drove to the hospital emergency room. The doctor on the night shift was sympathetic but admitted he wasn't qualified to examine a child for sexual assault. He did call Children's Hospital to schedule such an appointment there but the earliest available opening was in two weeks. The doctor also asked a police officer at the hospital to talk to Sandra, but Sandra wasn't certain at that time whether he was indeed an officer. He was wearing blue overalls and not a uniform, did not show a badge or even identify himself, and only asked two questions of her and left.

After Sandra and Melinda arrived at home, the police called at 3:00 A.M. to inform them that they could not come to their house because there were too many emergencies. Melinda's rape, the officer explained, could not be considered urgent since it occurred some time ago. About one week later, Sandra noticed a patrol car passing in front of her home. She ran out to the street and waved for the officer to stop. She demanded that he take a report of the rape. From the perspective of law enforcement, perhaps, there were legitimate reasons as to why nothing had been done thus far. From Sandra's view, nevertheless, it was a complete lack of caring by the police for what happens to "black families living in the ghetto."

For Sandra and Melinda, however, their ordeal was just beginning. James quickly discovered that Melinda had disclosed him when Louis, after he found out about the rape, stormed after James. The two engaged in a bloody fight. Thereafter and in the ensuing weeks until his arrest, Melinda was terrified that James would kill her for telling her mother. After the preliminary hearing and following James' arrest, James' family continued to threaten and harass Sandra and Melinda. When Sandra tried to seek some sort of protection, she was told by the police that something violent would actually have to occur before they could do anything.

When Sandra and Melinda first went to the district attorney's office, they were alarmed to meet the white female deputy prosecutor assigned to handle their case. All their fears about the white justice system and its attitude toward blacks had been confirmed up to this point. Fortunately, the deputy prosecutor was experienced and was somewhat astute in relating to victims and witnesses of varying racial backgrounds. A black female victims' advocate was also there to lend assistance.

Nevertheless, young Melinda boldly announced her opinion to both the prosecutor and the advocate that "the whites enslaved the blacks" and that they also kill black people. Melinda had been studying in school about the civil rights movement and the Reverend Martin Luther King, Jr. and his assassination. She also told them how she had been "bopped" on the head by some of her non-black classmates because she was "dark." She wanted to be called "African American" because her people should be treated better.

Eventually a modicum of trust was established between Sandra and Melinda and the prosecutor. This resulted partly from the advocate taking the time to meet with Sandra and Melinda on several occasions. The prosecutor, however, was also disarmingly frank: "I'm white. You are black. I'm going to get the job done" (N. O'Malley, personal communication, January 23, 1990). A jury trial resulted in a conviction, and the defendant received a 13-year sentence out of a possible 15-year maximum.

Sandra, nonetheless, was still bitter that it was only her persistence that initially produced the response from the criminal justice system. Although she was distressed when she first learned of Melinda's rape, she knew that it was a crucial breakthrough for her daughter to reveal what had happened. But all this, in her eyes, was unimportant to those from whom she sought help. Sandra also believed strongly that the white public defender at the trial argued his case along "color lines." When she was on the witness stand, she felt that his cross-examination was meant to minimize the seriousness and effects of crime in the black community. He insinuated that she had abandoned her child to the mercy of perverts while she was selling her body on the streets! He seemed to argue that crimes such as child molestation are "supposed to happen" in the black ghetto.

In discussing Sandra's impressions with the deputy prosecutor, I was told that the defense attorney did not make any direct racial remarks and that Sandra had never mentioned these feelings to her. The prosecutor mentioned that the defense attorney had a reputation for generally demeaning rape victims, minimizing their trauma, and discrediting their testimony. We both agreed that a more adequate preparation of Sandra and Melinda about the public defender's style would have helped to offset the impression of racism that was very distracting and painful for them.

In some ways, it was less important whether the defense attorney was in reality prejudiced. It only mattered that Sandra and Melinda were vulnerable to what might have been interpreted as racial remarks and innuendos. The prosecutor admitted that there were early signs of Melinda being "hung up on racial issues." This should have been the cue to the prosecutor to at least give special attention to certain areas of the prosecution and court process that might raise concerns. Because Melinda herself had been blunt about racial matters, a simple adjustment to the usual witness preparation could have been made in order to confront and hopefully defuse issues of race.

Melinda's terse comment that "whites enslaved the blacks" indeed has the potential for being affixed as a description of the criminal justice system itself. This was Elizabeth's viewpoint. Her 13-year-old daughter, Tammy, was stabbed to death by a white man that Elizabeth had met at an adult night school (Plank, 1989, p. 15). Elizabeth, 31, and this fellow student had exchanged telephone numbers. He subsequently came to visit her. Within 30 minutes after arriving at her home, he became belligerent and addressed Elizabeth with racial slurs. He then pulled out a knife and viciously began attacking her. Hearing her mother's screams, Tammy came running to her aid. The man whirled around and plunged the knife into Tammy six times. Turning again to Elizabeth, he stabbed her once more and then left the apartment. Tammy was dead. Elizabeth was in critical condition.

Police later arrested the man on murder and attempted murder charges. Elizabeth spent many weeks in the hospital. During that time her electricity and telephone services were terminated by the utility companies for non-payment of bills. This only added insult to the tremendous guilt she experienced for having caused her daughter's death by allowing a killer into their home. The criminal justice system Elizabeth felt, had driven the knife wounds and grief even deeper. It took one year for just the preliminary hearing to take place. To Elizabeth, the murderer and the court system shared the same disregard and disdain for blacks (V. Hart, personal communication, January 17, 1990).

But whites are not the only ones who enslave blacks. Virginia, for example, was molested by her stepfather for eight years, from the time she was nine until she was 17. When she became pregnant and gave birth to their child, the legal system intervened, and Virginia and the baby were sent to a foster home. The foster parents were a middle-class and middle-age black couple who provided a stable and nurturing home life. The husband was a counselor and spent many hours helping Virginia cope with her years of molestation. Virginia soon began attending community college, and there blossomed into a confident and articulate young woman.

After two years, the case against Virginia's stepfather finally came to trial. Virginia's testimony was crisp and composed. She did not waver or become distracted by the emotions of having to tell of the horror she had survived. The trial, nonetheless, ended in a hung jury. The vote had been 11 to 1 for conviction. The mistrial was caused by a black juror. This woman, in her fifties, refused to believe that a black girl who was raised in the ghetto and who had suffered such molestation could look and act the way Virginia did. The deputy prosecutor had mistakenly assumed that this juror would be sympathetic to Virginia. More incisive *voir dire* may have unveiled this woman's preconceptions and prejudices. Her vote had the effect of enslaving Virginia in her past rather than acknowledging the liberation that Virginia had achieved (V. Hart, personal communication, January 17, 1990).

Dying to Be Heard

Alejandro, or Alex as he is called by his family and friends, was the 15-year-old son of Julio Calderon, an information officer with the California Youth Authority. Alex was waiting with a friend at a bus stop in Newark, California, on Friday afternoon of January 12, 1990. At the same time, 13 angry teenagers were driving around the city in a van searching for another youth with whom one of the teenagers had an earlier confrontation. Failing to locate the youth, the teenagers noticed Alex at the bus stop. Alex had supposedly given one of the youths a dirty look the week before. The van pulled to the curb and the 13 boys piled out to descend upon Alex.

They repeatedly punched and kicked him. Somehow Alex struggled free to make a desperate dash for the sanctuary of a nearby 7-Eleven convenience store. But at the doorway he was knocked down by one of his attackers. A 14-year-old boy then pulled a knife, stabbing Alex three times. One of the wounds penetrated Alex's heart. As he lay dying on the pavement, the assault continued. He was kicked until there was not a quiver of movement left in his now lifeless body.

This was a tragedy that would be devastating to any parent. To lose a child at an early age is a prospect no parent would ever want or care to imagine. Julio described his son as a skinny kid who had always caused him far fewer worries than his older brother. Alex had a future. He was not a member of any gang. In fact, his mother had specifically instilled in him the attitude that he should not intentionally hurt anyone. He was thus a good role model for his young nieces and nephews.

The pain that Julio felt, however, went beyond the emotional anguish of losing Alex in such a senseless manner. At the sentencing hearing for one of his son's murderers, Julio made an impassioned plea to the court to send a strong message to the community that the criminal justice system would not condone such a killing. Justice would not be served, he argued, if the juveniles were given anything less than some term of incarceration. Otherwise, the juveniles would mock the courts and, worse, be fully initiated into the gang mentality of operating under separate rules than the rest of society. The courts chose instead not to incarcerate, citing that he would have a better chance at rehabilitation. Because this particular juvenile had no previous record, the hearing officer decided that he deserved another chance.

Alex's father was enraged. His son had lost his one chance in life. At the sentencing hearing for another one of the teenage defendants immediately following this first one, Julio made clear to the court that he and his family were being revictimized by the court. He had come looking for justice, hoping that there might be a deterrent value to a firm sentence. Julio had for many years been a political activist. He had especially worked hard to establish a power base for Latinos in California. He was part of "the system" because he had the vision to work within it to better the whole system. And now that very system had failed him and, ironically, the juvenile offenders themselves. The frustration that Julio felt was therefore more intense than those whose race and ethnicity have never made them feel like outsiders. Julio had long been an intelligent, articulate voice for his people. But now he felt that his words had failed at a deeply personal moment. Were his expressions of pain not enough to have any effect on the sentencing?

Juanita, Alex's older sister and a single mother of four at age 22, also testified at the hearing. When Alex died, Juanita told the court, her own life seemed to end. Her eldest child, a daughter just six years of age, cries for her uncle at night and asks when Alex will come back. Juanita can only say that Alex is "at peace." There are, however, no real peaceful moments for Juanita. Their family, in traditional Mexican custom, had stood by one another through many troubled times. There was *confianza* (feelings of security and warmth) among them and a trust that mutual support would always be there, but to explain this feeling of family warmth to others, informally or formally, is not commonplace. It required special courage for Juanita to expose her feelings of loss to a courtroom full of strangers, something she was willing to do for the sake of her brother.

Sadly, the court responded with terse cliches about understanding what the family was going through. The hearing officer interrupted Juanita at critical times in her statement. There seemed to be little awareness or appreciation for what it must have taken for Juanita to even make an appearance at the hearing. Juanita was in fact also representing her mother, who found it too emotionally difficult to be present. Afterwards, Juanita remarked that the hearing officer attempted to counter everything she had tried to say. She was particularly upset when the hearing officer stated that she knew what Juanita was feeling because she herself had grieved over the ill health and death of one of her colleagues several years previously. The hearing officer actually spent more time offering sympathy and explaining her own experience of loss than listening to Juanita's!

The results of the hearings were not only a crushing blow, but the process itself created immense frustration for the Calderon family. They felt betrayed by what had taken place. They had spoken words of careful thought from a veteran youth corrections official and words of the heart from a distraught sister. But the words were not truly heard. The Calderons experienced the injustice of Alex's death again and again.

The Rosales and Zuniga families went through a similar ordeal. On July 12, 1988, Karla Rosales, an eight-year-old student at Hawthorne Elementary School in Oakland, and her cousin, 10-year-old Rene Zuniga, were killed when a car struck them as they crossed an intersection by their school. Another cousin, Angela Rosales, age six, and crossing guard Magali Dominguez, 12, were also seriously injured. The driver of the car, Michael Brandon, who had poor vision and no driver's license, was speeding to the rapid transit station to board a train to his workplace. Near the school he passed a car that had stopped for the children, striking them in the crosswalk. A trial in November of 1989 was halted by the presiding Superior Court judge who granted a motion for acquittal on the grounds of insufficient evidence to prove the two counts of second-degree murder. He found that the prosecutor had not proven that Brandon showed a "conscious disregard for life" or "malice" when he struck the children. Later, a conviction on lesser charges was achieved.

On January 26, 1990, the Rosales and Zuniga families appeared at the sentencing hearing. Karla's father, Carlos, pleaded with the judge to impose the maximum sentence of nine years and six months. He told the judge that he and the other family members would have to suffer the rest of their lives because of the loss of their children. "When they died, we died with them," he said through an interpreter. "The children should not have died in that manner." The judge replied that the punishment had to be fair and that although the children's deaths were an irreparable loss, he was compelled to give the defendant the opportunity to reform. Brandon was sentenced to four years in state prison.

Carlos Rosales angrily complained, "There is no justice. We thought children were protected by the law, but it appears that is not true." Rene Zuniga's father, also speaking through an interpreter, added that they were being discriminated against because they were natives of Nicaragua. A member of the Hawthorne Neighborhood Association perhaps put it most dramatically:

> How can you get off that easy after killing two children? If someone had run over my kid, they would have to prosecute me. Maybe I'll get only four years and I'll consider that justice. (As cited in W. Jones, 1990, p. A-9)

For the Rosales and Zuniga families, their children are everything. They attempted to convey to the court the overwhelming impact on their lives of what the defendant had done in the cruel irony of his haste to make a living. They had been told by victim assistance counselors that it was their right to speak and the court's responsibility to listen (see also Alexander & Lord, 1994). They spoke in Spanish but the judge seemingly could not hear despite the interpretation provided. Karla Rosales and Rene Zuniga had given their young lives for their parents to have the opportunity to be heard in a U.S. court of law. Only for Michael Brandon was it a cheap price to pay.

RESTORATIVE JUSTICE

Restorative justice has been referred to as a new paradigm for community corrections. It is said to have "evolved out of a sense of failure and frustration with the current system and its detachment from the real problems of victims, offenders and communities" (Bazemore, 1994, p. 21). Offenders, for example, have been subjected to the varying and fluctuating correctional philosophies of retribution/surveillance or rehabilitation/treatment (p. 20). These approaches have been essentially closed and inadequate systems because they allowed very little victim participation or community involvement (Byrne, 1989, p. 487). A more balanced system requires a mission to be responsive to the needs of victims, offenders, and the community as equal clients, and this is the central value offered by the restorative justice model (Bazemore, 1992; Maloney, Romig, & Armstrong, 1988). As Bazemore explains, the primary concern of restorative justice is with repairing the damage or harm done by crime to victims, the community, and the offender (Bazemore, 1994, p. 21).

Actually, restorative justice, according to Gay and Quinn, is a return to the justice of old, which is "catching on anew in our society" (Gay & Quinn, 1996, p. 16). Ancient concepts and values long abandoned by the justice system and the emerging crime victims' movement since the 1970s have combined to form the foundation for restorative justice (Bazemore, 1994, p. 21). For minority crime victims, many aspects of this system of justice are already familiar. Their traditional methods of resolving matters and restoring community life can, in fact, contribute to the further development of the restorative justice model. As Umbreit has noted:

> Restorative justice…provides a very different framework for understanding and responding to crime and victimization…. Crime is understood to be primarily

against people within communities, as opposed to the more abstract concept of crime as being against the state. Those most directly affected by crime are allowed to play an active role in restoring peace between individuals and within communities.... In truth, the essence of what is now being called restorative justice is deeply rooted in the traditional practices of many indigenous people throughout the world, such as Native American, Pacific Island, Maori in New Zealand, and First Nation people in Canada. (1997, p. 35)

Victim Impact Panels

Victim impact panels are one key element of the restorative justice model (National Victim Assistance Academy [NVAA], 1997, Section 21–5-4). Crime victims address an audience of offenders and relate how specific criminal actions have affected them personally. These panels serve two purposes:

1. Offenders are provided with an in-depth understanding of the pain and suffering—both short-term and long-term—they have caused.
2. Victims have the opportunity to possibly deter future criminal behavior of the offenders and thus enhance public safety.

One of the leaders in the conduct of victim impact panels and training of those in the corrections system is Mothers Against Drunk Driving (MADD). The MADD victim impact panels are primarily for first and second offense "driving while intoxicated" (DWI) or "driving under the influence" (DUI) offenders. As Regina Sobieski, Assistant Director of MADD's National Victim Services Division, states, the members of the individual panels typically reflect the backgrounds of the offenders. "Drunk driving is a crime that doesn't discriminate—whether male or female, young or old; the color of skin does not protect you from the devastating effects of a drunk driving crash" (1997, p. 1).

Culture and belief systems are woven into the panel presentations. A Navajo woman, for example, participates regularly on the MADD Albuquerque panel. She introduces herself and welcomes the audience in her native language. She also proudly wears her traditional dress of turquoise and silver. Native American panel members, or people of non-Native American descent who address a Native American audience, generally use the word Creator rather than God in their references. Story-telling is also very important, and sufficient time is allotted for panelists' stories to unfold. The speakers recognize family ties by inviting everyone into a circle of significant others who will address the healing and responsibility for it together (Sobieski, personal communication, September 9, 1997).

When MADD conducts Hispanic victim impact panels, time is often scheduled for Catholic members to say the rosary and/or hold other rituals before or after the presentations. This acknowledges the strong influence of religion in the lives of many Hispanics. Panel members will thus often speak of the importance of faith for both victims and offenders. Celestina Gutierrez, a member of MADD in El Paso, Texas, for example, recounts this story of the death of her daughter at age 15:

One insensitive, careless, reckless man decided to drive at a high speed, running a red light…crashes into my poor innocent young daughter who was simply standing at the corner waiting to cross the street…. He carried her body on top of his car for about ten yards and as he shifted to the left again her body fell off his hood…. He never slowed down. He kept on speeding and screeching into the night making his getaway, leaving my poor daughter there to die…. She was my precious, prayed for baby girl…the only girl we had in our family of four sons. God granted us this last child, she was like a little piece of heaven sent from above, so her given name was "Celeste," which means of the heavens or heavenly. (personal communication, April 13, 1997)

Hispanic panel members also place emphasis on the effects on the entire family as the result of death and injury caused by drunk driving. Gutierrez tells how her daughter had been "the apple of her daddy's eye" and "the companion for my older years." When Celestina and Henry's daughter died, however, she says, "a part of us died, too." Celeste's death brought "disaster onto a whole family."

I, as her mother, lost the excitement that she and I shared in developing our business (a fashion boutique), so in the matter of three months, I had lost my business and with it went our extra income. My husband became listless. Our sons: two of them lost their jobs; our youngest son fell into so much depression; one of our twin sons went on the mission field to teach children in the orphanages of Romania. There he developed some type of anemia caused from the loss of his beloved baby sister. (personal communication, April 13, 1997)

The Gutierrez family, however, made a decision that they say has been "God's miraculous way of allowing us to share the gift of life which He first gave us." When Henry Gutierrez returned from the morgue where he was asked to identify his daughter's body, his wife could see the unmistakable pain in his eyes that told her the victim was indeed Celeste. Her husband later told her of meeting a doctor from the transplant donor foundation. The doctor had explained that if Celeste were to be a donor, she could help up to 60 other individuals awaiting transplant surgeries. Because Celeste was such a caring and giving person, Mr. Gutierrez decided to sign the consent papers.

Since that day, I thank the good Lord for having touched my husband's heart in making such a wonderful, but difficult decision. A decision which, in the span of three years, has indeed given a second chance at life to as many as thirty persons across the nation. A decision which has become our blessing…. Celeste being a donor allows me to feel that she lives on. (Gutierrez, 1997, p. 3)

Hispanic panelists, moreover, usually employ tangible items as visual reminders to, literally, bring home their message. These include, for example, the homicide victim's clothing, shoes, or favorite possessions that will bring life to that person as a real family member who is now deceased. The above cultural moorings and common values assist MADD in forging a bond between the panelists and their listeners.

Native American Justice Systems

In 1994, President Bill Clinton directed federal agencies to relate to Indian tribes on a government-to-government basis when tribal government or treaty rights are at issue. The President stated that "respect for the rights of self-government due the sovereign tribal governments" shall be implemented by executive departments in a knowledgeable and sensitive manner (Clinton, 1994). As Kristine Olson, United States Attorney for the District of Oregon, has commented: "One of the most important parts of self-government is the power to create and administer an independent justice system" (1997, p. 1).

The U.S. criminal justice system, according to Ada Pecos Melton, director of the American Indian and Alaskan Native Desk at the Office of Justice Programs, U.S. Department of Justice, has its "roots in the world view of Europeans and is based on a retributive philosophy that is hierarchical, adversarial, punitive, and guided by codified laws and written rules, procedures, and guidelines" (1995, p. 126). The vertical power structure in the current system is upward, with authority and decision making limited to a few. It focuses on one aspect of a problem—the criminal act involved—and this is addressed through adversarial fact-finding and argument (p. 126). The symbol for this system of justice is the triangle as a pyramid of power (The Judicial Branch of the Navajo Nation, 1997, p. 18).

In contrast, Melton states, the indigenous justice system is based on "a holistic philosophy and the world view of the aboriginal inhabitants of North America" (p. 126). This system is guided by unwritten tribal laws, traditions, and practices, all of which are learned by example and through the oral teachings of elders.

> The holistic philosophy is a circle of justice that connects everyone involved with a problem or conflict on a continuum, with everyone focused on the same center. The center of the circle represents the underlying issues that need to be resolved to attain peace and harmony for the individuals and the community. The continuum represents the entire process, from disclosure of problems, to discussion and resolution, to making amends and restoring relationships. (1995, p. 126)

The methods used in the indigenous justice system reflect restorative and reparative principles. The victim, the offender, and the community need healing and renewal. To restore the well-being of the victim and to regain trust and dignity, the offender must make amends through apology, asking forgiveness, restitution, and other demonstrations of sincerity. Corrective intervention requires also the involvement of families and elders or tribal leaders to define the boundaries of appropriate behavior and the consequences of misconduct. This system reveals that law and justice are "part of a whole that prescribes a way of life" (Melton, 1995,

p. 127). This means, explains Melton, that restoring spirituality and cleansing one's soul are essential for all those involved. Prayer therefore occurs throughout the healing process. Sweat lodge ceremonies, fasts, and purification are also employed. In the U.S. justice system, in contrast, the separation of power is tantamount, and the separation of church and state are crucial doctrines that ensure justice occurs everywhere, uncontaminated by politics and religion. Such separation is difficult and often impossible for tribes to follow.

The communal nature of indigenous justice is symbolized by the circle, showing equality in relationships and commitment to consensus (The Judicial Branch of the Navajo Nation, 1997, p. 18). It is further seen in the "distributive aspect" of offense whereby an individual's offense is generalized to the offender's wider kin group. Law is linked, in other words, to life within elaborate kinship relationships and tribal divisions in longstanding communities. In several Pueblo tribes, for example, one is born into one of two *moieties* (tribal subdivisions), decided by patrilineal lines. Membership is generally not changed except through marriage for a woman, through adoption, or through a mother's remarriage for a man. The kinship bond governs then from birth, through life, and death. The group or extended family, accordingly, shares responsibility and blame for the crime and is held accountable for corrective measures and repair of relationships. It thus becomes a resource for resolution, protection, and compliance in its accepted ownership of the problem.

Among the Sioux, all those within the kinship network, including adopted outsiders, are "relatives." DeMallie (1994) explains that the *hunka* (the adoption ceremony) was a ritual mechanism for formalizing such a relationship. In the book *Speaking of Indians,* Deloria reported a case in which a murderer was adopted by the family of the man he had slain. The ultimate outsider was thereby incorporated into the kinship network as a means of atonement (DeMallie, 1994, p. 131).

The forums for addressing wrongs committed and adjudicating criminal acts differ according to tribes and are used in varying combinations:

- *Family forums* are family gatherings and talking circles, facilitated by family elders or community leaders, and based on traditional laws, sanctions, and practices. The victim may speak on his or her own behalf or assisted by family members. The accused also speaks or is represented through a spokesperson. Adherence to agreements is monitored by the families.
- *Community forums* follow more formal protocol and are mediated by tribal officials but mirror in many ways the process of family forums.
- *Traditional courts* incorporate some modern judicial practices such as written complaints and judgment orders but are guided by customary laws and sanctions and presided over by tribal heads. Non-compliance by offenders may result in arrest and confinement.
- *Quasi-modern tribal courts* are based on the Anglo-American legal model, employing written rules and procedures, punitive sanctions, and appeal processes. Lay judges preside.
- *Modern tribal courts* parallel U.S. courts and are presided over by judges trained in law.

Tribal courts, however, often use family and community forums and other indigenous methods of tribal law for matters such as sentencing alternatives, sentencing practices, or victim–offender mediation (Melton, 1995, pp. 129–130).

Indigenous methods include the Traditional Dispute Resolution Research Project and Peacemaker Program of the Northwest Intertribal Court System and the Apache Mediation Center of the White Mountain Apache Nation. The most favored model, however, is Navajo Nation Peacemaking, which is used alongside U.S. justice procedures. As Justice O'Connor writes, "The Navajo Peacemaker Court is now an active, modern legal institution which incorporates traditional Navajo concepts into a judicial process…[and] successfully blends beneficial aspects of both Anglo-American and Indian traditions" (1996, p. 13).

Peacemaking procedures are led by the *naat'aanii,* the traditional Navajo leader who is called "peacemaker" in English. The naat'aanii are chosen for their reputation and respect by each of the Navajo Nation's 110 communities or chapters. There are over 250 peacemakers, many of them women, who invoke the Spirit in the adjudication process with prayers intended to create a right attitude among participants, and bring together ceremonial wisdom and traditional lore (The Judicial Branch of the Navajo Nation, 1997, p. 10). The peacemakers teach the parties to address the problem and make decisions *with,* not for, them. The process is not mystical or mysterious. The values and principles are based on Navajo common law, and the setting promotes discussion to find the causes of problems and to build consensus to deal with them in practical ways (p. 10).

Navajo peacemaking is notably used in cases of family violence, driving while impaired, and assaults. Sessions are held in courtrooms, court meeting facilities, chapter houses, homes, or traditional hogans. Peacemaking is not considered "alternative dispute resolution" or mediation (p. 14). It involves relatives, friends, neighbors, and anyone with even a marginal interest in what has occurred. *Nalyeeh,* the outcome of peacemaking, focuses on feelings, relationships, and future conduct. This may include compensation. Vincent Craig, the Chief Probation Officer of the Navajo Nation courts, recalls an incident of a young woman who had been sexually molested who was asked what she wanted from the perpetrator. Her response was: "Six horses." Horses are valuable to Navajos, and the compensation she demanded is said to be customary in sexual assault offenses (p. 15).

In cases of domestic violence, Navajo women have the choice of traditional peacemaking or modern restraining orders. They most often choose peacemaking because threatened recourse to justice officials is not a deterrent in remote, isolated areas. These women (and their batterers) must continue to live in their small communities. Peacemaking addresses the problems underlying an offender's actions, and has proven more effective because it requires the direct attention and involvement of others, which helps ensure the safety of the women (p. 18).

The legitimate right of Native American judicial systems to exist alongside U.S. judicial courts was recognized in 1993 in the Indian Tribal Justice Act, which declared that "traditional tribal justice practices are essential to the maintenance of the culture and identity of Indian tribes" (25 U.S.C. Sec. 3601[7]; see also The Judicial Branch of the Navajo Nation, 1997, p. 2). On June 1, 1995, U.S. Attorney General

Janet Reno, moreover, instituted a new policy to reaffirm Native American nations' sovereignty by establishing the Office of Tribal Justice and supporting Indian justice systems through the Tribal Courts Project (The Judicial Branch of the Navajo Nation, 1997, p. 2). The future of tribal systems of justice, however, will depend on "its integrity, authority, power, and meaning" to Native Americans (Melton, 1995, p. 133).

> The strong adversarial features of the American justice paradigm will always conflict with the communal nature of most tribes.... The many intrusions to the tribal way of life have interfered with the natural evolution of the indigenous justice paradigm, but while slowed, it has never stopped. The tribal resurgence to strengthen and retraditionalize their judiciaries has rejuvenated the evolutionary process. While mainstream society is in the midst of shifting from a retributive justice model to a restorative one, many tribes are strengthening their indigenous paradigm. In doing so, they are empowering themselves to provide a justice system that has meaning to the people they serve and the power to perpetuate what was preserved by the ancestors and passed on by the elders as testimony of their commitment to the future of tribes. (Melton, 1995, p. 133)

Ho'oponopono

Hawaiian culture has relied on shamans, known as *kahunas* (Sheikh, Kuzendorf, & Sheikh, 1989, pp. 473–475). There were kahunas for different aspects of living in order to safeguard *lokahi* (harmony) between humankind, nature, and the gods. The expertise of kahunas involved ceremonial rites, counsel of leaders, sorcery, herbal medicines, and crafting of certain implements. According to Leslie Kuloloio, a modern day kahuna on Maui, the *kahuna lapa'au* (healer) was also called on to conduct a traditional Hawaiian method of resolving conflicts and maintaining accord within the extended family called *ho'oponopono*. Ho'oponopono symbolizes the primary values with which Hawaiians regard relationships—cooperation, sharing, generosity, patience, and interdependence (Ogawa, in press).

The Hawaiian metaphor of a tangled net illustrates how problems within a family or group affect not only the persons directly involved but also others. As E. Virginia Shook of the University of Hawaii writes: "The family is a complex net of relationships, and any disturbance in one part of the net will pull other parts. This metaphor reinforces the Hawaiian philosophy of the interrelatedness of all things." (1985, p. 11).

Mary Kawena Pukui, a *kupuna* (elder) who has been the inspirational and knowledgeable guide for the reemergence of ho'oponopono in modern times, calls it the "thrashing out of every grudge, peeve, or resentment," and searching the heart for "hard feelings against one another." In this endeavor one must have the courage to ask for and to offer forgiveness in order to restore and maintain good relationships (Pukui, Handy, & Craighill, 1972, p. 61).

Ho'oponopono is usually led by a senior member of the family or a respected outsider such as the kahuna lapa'au. It is opened with a *pule* (prayer) to the *'aumakua* (ancestor gods) or to God to request assistance for and blessing on the problem-solving process. As Shook states, "Prayer lays the foundation for sincerity and truthfulness, necessary conditions to be maintained throughout" (1985, p. 11). The kahuna identifies the nature of the problem to be discussed and emphasizes the pooling of strengths for a shared purpose. The leader handles any resistance from a particular member by reaching out to the person.

Focus is next on the specific problem or *hala*. The persons involved are considered bound together in a negative entanglement called *hihia*. The seriousness of this entanglement is that the initial hurt is often followed by other reactions and further misunderstandings until a complex knot of difficulties has evolved. It is the leader's responsibility to choose one of the problems and resolve it through *mahiki* (discussion). Successive layers of trouble are uncovered and resolved until the relationships are again free and clear.

In this entire sequence the leader prevents individuals from directly confronting one another in order to avoid emotional outbursts that could escalate the problem and discourage its solution. Each person directly or indirectly affected by the problem is, however, asked to express his or her *mana'o* (feelings). This is done with honesty but also self-scrutiny to avoid blame and recrimination. If tempers do flare, the leader can declare *ho'omalu* (a cooling off period of silence). Members can then reflect on the purpose of the gathering and allow their emotions to subside.

After all discussion there is confession of wrong-doing and the seeking of forgiveness. Any forgiveness asked is expected to be granted. Any restitution necessary is agreed on. Those who had been in conflict are expected to *kala* (release) the problem, which is now *oki* (cut off).

Shook provides this excellent description of the final phase of ho'oponopono:

> The *pani* is the closing phase and may include a summary of what has taken place and, importantly, a reaffirmation of the family's strengths and enduring bonds. The problem that has been worked out is declared closed, never to be brought up again. If other layers of the problem need to be worked out, the final *pani* is postponed. Sometimes *ho'oponopono* may take many sessions. Each session has a *pani* about what has been resolved and includes a closing prayer, *pule ho'opau*. After the session the family and leader traditionally share a snack or meal to which all have contributed. This demonstrates the commitment and bond of all who participated and provides a familiar means to move from the formal problem-solving setting to normal daily routines. (1985, p. 12)

Although it is culture-specific in its history, use of Hawaiian language, and genesis in Hawaiian cultural values—spirituality, family life, and harmony—ho'oponopono is clearly a restorative process that is informative to all group processes that endeavor to soothe differences and right social errors. One of the leading proponents of using ho'oponopono by extending it beyond the Hawaiian culture is Lynette Paglinawan, a social worker in Honolulu. She has adapted variations of ho'oponopono for groups of unrelated individuals and non-Hawaiians. Other Hawaiian and some non-Hawaiian leaders, social workers, and counselors are also using ho'oponopono in youth drug prevention programs, marital counseling, mediation of disputes, delinquency programs, and dysfunctional family intervention.

6

REDESIGNING VICTIM SERVICES

Way of All the Earth

Endless Horizons, Boundless Depths, Infinite Sphere

John S. Dunne (1972), in his seminal book *The Way of All the Earth,* describes the spiritual adventure of our time period as "passing over" from the standpoint of one's own culture to that of others, followed by an equal process of "coming back" with sympathetic understanding and new insight. This odyssey is a way of examining one's own life and of learning from a broad range of human experiences.

Passing over and coming back, however, are not simply experiments but a way of life. It is like peering at the night sky and seeing no discernible boundary but realizing that one's vision is limited and the most distant stars fade from view. The depths of the heavens are boundless.

Journeying toward the horizon on a round earth, one also discovers that there is no final horizon. The earth, in Dunne's words, is an infinite sphere where the center is everywhere and the circumference is nowhere. No one culture, that is, contains either the sum total of wisdom or the final word on the creative course of humankind.

Chapter Overview

- Multiculturalism in Victim Services
- Minority Mental Health Systems
- Culturally Competent Approaches

Minorities typically underuse crime victim services. This is often attributed to some deficiency on the part of minorities, including lack of sophistication, education, or awareness. Such a perspective fails to recognize that minorities often view existing services as unresponsive to their needs and misinformed concerning their preferred traditional practices and beliefs. The major responsibility, after all, for delivery of and accessibility to services rests with providers and not with their clients.

This chapter begins by considering prejudice, stereotypes, and racism and their effects on providing services to minorities. Some of the major tenets of cross-cultural counseling are also discussed. Differing cultural definitions and systems of mental health are then described, along with examples of important approaches to counseling and assisting minority crime victims.

MULTICULTURALISM IN VICTIM SERVICES

Sincerity and empathy are powerful tools in serving minority crime victims. Personal sensitivity, however, cannot successfully cross the "cultural chasm" (Draguns, 1990) without cross-cultural knowledge and the ability to respond and adapt to the specific cultural context and circumstances (Cushner, 1996, p. 238).

Color Blindness

Many of us possess a variety of perceptions concerning those of a different race or culture. Charles Ridley (1989) provides a synopsis of these perceptions. Prejudice, Ridley explains, is literally a preconceived judgment or opinion, usually unfavorable, based on insufficient knowledge or spurious justification. It is part of a more generalized process called stereotyping. When we stereotype we simplify the characteristics of a race. Many of our stereotypes are inaccurate but not necessarily negative. Prejudiced people stereotype, according to Ridley, but not all who stereotype are prejudiced.

Stereotyping does become faulty, however, when it assigns characteristics that are assumed to indicate some manner of genetic or cultural inferiority, or when it becomes dogmatic and nonreceptive toward information that is new or perhaps contrary to previously held ideas. As Sue and Sue have written, "the danger of stereotypes is that they are impervious to logic or experience" (1990, p. 48). Ethnocentrism, for example, is the belief that one's own race or culture is the standard by which all others must be evaluated and judged. The best interests of one's own group are thus safeguarded and advanced—not always but many times at the expense of the well-being of other groups. Ethnocentrism, in other words, is not itself racism but may very well lead in that direction.

Racism is *multifaceted* in its forms and consequences. Any behavior or pattern of behavior, argues Ridley, that systematically denies access to opportunities and privileges to one social group while perpetuating these for another social group defines racism. Both individuals and institutions can be racist. When individuals or institutions act overtly (i.e., openly) in a racist way, there is clear and obvious intent to discriminate, harm, or exclude. But an individual's racist motives or an institution's racist policies can also be covert (i.e. hidden behind a facade of reasonableness and decorum). The same motivation of racism, for example, may underlie the lack of expenditure of funds and minimal programmatic effort to serve minorities as well as the direct refusal to do so.

A person or institution may furthermore *unknowingly participate* in racism. Even with good intentions, a service provider may say or do things that belittle or demean a certain racial group. Minority members have heard the refrain, "I haven't noticed that you are different. We are all humans. Our agency doesn't care if you are black, green, or purple." This approach is termed *color blindness.* The adverse result of color blindness is to "abstract" minority persons from the specific conditions of their history and experience and disregard the "central importance of color in the psychological experience of the client" (Ridley, 1989, p. 62). There is also the simultaneous neglect of the "undeniable influence" of the service provider's whiteness or other racial background upon the person being assisted (p. 62).

Unknowing or unintentional racism is therefore the most insidious. Whether from anxiety about appearing impartial, insecurity about personal views on race, or oversensitivity to the possibility of offending a minority client, avoiding culturally relevant factors and issues prevents effective service. Ridley correctly draws our attention accordingly to a *behavioral* understanding of racism.

Mistakenly, racism is often equated with prejudice, and solutions to the problem are generally limited to attitude change and consciousness raising. Certainly, these concerns are important. However, such a focus distracts from the
more basic problems of identifying and modifying the specific types of behavior that systematically produce adverse consequences for ethnic minorities.
(1989, p. 61)

All providers and agencies therefore need to scrutinize not only what they
think and feel about minority victims but also the particular ways these victims are
being served. Each service provider should develop its own "Personal Inventory
on Cultural Sensitivity" and "Survey of Agency Services to Minorities" instru-
ments that highlight and evaluate the racism profiles of individuals within their
organizations. Again, very few crime victim service providers or groups are bla-
tantly racist. A rift can easily develop, however, between persons who assist
minority victims, particularly minority professionals and their agencies, and others within the same field. The warehouse of values by which we conduct ourselves
is full of negative stereotypes, underlying prejudice, and unwitting racism. Pre-
tending or attempting to be color-blind is effectively the same as ethnocentrism.
The range of ethnicities in our culture still exists. What matters, therefore, is
whether or not our "ethnoprism" reflects this reality.

Cross-Cultural Counseling

The effectiveness of counseling for minority victims of crime can only derive from
the cultural appropriateness of the treatment being offered. How the victim identifies the most important aspects of a crime's impact and how these are addressed
by the methods and goals of a particular therapy must correspond. Jerry Tello, in
his article entitled "Cultural Competence in Working with Latinos," provides this
insight:

Typically, one may hear service providers…minimize cultural differences by
stressing the similarities between ethnic groups. Statements such as, "We all
have feelings, the same emotions, want the best for our children and therefore
are all alike," or "You really just have to look at each family or person on an
individual basis rather than looking at their culture and community," are often
heard…. Although these and other such remarks merit discussion, these points
cannot and should not negate cultural differences based on traditions, customs, history and socio-economic experiences. What it does demonstrate is the
service provider's inability to understand and articulate these differences.
When this occurs, the service provider may attempt to further justify his own
position by minimizing the role of culture. (n.d., p. 3)

Tello is aware that the role of culture must be balanced by considerations of the
individual's unique circumstances and personal resources. As Roll, Millen, and
Martinez have pointed out, "there are some ways in which any particular Chicano

is like all other Chicanos and there are some ways in which a particular Chicano is like no other Chicano" (1980, p. 165). There is no universal human approach to counsel persons who suffer, but there is also no one method that will suffice for all persons *within* a specific culture. The competent service provider is therefore one who learns about other cultures, continues to assess whether the various communication styles and counseling methods are adequate, and is flexible enough to adjust to these on a case by case basis (Sue & Zane, 1987, p. 37).

Many therapists have been reluctant or resistant to practice with such openness. They adhere to a set of Western European-based cultural values that govern their notion of normality, structure their expectations toward clients, and undergird their definition and regimen of cure. Their basic model is a *psychological* interpretation of trauma and suffering, with the therapeutic goals of healing emotional wounds and maintaining a healthy state of mind. The techniques employed to accomplish these goals include *verbalizing* underlying fears and conflicts and providing *symptom relief* by prescribing medications (Eth, 1992, p. 105; Lee & Armstrong, 1995, pp. 447–448).

This system of mental-based health, however, has proven inadequate and restrictive for many persons in the U.S., especially minorities. There are many cultures that do not isolate physical, emotional, and spiritual factors in health and illness. Trauma affects the whole person and not just one aspect of life (Sheikh, Kuzendorf, & Sheikh, 1989, p. 472). Different cultures therefore have unique "idioms of distress" to publicly communicate subjective discomfort. Southeast Asian refugees, for example, often complain about body dysfunction such as headaches or chest pains when experiencing depression (Nishio & Bilmas, 1987, p. 343). Asians, in general, experience and report stress psychosomatically (Root, 1985). Western psychiatry would have the propensity to minimize these physical complaints as hypochondria, the product of imaginary ailments. This diagnosis would confuse Asians who do not make the same mind–body distinctions. Vital information affecting treatment could therefore be lost through such misunderstandings.

Ilola (1990), for example, summarizes cases of Hmong refugee deaths attributed to "Hmong sudden death syndrome" or "nightmare death." The cause of this death is generally inexplicable in terms of biological or pathological etiology; it occurs during sleep and is found most frequently among the Hmong, but also occurs among Laotians, Cambodians, and Vietnamese. Somatization of distress caused by survivor grief, severe culture shock, and war-related experiences are thought to be factors. Even with bilingual translators, Western psychotherapy seems not to help. Instead, a shaman from the community can help bring the problem under control in a relatively short time.

The term *shaman* is derived from the Russian *saman* meaning "ascetic." The concept of shamanism is at least 20,000 years old and encompasses the idea of priest, healer, and magician. Shamans are found in all continents and share remarkably similar practices (Sheikh et al., 1989, p. 472). Shamanistic approaches are radically different from most dominant beliefs of Western physicians and mental health practitioners.

Modern scientists generally look upon the body independently of the spirit. Disease is an external agent, something against which one should protect one-self; failing that, disease is something that should be removed or destroyed through technological intervention. The shamans not only knew of no reason to isolate the spirit from the body, but they even recognized the danger of doing so.... In other words, disease was a concrete manifestation of a spiritual crisis. (Sheikh et al., 1989, pp. 472–473)

Much of Western psychiatry, in contrast, is awkward in its evaluation of the validity of the spirit realm (Sharma, 1989, p. 517). Deference toward or communication with this realm is at best likely to be regarded as unusual. An eight-year-old Puerto Rican girl, for example, was referred for psychological testing because she was "hearing things" (the collision of drinking glasses in a closed refrigerator) and "seeing things" (a woman sitting on her bed at night). A therapist believed the girl was hallucinating. In Puerto Rican culture, however, this girl's sense of the spirit world was not considered a deficit but rather a highly valued faculty for discernment. The results of the psychological testing, in fact, revealed no evidence of psychopathology. Erwin Parson, an expert on post-traumatic stress, emphasizes the role of ethnicity in counseling.

All ethnically focused clinical, sociological, anthropological, and experimental studies converge to one central conclusion regarding ethnic America: Ethnic identification is an irreducible entity, central to how persons organize experience, and to an understanding of the unique "cultural prism" they use in perception and evaluation of reality.... Thus, the client's ideas, feelings, beliefs, values, gestures, intonations, perceptions, and evaluations, can only be understood within the patient's ethnocultural context. (1985, p. 315)

Cultural differences in behavior, however, have been often misinterpreted as pathological rather than understood as different but realistic responses to a situation. As Casas and Vasquez warn, "The interpretation of behavior in terms of the counselor's values rather than those of the client can result in erroneous assessment and diagnosis and potentially ineffective or destructive intervention" (1989, p. 158).

The Sioux, for example, practice a form of self-treatment called *wacinko,* usually translated as "pouting." Wacinko is a sort of "time out" by which the individual intentionally sets aside active and nonproductive involvement in a stressful situation. This practice has been frequently misdiagnosed as a reactive depressive illness and a maladaptive form of withdrawal when, in fact, it is a solution to a problem rather than its cause (Trimble & Fleming, 1989, p. 187). As Blue and Blue have found, Native Americans may simply wait out the circumstances of an intransigent problem because they trust that a resolution will naturally occur. This "waiting for something to happen" may *appear* to be a state of depression or withdrawal, but is actually a culturally expressive form of healing. Passivity in the context of Native American culture is not hopelessness but hopefulness (Blue & Blue, 1993, p. 20).

Similarly, in Asian culture there is an emphasis on harmony with the natural flow of life events. In Zen philosophy a person is to be *unsui*, like "cloud-water" (Kapleau, 1989, pp. 10–11). Clouds drift freely, forming and reshaping according to the dictates of atmospheric conditions and their own nature. In like manner, water adapts to its circumstances, becoming round in a round vessel and square in a square one but always retaining its identity. In a river, for example, water travels toward its destination, the sea, encountering obstacles and obstructions but finding ways to continue on its path. A person likewise meets challenges and problems but, by remaining purposeful, is able to persevere (Kapleau, 1989, pp. 10–11; Ogawa 1996, p. 7; Reynolds, 1989, pp. 181–182) Westerners have misconceived this acceptance as fatalism or resignation. Acceptance, however, is not surrendering one's aspirations or languishing in defeat. It is, instead, the careful identification of what is and what is not under one's control and directing one's behavior accordingly. It is only the locus of attention and effort that changes, not the will or desire to live well.

The accurate recognition of psychopathology necessitates, in other words, a respect for and an understanding of the unique ways various cultures deal with life problems. As Casas and Vasquez argue, "the question is no longer *whether* counselors are personally and professionally encapsulated and biased but *to what degree and in what ways.*" Failure to admit this bias and to disregard the cultural values of minority clients have led minorities to see counselors not as "benign helpers" but as agents of social oppression whose primary function is to assure conformance to the majority culture's values (Casas & Vasquez, 1989, pp. 161–162).

Even feminism, which has contributed much to the rethinking and reformulating of how persons view and treat one another, must reorient itself to include non-white perspectives. Julia Boyd, a black psychotherapist, has written:

> Feminism that denies freedom of ethnic and cultural differences is not feminism; therapy that covertly denies the validity of a woman's ethnic and cultural experiences is not therapy.... Many white feminist therapists forget that they were white long before they chose to become feminists or therapists. Being a feminist therapist does not negate the societal privilege that is inherent in being born white. As Elsie Smith says in her 1981 piece in the *Journal of Non-White Concerns*, it is nurtured by generations of "hand me down" hatreds. White feminists who exercise race privilege on a daily basis often lack awareness that they are doing so. (1990, pp. 231–232)

The results of failure to account for cultural differences have occasionally been near tragic or even fatal. In order to ease the mourning of Hmong children in St. Paul, Minnesota, after the death of their Headstart teacher, Charlotte Bell, her family tucked a card with the children's photographs into the casket before it was buried. The Hmong parents, on later discovering what had been intended as a comforting gesture, urged that the casket be exhumed. The Hmong believe that if you are still alive but your photograph or some other personal artifact, such as hair, is buried, your own spirit will leave your body. Bell's family graciously agreed to the exhumation without condescendingly ignoring it as a bothersome superstition.

The outcome of misunderstanding cultural differences was not so fortunate for a Vietnamese father who was mistakenly accused by child protective authorities of abusing his son. He had cared for his sick child by practicing *cao gio* (coin rubbing), the traditional Vietnamese technique of pressing heated metal coins forcefully on the body to reduce fever, chills, and headaches. The lesions from rubbing the child's skin resembled trauma inflicted by intentional injury. The father—feeling overpowering grief, confusion, and humiliation over the investigation and accusations—committed suicide (Korbin, 1980, p. 24).

Steve Shon, a psychiatrist, warns against the hazards of ethnocentric therapies: "What's fairly clear is that the mental health system has to change in order to accommodate itself to different kinds of people" (Nakao, 1990a, p. A-12). This change may not come easily. Both subtle and blatant stereotypes of minorities are held by many practicing therapists. One study found that a number of therapists had negative attitudes toward Hispanics, characterizing them as "lazy, dumb, dirty, and overemotional." Another study reported that white counselors are more likely to be influenced by stereotypes than are minority counselors (Casas & Vasquez, 1989, p. 161).

Relatively few mental health or social work professionals, in fact, have extensive training and experience in cross-cultural counseling methods. The American Psychological Association's Subcommittee on Culturally Sensitive Models within the Board of Ethnic Minority Affairs conducted a nationwide survey in 1990 and found that only 4.2% of the graduate psychology programs offered culturally relevant training in a comprehensive format. The Center for Social Work Research at the University of Texas, in a 1995 survey of social work programs, found a similar situation:

> Even though many of these graduate programs offered diversity courses that examined the history, culture, experience and practice issues germane to work with different cultural and ethnic groups in the U.S., these courses were rarely required for graduation. Only 5 of the 57 programs (9%) responding to the survey required all students to take a course on cultural diversity. (Center for Social Work Research, 1995, p. 2)

It is hardly remarkable therefore that just since the 1960s have books on multiculturalism in counseling been written (Pedersen, Fukuyama, & Heath, 1989, pp. 3, 39). There have been, for example, relatively few books describing non-Western counseling methods' suitability for Western clients. Morita and Naikan therapies, both indigenous to Japan, are major modalities in the East. They were briefly introduced to the United States in the 1930s, but not until the 1980s and 1990s did they gain some popularity (Reynolds, 1976; Reynolds, 1989). This author has adapted Morita and Naikan approaches to the counseling of violent crime victims, including rape victims and battered women (Ogawa, 1986; 1988a; 1989; 1996). Only through such efforts will we be able to identify those counseling methods that are culture-specific and those that are more readily transferable between cultures. Transcultural counseling (Sharma, 1989) provides a major avenue for understanding not only other lifeways but also evolving our own. It highlights the fundamental linkages of humanity in a practical and useful manner.

Victim service agencies, in making referrals for treatment or counseling, must, in other words, be cognizant of the level of awareness and experience individual practitioners have in treating diverse populations. An agency's own commitment to culturally sensitive treatment is partially demonstrated by the racial diversity of its administrative and especially its direct service staff relative to the composition of its client population. There may be justification why an agency does not have any minority staff members or the presence of only a token representation. A survey in 1993, for example, found that in 25 accredited marriage and family therapy graduate programs, only 3% of the master's and 2.7% of the doctoral students were African American (Hardy & Laszloffy, 1994, p. 13). If minority staff members are not available, cultural sensitivity will be developed by other means that meet the needs of minority victims. These include:

- minority volunteers
- a systematic referral system
- protocols to guide non-minority staff
- periodic training
- culturally sensitive written materials
- on-call translators

It must not be presumed that service providers of the same racial or ethnic heritage as their clients will always be preferable. A counselor's close and favorable cross-cultural contacts are likely a greater predictor of effectiveness than identical race and ethnicity. Clients, according to one study, desire their counselors to have more education but similar attitudes and values, to be older but compatible in personality, and *lastly* to be of the same ethnicity (Sundberg & Sue, 1989, p. 347). A bilingual and bicultural counselor is not, in Tello's terms, implicitly "biculturally competent." Partaking of two cultures is not the same as possessing the skills to assist a minority client to function in meaningful and healthful ways across cultures.

Julia Boyd contends, in this regard, that black women have become "masters in the art of being bicultural" because they have had to adopt certain behaviors and mannerisms of the white culture in order to survive. Boyd illustrates this by giving an account of her experience in treating a young Southeast Asian woman for depression. This client had been treated unsuccessfully in the past by another therapist, but her physician advised her to try counseling once more. She came to Boyd not expecting any real help but rather to fulfill her promise to the physician that she would make the appointment. This is Boyd's description of her approach to a client of another culture:

> During our first interview, I obtained a full family history, which included a detailed history of her family life prior to coming to the United States. In taking the history, I encouraged the woman to elaborate, which allowed me to gain some insight regarding her world as she experienced it. After the first interview,

I began doing my homework, which was to network with other Southeast Asian women and to research material that would help me know my client as a bicultural person. During subsequent sessions, as she related information concerning her depression, I was able to shape the therapy into a context that included some of her traditional ethnic values, such as family loyalty, and a circular concept of harmony between self and nature. In listening to this Southeast Asian woman, I was able to glean information regarding her lifestyle, her needs, her wants, and her disappointments; many of which were not the same as mine. However, I was able to recognize that her depression was in some part linked to an ethnic and cultural deprivation she experienced living in the United States. (1990, pp. 232–233)

Boyd bothered to study and address the cultural context of the emotional needs of her client. In doing so, she adopted a constructive counseling format between her client and herself.

Any counselor must guard against both the anxiety of not being able to meet the needs of a client and the overconfidence of believing prior knowledge is sufficient. In counseling a minority client, these impediments are overcome not by dismissing cultural issues because of adherence to conventional counseling theories or by overlooking significant psychological problems in favor of cultural interpretations. The minority client is best served when the counselor empathizes with what is both culturally *and* individually relevant to the client's situation. The box below details service provisions that meet the critera of cultural sensitivity for all clients.

_____ Culturally Sensitive Public Service Provisions _____

For victim service agencies to be sensitive to the needs of minority crime victims, the following are required:

- Service providers must begin acknowledging that there are different and equally valid cultural definitions concerning personal well-being and recovery from traumatic events.
- Providers must also support the sophisticated and varied approaches to mental health that exist in minority cultures and take these into account when offering minority victim services and referrals.
- There must be extensive cultural awareness training and competency testing that gives staff the capacity to understand persons whose thinking, behavior, and modes of expression are culturally different.
- Professional staff must develop multiethnic teamwork responses as a primary resource and tool for implementing and monitoring effective services.
- There must be in place a cross-cultural perspective that will incorporate and benefit from the principles and methods of other cultures.

MINORITY MENTAL HEALTH SYSTEMS

Latino Cultural Values

Crime victim services for Latinos entail more than having established programs made accessible through the hiring of Spanish-speaking individuals or by "Latinizing" programs with cultural frills and displays. The elements of appropriate service are those that select Latino practices and beliefs to shape the style and content of outreach, education, and treatment.

Lilia Hernandez, a therapist with the Family Stress Center in Chula Vista, California, for example, calls Latinos the "worst planners" but the "best improvisors" (L. Hernandez, personal communication, 1990). The white value of holding to rigid schedules is not as important to Latinos as are other concerns. Hernandez tells of a Mexican male who was always late for the weekly group sessions for parents of sexually molested children. Rather than come directly from work to the meetings, he chose first to bathe and change into clean clothes at home. Making himself presentable was of more importance than arriving at a designated time. Hernandez accepts this man's reason without upset, simply begins the meetings whenever most of the parents arrive, and does not interpret coming late as avoiding attendance or being disinterested (L. Hernandez, personal communication, 1990).

Ignacio Aguilar is also a California therapist serving the Latino community. He integrates the symbols and forms of the Latino culture to assist his clients, including homicide survivors, abused women, depressed and anxiety-ridden persons (Haldane, 1990, p. 1). Dichos and folklore, traditional Mexican music and dance, poetry and crafts, the Aztec calendar, and role-playing modeled after modern Spanish-speaking *novelas* (television soap operas) are all conspicuous in his approach. By relying on culturally recognizable forms, Aguilar removes the hurdle of his clients having to understand and conform to a therapy foreign to their experience. This approach, because it is structured around those things encountered or occurring in his clients' daily life and honored within their cultural history, brings its own affirmation and uplift and creates a more natural therapeutic setting.

Some of the cultural traits of Hispanics that must be recognized in providing counseling or social services have been summarized by Casas and Vasquez:

1. Often display a great concern for immediacy and the "here and now."
2. Frequently attribute control to an external locus, such as luck, supernatural powers, and acts of God.
3. Favor an extended rather than a nuclear family support system.
4. Often take a concrete, tangible approach to life rather than an abstract, long-term outlook.
5. With authority figures, try to practice a unilateral communication pattern that uses limited eye contact, deference, and silence as signs of respect.
6. Try to develop multilingual communication skills, using English, Spanish, and "Spanglish," a hybrid of the two. (1989, pp.165–166)

Alongside adaptations of Latino culture for mental health treatment or counseling services are *curanderos* (folk healers). These folk healers are able to dispense a wide assortment of cures according to the gifts of healing given to them. *Susto,* for example, is the result of a traumatic experience, usually experienced by children but also suffered by adults. In Mexican culture a curandero customarily treats this affliction by *barriendo* or "sweeping" over the person, who is lying on his or her back. This sweeping may be done with a broom, an egg, or a bundle of herbs, and may be accompanied by reciting a creed (West, 1989, pp. 139–140).

Most ailments are interpreted by curanderos as occurring in the natural course of life. There are some, however, that come from the willful intent of someone to harm. One of these is the dispensations of *brujos* (witches). Curanderos are then called on to counter such hexes. Because of such powers of good, curanderos are revered and gain reputations that span time. Don Pedro Jaramillo of Texas, for example, was a lowly shepherd who, while severely ill and unconscious for days, was given his gift by God. When he awoke, he pledged to devote himself to help those who suffered. Since his death, his saintliness has been honored by many, including other curanderos:

> On each of their altars, an essential piece of equipment for every curandero, is a picture of Don Pedrito. It is possible that they may not have an image of the Virgin there, but not to have a picture of Don Pedrito... "*Ay no!*" one says with pain in her voice, "*Es imposible!*" One curandera...in South Texas had a special altar for Don Pedrito. She prays first to him and then to the Virgin. (West, 1988, p. 141)

Nonetheless, the Catholic Church has been a central and formative institution within Latino culture. At times, its teachings have seemingly shackled Latinos with doctrines that have stigmatized some victims of violent crimes. A 13-year-old Mexican American girl, for example, had been severely beaten with an electrical cord by her mother. She had begun to receive phone calls from boys at her school. This was strictly forbidden by her parents. She had been warned that she was too young to be talking to boys. Earlier the evening of the beating, two boys were riding their bikes past the girl's house and stopped to talk with her. Her mother, stepping out from the front door, saw her talking to the boys and became furious. She dragged her daughter by her hair into the house. She then took an electrical cord and began to whip her. The boys outside, hearing the commotion, became frightened and called the police.

Although the daughter had red swollen lash marks all over her face and body, the police had difficulty explaining to the family why this was illegal and the mother was being arrested. The girl's father quoted several Bible verses to show that God had given parents the responsibility of disciplining disobedient children. God, he said, expected his wife to punish their daughter because he had not been home to do it himself. The police tried to explain that teenagers have a natural interest in relating to one another and that their daughter's talking to boys did not warrant a beating.

The daughter was not upset with her mother. She felt guilty and even said it was her fault. She said that she should have pretended not to have seen the boys and gone into the house. Her four sisters, all younger, added that they all get spanked and that it was the sister who was in trouble because she had made their mother mad. The family were all regular churchgoers and believed that the criminal justice system was interfering in their religiously supported actions. As the police later discovered, so did their priest (H. Thueson, personal communication, 1997, July 11, 1997).

Latinas, moreover, who have been victims of rape have experienced considerable internal conflict about seeking help.

> The idea of rape as God's punishment for previous sin relates to the equation of rape with the sexual act. This concept arises directly from the Catholic Church teachings which emphasize a woman's virginity and purity of mind and body. Thus, her sexual behavior and attitudes may tend, traditionally, to label her as one of two extremes—as "madonna" or "whore." (Destito, Santiago, & Darder, 1985/1986, p. 90).

Angelo Ginorio, of the Women's Information Center at the University of Washington, and Jane Reno, clinical supervisor at Consejo in Seattle, describe how the veneration of the Virgin Mary is directly related to this assigned gender role of *marianismo.* The only acceptable reason for not being a virgin is motherhood. The married woman who has been raped is therefore disgraced and loses respectability because the sexual act was not with her husband. Similarly, the marriageability of the single woman who is raped is jeopardized. It is *her* reputation that is tarnished because her virginity is lost. The Catholic Church in its attempt to sanction sexual mores and family life has, in other words, brought confusion to Latinas' formation of their self-concept as women and what is deemed their responsibility in the wake of sexual assault. As Ginorio and Reno explain:

> Because for so many women the Church has been the only avenue for participation and expression outside of the family, we have looked to the Church for leadership and support to help in establishing our identity as women. However, our moral and religious beliefs have often been a powerful impediment to change.... The religious stance on sexuality, rape, abortion and birth control has not made it possible to openly and frankly confront these issues so central to women's lives—neither in the privacy of the family nor in the public forum of society. (1985, p. 2)

Many Latino victims of crime, notwithstanding, do call upon the Virgin Mary and saints for intercession, consult priests, and attend mass both regularly and on special occasions (such as the Memorial Mass for a deceased loved one). The Catholic Church provides a theology to alleviate suffering, rituals for guidance and release, and a social setting for emotional support. When the Church, moreover, takes an *active* part in serving in, organizing, and leading programs designed to assist Latino crime victims, it provides these victims with an all-encompassing source of practical and spiritual help. Catholic Social Services, for example, has sponsored counseling programs for child molestation victims across the country. In Los Angeles, Brother Modesto Leon has guided mothers of slain youth to find mutual support. These mothers tell their stories to gang members and others in order to salvage lives and prevent more violence in the barrios. It is evident through these and other programs that the church's message of redemption is meant also for crime victims.

Black Churches

The mental health system available to the black community has often been the extremes of hospitalization and incarceration. Black males, for example, have been consistently overly diagnosed as suffering from serious psychoses and schizophrenia. African Americans thus have "a deeply rooted and long-standing distrust of American psychiatry" (Maultsby, 1982, p. 39). Problems are kept within the family and remedied in the home. To invite the attention and scrutiny of outside authorities could mean being locked up for "acting crazy." Outside agencies and practitioners are usually sought only in desperation or emergency. It is during these crisis situations, however, that there is even less chance that the mental health system will be prepared to adequately respond. African Americans, in other words, have been ill-served and underserved recipients of mental health delivery. As Boyd states of its effect on black women:

> Generational teachings regarding trusting others outside the ethnic and cultural community have been strongly enforced by family and respected community members. From early childhood, black women have been taught that personal disclosure outside the community is synonymous with treason. This strong devotion to non-disclosure has for many years silenced black women in personal crisis. (1990, p. 227)

The story of Clementine Barfield of Detroit, Michigan, is extraordinary and inspirational in this regard. Barfield is the founder of an organization called Save Our Sons and Daughters (SOSAD). On July 17, 1986, Barfield's son, Derik, was shot during an argument. His murder was not spectacular, given the fact that 30 other Detroit teenagers were killed by handguns that same year. His death went virtually unnoticed by the public, filling only three brief paragraphs in the newspaper. But Barfield and six other mothers of slain youths would not let their children's deaths be forgotten. In early 1987, they and 90 other Detroit residents organized SOSAD with the dual purpose of comforting grieving families and working to prevent violence by and against the city's young people. As Barfield has stated:

> In the black community, bereavement support is not something we normally reach out for. The norm is for people to lock themselves in their house and feel

like they're the only one who feels this badly. But we have over 130 families in SOSAD, families that have reached out. Wherever I go, kids are stopping me and saying, "You're that lady about the kids getting killed." (As cited in Irwin, 1990, p. C1)

SOSAD is developing chapters in other Michigan cities and has received requests for organizational assistance from Milwaukee, St. Louis, Atlanta, Los Angeles, San Francisco, Columbus, and Omaha. Barfield says it has taken "a lot of love and a lot of commitment" to start and sustain SOSAD (p. C1). She has tirelessly attended funerals two or three times a week. Yet the sound of so many mothers crying over their murdered children has spurred her to look even more deeply for *solutions*. On a certain morning, she is busy planning a week-long antiviolence program at a local high school and an anti-drug march through several neighborhoods. That afternoon, she accompanies another mother to the state juvenile prison to visit the young killer of the woman's son. The woman wants to talk to the teenager about straightening out his life. Barfield's own recovery has been a difficult one, but SOSAD has given her a worthwhile purpose.

I can't heal as long as I talk about it every day, so the healing process is not just something I can work through. But I know I've been instrumental in helping some children, and it helps to know I haven't lost my son for nothing. (As cited in Irwin, 1990, p. C1)

There have also been traditional institutions within the African American community, especially the church, that have rendered a variety of social and other services (McRoy, 1990, pp. 12–13). The black church has historically played a vital function as a gathering place for blacks. Although it has generally been ignored, it has thus been undisturbed by the larger white society. Leigh and Green provide this summary:

The Great Awakening, a religious revival which began in the North during the mid-1700s, sent traveling preachers (usually Methodist and Baptist) throughout the country. They carried their evangelistic message to both Blacks and whites and inspired the rise of Black preachers on estates and in cities throughout the South. This led to the proliferation of Black churches…and the desire to control their own congregations led to splits such as that which resulted in the founding of the African Methodist Episcopal Church in 1816.

After Emancipation, the "invisible" churches of the plantations became more open and visible…to provide significant services to the Black community. Churches were the center of educational activity at a time when schools were either unavailable or closed to Black students. Leadership skills were developed in the operation of churches. Ministers enjoyed high prestige not only as spiritual advisors but as highly visible community activists. Mutual aid societies and benevolent associations were established…in order to provide health and welfare services to those in need. (1979, p. 135)

The black church today is primarily Christian, including membership within the large mainline denominations and smaller independent movements. It also has an important Muslim presence and some traditional African religious practices. The black church continues to take seriously its role in the community. The Shiloh Baptist church in the inner city of Washington, D.C., for example, has independently constructed a multimillion-dollar Family Life Center that offers counseling, tutoring for young people, child day care, recreation, and senior citizen activities. In Oakland, a group of black ministers formed a corporation to renovate a motel— the notorious site of prostitution and drug-related crime—into one and two bedroom units for low income families.

Crime prevention and victim support are also increasingly on the agenda of black churches and ministers. The Reverend Cecil Williams, pastor of Glide Memorial United Methodist church in the Tenderloin area of San Francisco, for example, is at the forefront of a campaign to keep illicit drugs, specifically crack cocaine, away from African American children. Marches through the city's housing projects have reverberated with shouts of "Up with hope, down with dope." Black churches in the East Bay have initiated neighborhood meetings in the wake of surges in violent crimes or to periodically quell hostilities arising from the misconduct of law enforcement officers. Black ministers in Los Angeles have convened peace talks between rival gang leaders in order to suppress their activity and save lives. Individuals like Veronica Wilson, a young adult leader with the United Church of Christ in Southern California, coordinate outreach to sexual assault victims from a center sponsored by the Southern Christian Leadership Conference.

In the city of Memphis, Tennessee, Dr. Katherine (Kitty) Lawson, an African American ordained minister at Abundant Grace Fellowship, offers support to homicide survivors. Dr. Lawson founded Victims to Victory in 1995 in response to her ministerial outreach to a church family tormented by a double homicide. Drug dealers, apparently enraged to discover they had broken into the wrong apartment, killed a young couple and locked their three-year-old daughter in the closet with her father's bloodied body. "We knew we had a responsibility to support and minister to the child, as well as to the woman's parents, who were also members of our church," stated Dr. Lawson. Immediately the church set up a fund for the child's future education and counseling needs (as cited in Beane, 1987, pp. 8–9).

Dr. Lawson started Victims to Victory so that homicide survivors would have a "balm for their wounds" and a place where faith would be the "foundation for healing" (Beane, 1987, p. 9). Dr. Lawson, a trained psychologist, provides individual counseling for the program, refers victims to other therapists, and facilitates the homicide survivor support groups. She calls Memphis "a city of churches," where the church, particularly in the black community, has been the traditional source of trust for those seeking help. During the period from 1996–97, Victims to Victory served 137 homicide survivors. Of these, 126 were African Americans, reflecting the majority population of the city of Memphis (K. Lawson, personal communication, September 16, 1997). "People came with such agony," says Dr. Lawson. The survivors who participate in the group sessions are primarily women and children. Men who attend usually accompany their spouses. Outreach to men includes a lending library of grief books, social events such as picnics, and publicity through local newspapers.

Eighty percent of the operating funds for Victims to Victory is from state-administered federal Victims of Crime Act (VOCA) monies. The government is now acknowledging that the church is a natural system of support for African Americans and a place where their spiritual and counseling needs are not separate. Americans generally have called upon clergy and religious leaders during times of personal crisis (Chalfant, Heller, Briones, Aguirre-Hockbaums, & Farr, 1990), especially after the death of someone close (Verhoff, Kulka, & Douvan, 1981). For African Americans the church has undoubtedly been the most influential institution in their lives for its ability to merge their innate African spirituality with Christianity, serve as the base for socialization and community life, and sustain them through enormous life traumas, including victimization (Butler, 1995, p. 39). In 1997, Dr. Lawson, buoyed by the ministry of Victims to Victory, launched efforts to establish a Memphis branch of Neighbors Who Care to minister to all types of crime victims.

Not only does the black church continue to offer solace and hope, it also remains a stable community organization for social and civil rights activism. Black churches are known for spawning political activists whose lives have been devoted to serving black communities. Adam Clayton Powell, Jr. was a preacher when he became the first black Congressman in 1945. William H. Gray III, the majority whip in Congress during the 1990 session, began his career in a pulpit in Philadelphia. Martin Luther King, Jr., Ralph Abernathy, Malcolm X, Andrew Young, and Jesse Jackson have also been lauded as both religious leaders and significant U.S. political figures.

In early 1996, therefore, a sharp rise in the number of arson attacks on African American churches, especially in the southern states, caused alarm in the black community. A series of these fires had been set around the time of the Martin Luther King, Jr. holiday (National Church Arson Task Force [NCATF], 1997, p. 5). In June 1996, the President formed the National Church Arson Task Force to investigate the fires. The Bureau of Alcohol, Tobacco, and Firearms (ATF) and the Federal Bureau of Investigation (FBI) worked with state and local task forces to investigate 429 incidents of arson and bombing that occurred between January of 1995 and May of 1997. Of these incidents, 162 involved African American churches—three quarters of them located in the southern United States (NCATF, 1997, p. 7). Of the 81 suspects arrested for arsons at the black churches, 55 were white, 25 were African American, and 1 was Hispanic (p. 8).

The arsons, of course, had raised concerns about an increase in racially-motivated crimes. President Clinton stated that the fires "offended every citizen who cherishes America's proud heritage of religious and ethnic diversity" (Sobieraj, 1997, p. A7). Macedonia Baptist Church in Manning, South Carolina, for example, was burned on June 21, 1995, by four ex-Ku Klux Klan members. The Church of Christ in Henderson, Nevada, was burned on September 19, 1996, by a white male after a failed burglary attempt because, he stated, its members were African Americans. The Mallalieu Methodist Church in Meridian, Mississippi, was burned on December 11, 1996, by three white teenagers who defaced the communion altar and walls with racial epithets. The motives of all of the apprehended arsonists, however, have been varied.

The motives do include blatant racism or religious hatred, but also financial profit, burglary, and personal revenge (NCATF, 1997, p. 15). Black churches understandably wondered about the direct involvement of organized hate groups, such as the Ku Klux Klan, and a national conspiracy. The arsonists have instead primarily acted as individuals, approximately 70% of whom were young males under the age of 24 (p. 26). These facts do not necessarily lessen the impact of church arsons on black churches. Whatever the specific reasons for the attacks, the center of community life for many African Americans was affected. What has been heartening is that over 15,000 volunteers came forward to help in the rebuilding process for many of the church structures. The U.S. Department of Housing and Urban Development forged a coalition with the National Council of Churches, the Congress of National Black Churches, Habitat for Humanity, local financial institutions, and other groups to coordinate resources. As Elisabeth Miller, a 17-year-old from Great Falls, Virginia, who traveled to Boligee, Alabama, to help rebuild Little Zion Baptist Church said, "At first I came here with the knowledge that I was to rebuild churches. What I did not realize was that I was also here to rebuild the hopes and trust of the suffering community" (p. 9).

Asian American Orientation

The stigma attached to mental illness has prevented many Asian Americans from seeking professional counseling. Self-worth, in Asian tradition, evolves less from individual well-being than one's value and place in a group or society. To cause embarrassment or disgrace to one's family, community, or race jeopardizes this essential relationship to others. To admit personal problems or inability to cope with crises must therefore be done with utmost care.

One way to offset the fear of public disapproval is for service providers to insure confidentiality. But shame is only one reason that Asian Americans have not sought Western modes of treatment. Asian cultures are not oriented toward individual psychology. As UCLA professor Harry Kitano writes:

> Discussions of feelings or of psychological motives for behavior and analyzing behavior from a psychological frame of reference are not common in most Asian-American homes, even those of the second and third generations. Disturbed behavior is often viewed as the result of a lack of will, supernatural causes, or physical illness.... Hard work, effort, and developing character are presumed to be the best "cure" for most disturbances. (1989, p. 146)

Verbal disclosure or assertiveness, in other words, is less valued than correct behavior and productive activity. There is congruence with the adage "Actions speak louder than words." Most Asians are taught to be task-oriented rather than emotion-led. Applied to counseling, a formal structure and directive approach is thus preferred (Sue & Zane, 1986). Therapy sessions for Asians should delineate goals, assign practical exercises, and be limited to a brief rather than extended period of time. This task orientation is clearly seen in the esteem with which most Asians view education. There is a stigma attached to *not* pursuing education if the opportunity exists. A number of therapists who serve Asian communities have thus worked and renamed their programs "life education." Instruction or classes are held instead of therapy sessions. These are not just cosmetic adjustments but reflect the belief that therapy essentially involves *re-educating* the person. The model of teacher and student has been readily and historically accepted by Asians.

Similarly, those who are consulted in the Asian community for personal difficulties carry a familiarity and respect based on a high degree of status. This credibility is *ascribed* because of age or position, or *achieved* because of special skills or wisdom. This reliance on authority and superiority as a respected individual establishes the client's confidence in seeking help. In the aftermath of the shooting of the schoolchildren in Stockton, for example, the Cambodians depended on their Buddhist beliefs and ceremonies and the ministrations of their priests. There would have been no stigma placed on them for receiving help from mental health agencies because the crime had affected the entire city. Their method of coping, however, was to form a bond as a people, and this included their shared religion.

In San Francisco, Bertie Moo, a mental health department supervisor, has long been active with the city's Cambodian and Laotian residents. When she inquired what would be most helpful to bring counseling services to their community, the Southeast Asians told her to have the city help them to build a temple. Moo lobbied for the city's assistance but, not unexpectedly, was refused. The opening of a neighborhood clinic was more suitable from the city's perspective. In effect, the city was separating mental and spiritual concerns. To the Southeast Asians, however, locating a multiservice clinic within, or at least adjacent to, a temple would integrate the two in way that would be a culturally acceptable and necessary means of service delivery.

Indian Shamans

Native Americans also do not segment life. Religion, for example, is not something they participate in; it is something that they live. Native American ceremonies and rituals are therefore only the "special occasions and expressions of a greater universe of sharing and belonging" (Coyote, 1988, p. 7). As Carl Begay, a Hupa-Navajo shaman, explains, everything in the world is alive. One literally converses with the rocks, hills, and animals, and receives messages from the wind, the river, and the sky. When one forgets this path of Oneness, it is often brought back in dreams (Begay, 1990).

Begay recalls his own dream of a woodpecker during the time his mother was seriously ill. The woodpecker spoke to him saying, "Help me and I will help your mother." The next morning, Begay did not remember the dream but as he was tanning skins by his uncle's trailer, a blue jay flew beside him and perched on the table. Looking up, Begay noticed the flock of crows chasing the blue jay. The blue jay had apparently gotten too close to the nests of the crows. Begay gathered a handful of pebbles and hurled them into the air to scare the crows away. When he turned toward the blue jay, it was no longer there. He suddenly realized the dream he had the night before and went to telephone his mother's house. *She was fully recovered* (Begay, 1990).

Fleming, writing to instruct service providers in Indian country, describes the dreams as important indicators of the symbols that permeate every aspect of Native American life:

> In response to why an Indian client sought him out, an American Indian psychotherapist was told, "We heard you did dreams." For many Indian persons, great respect is given to the phenomenon of dreams and to their importance, not only to the individual but also to the family and the tribe. (1995, pp. 162–163)

Florence Shipek, an expert on the Luiseno Tribe of Southern California, explains that shamans hold the essential knowledge concerning the natural cycles and forces of the wholeness of life. Traditionally, there were shamans who were regarded as priests because they guided the personal lives of tribal members at times of life crises, purification, marriage, and death. There were shamans regarded as scientists because they had complex knowledge of ecology, animals, farming, and food. There were also shamans regarded as doctors who cured diseases and prescribed medicines. The shamans, in other words, were multidimensional individuals responsible for the well-being of their people.

The practice of shamanistic powers, however, is usually reserved for specific locations because tribal identity is rooted to a particular space and topography. As Jack Norton, a Hupa-Cherokee and professor at Humboldt State University, believes, "You do not know *who* you are until you know *where* you are." The mountain "ridge walkers" of northwestern California, for example, traverse spiritual paths along only specific ridges (Norton, 1990).

During my conversation with Floyd Buckskin, an Achumawi ceremonial leader, at a conference on Native American shamanism, we were politely interrupted by a professional photographer, an older European American woman. She was visibly excited about a project that she had in mind to take photos for a calendar of the different places that were sacred to Native Americans in California. She wanted Buckskin to be her guide in traveling to these sites. With admirable gentleness and a smile, Buckskin thanked the woman for her interest but declined her invitation by saying the spirits were very strong in certain places. Entering into these areas could prove to be harmful to her. At one of these places, Buckskin himself had experienced a powerful and ominous presence that would not release him. He was finally able to leave, knowing that if he ever returned there he would never again be able to do so.

Buckskin, therefore, has limited many of his shamanistic rituals to Mt. Shasta. He periodically journeys there with Native Americans who need his counsel, chants, and healing methods. He is also concerned for those not of Native American descent who have found crystals in sacred places such as Burney Falls. Crystals are looked upon by Native Americans as the semen of evil spirits. They have powerful uses but only if gathered and used properly.

Relocation of Native American tribal peoples has then far-reaching consequences that affect not only their lifeways but separate them from the places of their life source. What has set apart the Pueblos, for example, from other Native Americans is that they have never been removed from their homelands. Ortiz explains that this has allowed a cultural similarity among Pueblos reaching back to prehistoric times. The Pueblos have a strong sense of place that is important to their enduring identity (1994, p. 296).

Intertribal unity is welcomed by most Native Americans as important for political survival and ethnic pride as long as they do not threaten the continuity and strength of different Native American cultures and their separate birthplaces. As a Karok shaman lamented, without a land the children of the Creator are left in darkness and all will become like the "off-colored white people" who are lost in their wanderings (Buckskin, 1990).

In a draft document dated April 15, 1990, for the purpose of recognizing the important role of shamans, the National Association of Crime Victim Compensation Boards, through its Native American Advisory Committee, stated:

> Programs should consider compensation for traditional Native American medical and mental health treatments, which may be the most effective treatment of choice for some Indians. (1990, p. 1)

The Association also recommended that state compensation programs should actively seek information regarding Native American healing practices within their jurisdictions and should allow for costs for traditional Native burial practices. The recommendation included a partial list of Navajo ceremonies to illustrate the integrity and variety of shamanistic practices—*Ho'zhoo'ji* (Blessing Way), *Too'ee* (Water Way), *Atsa'ji* (Eagle Chant), and *Inaa'ji* (Life Way). The state of Arizona now allows compensation for such rites. It is a goal of the Association that all states adopt a similar culturally sensitive approach and understanding.

CULTURALLY COMPETENT APPROACHES

Exodus from Hostility

Dang was a 55-year-old Vietnamese refugee who after three years of instruction was still unable to speak English. Prospective employers shunned him because they assumed he lacked sufficient motivation and intelligence. Vocational counselors, believing that Dang was suffering emotional distress because of his unemployment and failures to assimilate, referred him to a therapist at a refugee center. The therapist saw obvious signs of major depression. He learned from Dang's history that he had been a former government official who was imprisoned in Vietnam for four years. During that time, he received numerous severe beatings to the head with a thick bamboo rod. These blows resulted in deep lacerations and episodes of unconsciousness. On other occasions, his captors immersed his head in

water and gasoline until he again would lose consciousness. There were also prolonged periods of starvation and confinement under squalid conditions.

The damaging effects of torture and deprivation were apparent in the chronic
facial skin rashes and diarrhea, frequent lapses of memory, and mental confusion
that Dang, as well as the other captives, suffered. His depression and other symptoms were properly diagnosed by the therapist as post-traumatic stress disorder.
Medication helped in elevating Dang's mood. Neurological evaluation, however,
indicated that his central nervous system suffered such heavy assault that there is
permanent impairment to at least one area of his brain's functioning—the ability
to learn a new language.

Dang, like many other refugees from war-torn countries and oppressive
regimes, has been scarred by incredible atrocities and mayhem. Accounts by refugees from Southeast Asia and Central and South America testify to a shocking litany of maltreatment, including sexual abuse, mutilation, burning, electrical shock,
bondage, hanging, and disfigurement. Prior to their exodus from their countries,
many of these survivors experienced brutal labor camps and torture prisons. Some
were detained for the slightest of reasons. Many others witnessed the execution of
neighbors and barbaric cruelty to their loved ones. A refugee from Guatemala
gives this account:

> The government's army suspected that the Indians in the mountains were col-
> laborating with the guerrillas. Some people did, but many of us were Christians
> and only wanted to live peacefully. But the army said, "We have to teach you
> how to respect the government. They pushed forty people—men, women and
> two children—into a house that they used as a prison. One old lady came to the
> soldiers and begged, "Please let go of my son—he is innocent." The soldiers said,
> "You, too. Go inside." Then they poured gasoline on the house and set it on fire.
> Hours later, only ashes remained of the people. (As cited in Santoli, 1988, p. 151)

During the process of escape, refugees have also been extremely vulnerable to
victimization.

> Luong Bot Chau...and her husband, along with over two dozen refugees, had
> sailed away on a small, thirty-foot vessel. Off the coast of Thailand, their boat
> was attacked by Thai pirates. The pirates chopped off one of her husband's fin-
> gers to get his ring and then tried to slit his throat. "But the knife they had was
> too blunt," she said later. Instead they clubbed him to death and threw his
> body into the sea. Then they dragged the young girls up to the deck and sys-
> tematically raped them. "We heard them scream and scream," Luong Bot Chau
> cried. (As cited in Takaki, 1989, p. 451)

For many, the victimization has continued in both refugee camps and in the
countries of their resettlement, including the United States. A number of Southeast
Asian refugees, for example, have been resettled in poor areas and government-
subsidized housing occupied by other minorities. Some members of these minorities

feel displaced by the new arrivals and vent their anger through racial taunts, vandalism, or physical attacks. A 38-year-old Hmong refugee, for example, was returning to his home in a public housing project in Southern California. He was surrounded by three non-Hmong residents who previously had openly expressed their hostility toward the Hmong. When the refugee refused their demand for money, he was grabbed by two of the men while the other prepared to attack him. Managing to free himself, he leaped onto a nearby truck and then to the roof of a house. One of the men obtained a shotgun and fired two rounds, seriously wounding his victim.

In general, refugees usually suffer a series of disastrous events rather than a single victimization. They have become "stress-primed" to a world of violence, a realistic posture under threatening circumstances. Counseling refugees who have been victimized by violent crime thus requires particular skills and sensitivity. Joseph Westermeyer of the University of Minnesota states that "neurological, psychological, genetic, familial, social, and cultural factors interact to produce complex cases requiring an array of phased interventions, oftentimes involving multiple professionals and agencies" (1988, p. 16). He therefore cautions that counselors must be willing to devote an extended period of time when assisting refugees and must be caring listeners who do not abandon refugee clients during the sometimes protracted course of their recounting of traumatic histories.

Cultural psychiatrist D. David Kinzie furthermore emphasizes the need to gather basic information in five areas of the individual refugee's life:

1. life in the homeland, including education, socioeconomic status, health, family relationships, and war-related problems
2. experiences during escape
3. life in the refugee camp
4. adjustment to the United States
5. current problems and worries about the future (As cited in Lefley, 1989, p. 259)

This information reveals the incidence of stress and the manner of coping and adaptation. As Richard Mollica of the Indochinese Psychiatry Clinic in Massachusetts adds, all refugees have some trauma story that has been imprinted on their memory. It is this story that forms the initial centerpiece of treatment. The refugee client becomes the storyteller and the counselor the listener. This intimate sharing allows the refugee to turn from the hopelessness and despair of past trauma toward the reality of the present.

> The importance of storytelling cannot be underestimated.... The untold trauma story keeps him stuck in the past.... The storytelling begins to give flexibility to what was rigid and fixed in time. The past which was fixed in the present releases the present to new experiences. The past also becomes a future, a future of the past and present. (Mollica, 1988, p. 311)

Harriet Lefley of the University of Miami agrees that refugees need to identify and build on the practical living skills and personal resources that they have previously gained. Counselors, she argues, assist refugees, who have "unfortunate pasts and demonstrably uncertain futures," when they guide them to apply these skills and resources to their present situation (including criminal victimization) (Lefley, 1989, p. 260). This is achieved in part through concentrating on specific day-to-day tasks and increasing participation in supportive community programs. Counselors, accordingly, should have knowledge of the individual needs and family circumstances of their refugee clients and close personal contact with refugee-oriented health, education, English-language, employment, religious, and social services (Lefley, pp. 260–261). It is important, however, to remember in working with these services that refugees in these organizations have also suffered. Counselors must be aware, for example, that bilingual interpreters whom they use may possibly experience strong feelings associated with their own past in the process of performing translation.

Knowledge of the trauma story of individual refugees is also helpful because refugees who have experienced certain forms of interrogation, torture, or violence may be fearful or resistant to procedures that appear similarly intrusive. A rape victim may have been previously sexually abused or terrorized, for example, by having objects forced into the vagina or rectum. Even if the counselor or advocate for this victim does not have prior knowledge of such occurrences, she (or he) should provide careful and sufficient explanation of specific aspects of the medical and evidentiary examination. The unavoidable induction of some pain or discomfort during such examinations should be especially mentioned.

Refugees share the common experience of being victims of hostility generalized upon their race, culture, class, or political group. They have been involuntarily uprooted from their countries under duress. Their exodus was a means of survival. As one refugee remarked, "We love our home country, but we fled because we love our lives more" (Santoli, 1988, p. 151). Not all refugees, however, experience symptoms of post-traumatic stress associated with past torture or frightful events. Some are sustained with hope and a sense of new beginnings. A refugee from Guatemala, for example, who had walked with his family through Mexico and illegally entered the United States, gives this description:

> We met a group of Kanjobal who fled after us. They said, "Please don't go back to San Miguel. The war and violence is still going on. Go forward." We were concerned how we would live in the United States.... Many Guatemalans use Mexican "coyotes" to guide them across the border, but many times these men take advantage of the people.... Sometimes there are robberies, murders. We decided to cross the border without a "coyote." The problem was that we ran out of food and water.... We looked horrible and felt like we were dying, especially the children. It was an act of God that we met an American man.... We couldn't understand his language, but he looked like a good man.... He gave us some water and green lime fruit.... This man saved our lives.... A few hours later, we approached the city of San Isidro.... Once there, we met...[a] Mexican who drove us...to Los Angeles.... It was eleven o'clock at night when we arrived. The lights were on, like a million stars. I said, "Thank God we are in Los Angeles." (As cited in Santoli, 1988, pp. 153–154)

Another Central American refugee, with similar high expectations, asks:

> I already feel like a North American you know, because I respect the law, and North Americans are very law-abiding. Also, I am a hard worker, and North Americans are hard workers too. So, I figure that a hard-working person who respects the law won't have too much trouble getting along in the U.S., right? (As cited in Heyck, 1990, p. 332)

Fort Mojave

The town of Needles, California, is not Main Street America. It is far from the glitter of the big city lights of Los Angeles and the dimmer glow of booming Riverside and San Bernardino. It is a remote outpost where summer temperatures approach a sizzling 120 degrees. Located near the convergence of the states of California, Arizona, and Nevada, it is within moderate driving distance from the gambling mecca of Las Vegas and its miniature clone of Laughlin. But prosperity is not something of which Needles can boast.

There is, nonetheless, a renewed sense of pride appearing within at least one segment of the local population of several thousand. Needles is adjacent to the home of the Fort Mojave Indian Reservation. The Fort Mojave tribal leadership and members cannot ignore the real social and economic problems that have withered their self-esteem in the past. Their chairperson, Nora Garcia, has stated, notwithstanding, that she has hope and optimism for the future. There are, for example, plans to develop farmlands and a program to address long-neglected health issues (N. Garcia, personal communication, 1990).

The Fort Mojave tribe, however, has only 836 total members living on 17.1 acres. Because of its relatively small numbers, geographic isolation, and status as a political anomaly, the tribe has suffered from inadequate resources, staffing, and services, including those related to crime victims. Fort Mojave, like many Native American tribes, has been forced to exist without the financial and technical capacity and without clear jurisdictional authority to fully exercise its sovereignty.

In one instance, a sexually abused child had to be transported 200 miles to a hospital in Loma Linda, the only place she could receive the necessary forensic and medical examination. In another case, a father abducted his child from his estranged wife who had custody, but no assistance was available to pursue the father and return the child. Until 1990, there was not even a child protective services worker in the community. An investigation could previously only be initiated when a worker arrived from elsewhere. The delay usually was a minimum of five days.

For a battered woman there is no shelter facility and few options to piece together a life of her own. The tribe found a trailer that could be converted into a makeshift shelter, but there was no one to organize and oversee its use. In matters of domestic violence and other assaults, there has also surfaced, more than occasionally, the attitude by some in law enforcement that "It's just a bunch of Indians doing their thing." Crime victims at Fort Mojave, in other words, experience an even more tenuous position than their already marginal lives as tribal peoples (N. Garcia, personal communication, 1990).

The most direct way to address the needs of these victims is also the one most laden with political roadblocks—the strengthening of sovereignty for Native Americans. In 1990, after a two-year study, the U.S. Senate Special Committee on Investigations of the Select Committee on Indian Affairs reported, not surprisingly, that the federal government had severely mishandled Native American affairs. The committee recommended that both the resources and functions of federal programs for Native peoples be assumed by the tribes. As Senator Dennis De Concini (D-Arizona), chair of the special committee, stated:

> The time has come to allow tribal governments to stand free—independent, responsible, and accountable. The billions now wasted on self-perpetuating federal bureaucracies will belong to the tribes themselves, to determine their own destiny. (As cited in Gardner, 1990, p. 2)

As Nora Garcia commented, it is one thing to say in public hearings and record in signed documents that Native Americans are entitled to govern their own lives, and it is another thing to make that an *achievable reality* through proper funding and actual policy. Garcia has the personal vision, commitment, and energy to seek and work for the betterment of her tribe. It is imperative therefore that her example, and the tribal leadership of other reservations, not be stifled by any bureaucracy, apathy, or paternalism that doles out funds and services in a manner that displays distrust of Native American leadership. As Trimble and Fleming summarize:

> In many cases the Indian client and local Indian communities have no sense of ownership in the service unit or community center and thus tend to view it as one more enterprise foisted upon them to meet their needs. (1989, pp. 183–184)

The manner in which funds are distributed for victim services in Indian country, in fact, has been criticized as another means of denying self-determination for Native American people. Installing state administrative bodies between Native American leadership and the federal government had created another layer of accountability and control. Barbara Goodluck Morgan, program manager for the Navajo Nation Victim Witness Program, had been required to submit proposals and reports to each of the three states over which the Navajo reservation spreads. In 1996, the Office for Victims of Crime (OVC) of the U.S. Department of Justice did, however, modify its Victim Assistance in Indian country (VAIC) program to recognize tribal sovereignty and the government-to-government relationship between the federal government and Native American tribes. Overall, since 1988, OVC has provided over $6 million in grants to support victim assistance programs and to improve the handling of child abuse cases in Indian Country (OVC, 1997a). These funds have provided direct services to victims on reservations, including the first Native American childrens' advocacy center, crisis hotlines, court-appointed special advocate programs, and emergency transportation and shelters. The OVC grants are a key recognition of the long-neglected needs of Native American crime victims.

The problems of providing services, nevertheless, are many and reflect the general history of Native American life on reservations. The Menominee Reservation in Wisconsin, for example, has a population of about 4,000. In past years, the reservation has suffered a 34% unemployment rate, a level of income half the national average, and a violent crime index 17 times higher than the rest of Wisconsin. There are few telephones or automobiles and no public transportation on the reservation, and the reservation itself is 150 miles from the U.S. Attorney's office where major crimes occurring on the reservation are prosecuted. The reservation was formed in 1854 by bringing together nine separate bands from locations around the state. Initially, there were differences in language and even physical appearance to overcome. Wendell Askenette, a tribal judge, who started the Menominee victim assistance program, describes the program as essentially one of crisis response. He worked diligently responding to emergencies, dispensing money for food or shelter and transporting people. He knew that such work was a treadmill of activity that would ultimately go nowhere unless there was overall improvement of reservation life itself.

Similar circumstances exist for the Fort Mojave tribe. In 90% of the reported domestic violence cases on the reservation, for example, the perpetrator was intoxicated with alcohol (see also Norton & Manson, 1995, p. 315). For Native Americans, generally, the abuse of alcohol has been linked to feelings of low self-regard and humiliation, conditions of poverty, and a sense of hopelessness and powerlessness. All of these factors are descriptive of how many Native Americans view their lives on reservations. In the words of Mary Crow Dog, a Sioux from the Rosebud Reservation in South Dakota:

> In the old days a man made a name for himself by being generous and wise, but now he has nothing to be generous with, no jobs, no money; and as far as our traditional wisdom is concerned, our men are being told by the white missionaries, teachers and employers that it is merely savage superstition they should get rid of if they want to make it in this world. Men are forced to live away from their children, so that the family can get ADC—Aid to Dependent Children. So some warriors come home drunk and beat up their old ladies in order to work off their frustration. I know where they are coming from. I feel sorry for them, but I feel even sorrier for their women. (Crow Dog & Erdoes, 1990, p. 5)

Needles is a place to pass through for those who find it. It is not a destination but a way station from and to somewhere else. But for the Native Americans at Fort Mojave there is nowhere else to journey. It is the land on which they must find their livelihood, raise their children, and gain their respect. Crime victims at the reservation suffer both from the violence itself and from inadequate services. Their circumstance is in large part understood by the plight of the reservation as a whole.

Compton Storefront

Their building has been burglarized four times in the previous week. Various items of office equipment and supplies were taken, but this is not unusual. In the past several months, cars from the rear parking lot have been stolen. The reception area windows have also been shattered by stray bullets from gangbangers firing on rivals attending the funerals of their slain members in the mortuary parlor directly across the street. The Sexual Assault Crisis Center, a project of the YWCA Los Angeles Compton Center, occupies a storefront along a busy commercial boulevard. Its location makes it highly vulnerable to the criminal elements. It also, however, communicates the center's commitment to be of service to that community.

Monica Taylor-Williams, the project's director, was raised in the Midwest by parents who were active in the civil rights movement. She is a young black professional who disregards the fact that assisting the area's minority rape victims does not translate into plush work settings and generous perks. She is far more concerned that the range of services received by these survivors is closely coordinated to their situation and needs.

Approximately 80% of the 400 rape survivors that the center sees each year are African American. The rest are mostly Hispanic. The center has adjusted its program of counseling, outreach, and information to fit the circumstances of these women. Group sessions, for example, not only require the center to schedule convenient meeting times but also to make arrangements for child care and transportation. In these sessions, the counselor is also less a facilitator than an educator. The women readily express themselves and share in the group because, according to Taylor-Williams, they frequently make use of the center's help only after other individual resources and avenues of coping have failed.

Group meetings are the primary means to impart basic information. Program brochures and pamphlets on sexual assault are made available but, at least initially, are only glanced at by the center's clients. Taylor-Williams and her staff have therefore depended on the meetings to more thoroughly explain their services, speak about rape and recovery, and instruct on legal rights for women.

The focus of individual and group counseling, however, is on immediate problems and practical solutions. Counselors know too well that the vague question "How are you feeling?" hardly taps the pain, anger, and frustration that the center's clients are feeling. Neither does helping clients become more in touch with these feelings solve the reality and urgency of daily living. The center's counselors are more apt to ask their clients "What are you *doing* today?" and "What are you *doing* tomorrow?" For some, Taylor-Williams points out, this may mean dealing with a drug or alcohol problem, or working on self-esteem, or simply replacing a door lock smashed by the rapist on entry.

In this regard, even the most fundamental needs must not be overlooked. One afternoon, when the staff was showing a video on child sexual abuse prevention to several young children whose mothers were in counseling, two boys became obviously distracted. They sat whispering to one another and stared at a little girl who was eating a snack. As the boys were disrupting the viewing, which at first annoyed the staff, they were taken aside and gently reprimanded. However, the staff discovered that the two brothers had not eaten for three days. Understandably, all they could think about and see was the delicious-looking cookie that the girl had been enjoying! Thereafter, the center's refrigerator no longer contained just staff lunch bags but also a ready assortment of kids' food.

The crisis of sexual assault, in other words, does not remove victims from their responsibilities or suspend other needs. On the contrary, it may complicate the meeting of these responsibilities or jeopardize fulfilling these needs. The Compton center's model therefore is to assist women through direct action or referral and, in a variety of ways, to improve their lives. It is not by accident that the center is strategically housed with other services offered by the YWCA, such as job planning, parenting skills training, and health and nutrition education. This approach reflects what Leigh and Green have argued is the most congruent manner to assist the black community:

> An exclusive focus on the mental state of the Black client…diverts attention from system and ecological sources of the client's problems…. The crises for which many individuals need assistance may require the worker to become an aggressive advocate in the job or housing market, or in dealings with other social service agencies where a response to client needs has been slow. (1979, p. 125)

Minority women come to the Compton center not because they seek to fortify themselves as they prepare for the criminal justice process. Less than half of the center's rape survivors have made police reports. They do not come because of public advertising or mass mailings—these have proven less than successful. They come because of some form of personal recommendation or word being spread in the community that the center staff is nonjudgmental and is ready to listen and render specific help.

Sense of Belonging

The therapist told Kim that she needed to "heal the child within her" (B. Masaki, personal communication, March 9, 1990). Kim, a Southeast Asian immigrant, listened in astonishment and became very nervous and agitated. She wondered how this white woman would know that she was pregnant when Kim herself was unaware. Even more, she did not want another child by her abusive husband. Noticing the look of anguish in Kim's face, the therapist hurriedly explained that the term "child within" was not to be taken literally. It was an expression from a popular Western therapy that meant the spirit of a child within someone.

After the session, Kim returned to the shelter where she had been residing for one week. There, she tearfully announced to a staff member that the spirit of the child she had lost through miscarriage several months earlier was distressed and trapped inside of her! It was many hours before Kim could be reassured that her fears were unnecessary. She still could not understand what the therapist had been trying to explain, but at least she was less upset about it (B. Masaki, personal communication, March 9, 1990).

This incident shows what can occur when therapists or service providers fail to be aware of the ways different cultures define their well-being. For Kim the very concepts of *individual* and *psychological* mental health were foreign. When the therapist had suggested in a figurative sense that Kim explore the "child within her," she had hoped to assist Kim in her self-discovery. She instead had alarmed and confused Kim. Asians have traditionally focused inward through meditation, asceticism, or reflection. These paths, however, are not usually for narrowly defined personal benefit but to restore harmonious relationships, increase productive work on behalf of family and community, and practice religious devotion.

Beckie Masaki, director of the Asian Women's Shelter in San Francisco, thus emphasizes that the Asian immigrant or refugee woman who has been battered first needs a sense of belonging. She no longer has her primary identity from her husband and his family. She is an oddity in the community. The final act of leaving her husband is almost always fraught with uncertainties for a battered woman. For an Asian woman there are also serious cultural issues that must be addressed concerning her sense of worth and respect among others. The shelter which seeks to serve Asian women must therefore lessen the isolation experienced by these women by providing a strong base of support (B. Masaki, personal communication, March 9, 1990).

Although to the Westerner the Asian Women's Shelter program, founded in 1988, may appear to be too protective or to not foster enough independence, its approach identifies the cultural moorings of its clients. Masaki's staff spends a great deal of personal time with the residents. This empowers these women because it directly addresses their need to intimately affiliate themselves with those who do not hurt or condemn them. The group counseling that occurs also creates a social setting for the shelter residents. Each woman's lonely and silent endurance of abuse is replaced with a common and expressed bond. This is especially important because most of these women come to the shelter after a protracted abuse has escalated (Ness, 1994, p. B-1).

The shelter, moreover, bans the presence of all men. This denotes that the shelter is a safe place to be with other women. It additionally allows the residents to see women in a variety of professions and occupations. When the pipes at the shelter are leaking, for example, the plumber called is a woman. When repairs to doors or windows are needed, the carpenter who does the work is a woman. The shelter also presently has a Korean nun living there as a resident manager. Although she does not conduct any formal services, she welcomes the residents to join her in periods of meditation and fasting. If Kim had persisted in believing that the spirit of a dead child was within her, then the ministration of a religious person would have facilitated her healing. This supportive network of women, in other words, helps to offset the residents' history of dependency on men and serves to implant new and positive role models for the children staying at the shelter.

The shelter, furthermore, assists these women to maintain and broaden their ties to their communities. One woman, for example, continued to attend services and social gatherings at her church. Another was introduced to a woman from her Southeast Asian community who had also suffered in an abusive relationship. The two women quickly befriended one another by offering mutual support and sharing childcare. Many of the women at the shelter are referred to services such as legal assistance and ESL classes. All of these women, in other words, are rebuilding their lives through gaining a new sense of belonging to a community of caring others. As one shelter resident said,

> At the shelter everyone is supportive and helpful. On top of food, clothing and a place to live, they were always there whenever I needed help. While I worked, the volunteers and staff helped with my children. Asian Women's Shelter helped me find permanent housing, a child care center and more. It is just like an extended family. (As cited in Yamamoto, 1991, p. 1)

Pais Libre

Teresa came from Honduras in 1981 as a single parent. She had left her native country to escape from the social disapproval and isolation she felt because she had a child out of wedlock. She believed that the United States was a *pais libre,* a free country in which women had more rights than in Central America. It was not long before Teresa, a young and attractive woman, met and married a small business owner of non-Hispanic background. Three days after the wedding Teresa received her first beating. Thereafter, whenever her husband was upset at a collapsed business transaction or even a minor domestic mishap, he would without hesitation or thought slap, punch, and kick her (anonymous, personal communication, 1990).

There were times when bruises covered Teresa's entire body. She would have to make embarrassingly transparent excuses to her friends and coworkers that she had clumsily fallen or had been too playful with her husband. Her husband also confiscated her paychecks so that she was financially dependent on him. The situation deteriorated over the years as her husband began to beat not only her own daughter but also the child from their union.

While viewing a Spanish-language television program one evening, Teresa heard a public service announcement describing how battered women could seek assistance. A white woman was speaking but her words were being translated into Spanish. The next day, Teresa telephoned the women's shelter that had been mentioned on the program. The shelter staff instructed her to seek safety and to call the police. Teresa instead decided to return to Honduras. Within three months, her husband had followed her and convinced her family that Teresa was lying about what had been taking place between them. Teresa's family offered minimal support because they believed that a woman should not leave her husband. Teresa, they reasoned, had already failed in one relationship—she had not married the father of her first child. She should not be permitted to fail again with the father of her second child. They insisted that she return to her husband.

Teresa's brother came to the United States with her to make certain that things went smoothly. For several months, under the vigilant eye of his wife's brother,

Teresa's husband was relatively docile. After the brother returned to Honduras, however, the beatings quickly resumed. Teresa called the police on several occasions, but each time the police arrived after her husband had already left their apartment. The police explained that they could do little because they did not witness the violence. They also felt that Teresa was not in any immediate danger.

One day Teresa's husband broke her arm. She had simply asked him for school lunch money, 35 cents, for one of the daughters. In great pain, but determined to make her case known, Teresa walked the several miles to the police station and threatened to sue the police if they did not treat her seriously. The police filed a report and she was able to obtain a restraining order. Days later, her husband forced his way into the apartment by breaking a window and attempted to rape Teresa. She screamed and fought back, which caused him to flee. Teresa, badly shaken, called the police. It was four hours before the police arrived. They did not take a report. The next morning her husband returned. Teresa called the police again. This time the police did take a report on forcible entry and attempted rape, but for months Teresa awaited word on the status of her case.

Teresa speaks little English but is taking classes to improve her language skills. She doesn't think that being Hispanic hindered her in communicating to the police, who were mostly white male officers and generally nice. She feels, nevertheless, that the police do not consider domestic violence to be very important. This makes her see the need to be more aware of services for abused women. Teresa, in fact, desired counseling for herself and for her children. She had been willing to find support in a group of battered Hispanic women, but when she had seen or heard the term "Chicana" associated with certain social service agencies, she had assumed that only Mexicans were welcomed.

Teresa explained her personal problems to the teacher of her oldest daughter, Carla, because the teacher had expressed concern that Carla's grades had fallen dramatically. Carla had also become defiant in the classroom. Teresa knew that both of her children were very nervous after hearing their father repeatedly swear that he would kill her. Carla, extremely fearful of her stepfather, begged Teresa, "Madre, what am I going to do with my sister when you are dead?"

Now on welfare, Teresa has been searching for a job. She is taking classes in the hopes of having a career in computer programming. She is now a single parent with two children. In some ways her life is more difficult than when she first arrived from Honduras. Still, Teresa continues to look on the United States as the country of unlimited opportunities. She only wishes that these opportunities would more obviously present themselves to immigrant Hispanic women. Until her husband can be stopped from abusing her, Teresa is yet to know the United States as truly *pais libre*.

Reaching for the Sky

It was 2:30 A.M., the Fourth of July holiday, 1970, in Chicago. Brenda had just left her friends' restaurant and was walking toward her car. The only persons she noticed nearby were two men casually talking in the dark (anonymous, personal communication, 1990). Brenda intentionally avoided any more glances at the men, hoping that she would then somehow be invisible to them. The gun barrel, however, pressed hard against her right temple just as she reached to unlock the door of her car, ruefully showed that thinking about safety had little effect.

The two men, black and in their twenties, forced Brenda into the front seat of her car. One of the men drove and the other kept the gun aimed at Brenda's midsection. After a few miles, they entered an alley and stopped. Brenda pleaded with the men not to kill her because she had two young daughters at home. "Do you have a kid?" she appealed to the one holding the gun. He muttered, "A son." Helpless and in tears, Brenda demanded, "How would you feel if he never saw you again?" The only response she received was being thrown into the back seat and raped.

A barking dog alerted a resident to investigate what was happening in the alley behind his home. Peering over his fence, he called out for the occupants of the car to explain what they were doing there. Naked, Brenda scrambled from the car and, with what must have been an incredible rush of adrenalin, leaped over the man's six-foot-high fence into his backyard! The man was naturally shocked but quickly brought Brenda into his home and found a blanket to cover her.

Brenda telephoned her girlfriend for help instead of her husband because she knew he would blame her for not coming home directly after work. The police were then summoned. A white police officer arrived and, as Brenda remembers, basically asked three questions: "What did you do to provoke them?" "Were you dressed in flimsy attire?" "What were you doing on the streets?" Brenda was incredulous. She was a middle-class home owner with a well-paying job. But she was also black, which, she realized, made her rape somehow suspect. And because it was a black-on-black crime, she found that its gravity was minimized. She therefore refused to be transported to the hospital emergency room for an examination that might humiliate her even more. She chose rather to go to her own doctor several days later.

The rapists were never apprehended. Brenda's marriage deteriorated. No sexual assault crisis centers existed at that time in her city. Friends didn't want Brenda to talk about what happened. She suffered alone, weighted with the hefty baggage of self-blame. Brenda's great uncle, however, who had been a real estate and insurance broker, had always modeled an upbeat attitude. His favorite expression and advice to her was "keep reaching for the sky and you will never hit the ground."

Brenda, accordingly, moved to California with her daughters and reestablished her life. She eventually completed college with honors, obtained employment in computer systems management, took a dream vacation to Hawaii, and purchased another home. Nonetheless, perhaps the single most important factor renewing Brenda's life, has been her volunteer work with a rape crisis center in Northern California. It was through the training and experience received there that she was finally able, after nearly 15 years, to accept that the rape had not been her fault, despite how she had been treated by the police and spurned by her husband.

As Brenda broke the code of silence, it not only unburdened her, it also allowed her adult daughter to finally admit that she too had been raped while on a date.

Her daughter, Raymie, had not revealed anything previously because she had been fearful of being criticized for allowing the man into her apartment. By listening to her mother talk about how she no longer blamed herself and seeing how her mother now counseled rape victims without judgment, Raymie permitted herself to freely express her experience. It was a moment of incredible love and understanding—a sisterhood between mother and daughter.

To Brenda's surprise some of her friends also began to share their own experiences as rape victims. But it was after her minister, a black woman, admitted to being raped that Brenda found a new meaning to her involvement as a volunteer. Her minister had also been raped years ago but had never reported the crime. She had guarded her secret until now. When Brenda began volunteering, it was for the personal satisfaction of helping women and children in crisis. It was apparent that she had, in addition, become an informal means of outreach from the rape crisis center to the black community in which she lived.

Within the black community the church has always been a symbol of hope, comfort, and strength. It is a place where there is no lack of volunteers because it is traditional and vital to whatever black community it serves. The parishioners also know precisely what is expected of them. As Brenda says, the only qualification to be a volunteer in the church is faith in God. This is one reason, Brenda believes, that there are not more black volunteers in rape crisis, literacy tutoring, or other critical problems facing the black community. Volunteers may be reluctant to participate in the unknown, especially where their likelihood increases of being exposed to intimidation or being disparaged by white persons they might encounter.

Brenda hopes that her own church might be a place to recruit more volunteers, particularly because of the sensitivity and leadership her pastor can lend. But for now, she suggests that those who are attempting to solicit volunteers in the black community must understand how blacks historically have been mistreated by agencies and groups outside the physical boundaries or essential "soul" of their community. They must also be able to clearly explain what a volunteer does in terms familiar to blacks. Brenda, for example, was trained by the multiracial staff of the center in which she volunteers. Racism was one of the topics studied. There was also role-playing of interracial situations to supplement the more general education on crisis intervention and counseling techniques.

Brenda completed her volunteer class on a Saturday. There was an immediate need for her services the next day when she worked the hotline and was called to the hospital to assist a 37-year-old black woman who had attempted suicide after being raped. Brenda was nervous about having such a difficult first case but entered the hospital room knowing that someone needed to be there for the woman. She was present during the interview by a young black police officer. Brenda thought he was too impersonal because he did not look directly at the victim when he asked her questions. She confronted him in the hallway afterwards. She later learned from the victim, however, that she preferred the way the officer conducted the interview because it made her less afraid should she see any disdain or disbelief that might be in his eyes.

Brenda's second hospital call was to assist with the rape crisis of a white teen-ager who was retarded. The girl's mother was distressed because she felt responsible for what had happened to her vulnerable daughter. She didn't care whether Brenda was black or white, only that she understood the pain she was feeling. Brenda of course could identify with what it was like to suffer from self-blame. She knew exactly what the woman deserved to hear.

Her willingness to volunteer, in other words, not only has benefited Brenda and the victims she counsels but also those to whom she is closely related. She is an example of a survivor who was helped many years after her victimization. She recognizes the pool of other black women who have concealed their rape and have thereby denied the opportunity to make a significant difference in the lives of others. When her friends ask her why she sacrifices seven hours each week from her busy life for complete strangers, Brenda has only to think of her own lonely struggle. The compassionate support she offers to other rape victims is for them to "keep reaching for the sky."

EPILOGUE

Our burgeoning numbers on a solitary planet press us ever closer toward one another and compel us to find a neutral meeting ground for our hatreds, fears, and differences. This meeting ground will take more than merely reasoned argument, the behest of our chosen or self-anointed leaders, or glib reminders that our children inherit an accumulated pile of their parents' discards, foolishness, and excesses.

All of us must search for those paradigms that are able to guide us in our racial and ethnic struggles toward pervasively inclusive results. The specific Native American ritual known as the sweat lodge is noted here as a ceremony that unites the resources available for this endeavor. The sweat lodge ceremony is regarded as a serious and sacred occasion in which spiritual insights, individual identity, physical and emotional healing, and a sense of connectedness with a meaningful community can be attained. As John Wilson explains:

> The interior of the lodge creates an encapsulated environment that produces feelings of claustrophobia and an urge to escape. The lodge is crowded since the members sit knee to knee in cross-legged fashion. There is not enough room to stretch out or alter one's posture of facing the pit. *The space is configured in a circle which links the group together; there is both physical and symbolic unity.* The group is bonded together in a common environment that is simultaneously a dark space void of light but full of stress and pressure generated by the heat, steam, and smoke.... Each participant must find a way to overcome the pain, suffering, and distress, while at the same time concentrating on the prayers and words of the leader and the other members.... Attention *alternates* between being self-focused in a *seemingly isolated state* of discomfort and listening carefully to the concerns, needs, pains, hopes and emotions of the other members... (1989, pp. 51–52)

The sweat lodge ceremony is not just a simple rite of purification. It has a long history as a complex cultural practice and a highly-evolved transformation process. Its physical challenges produce specific neurophysiological changes in the brain and nervous system. It is a group task that establishes social ties and personal responsibilities to the community. It is a powerful renewal experience that is said to "reattach one's major arteries" to the mother earth, reaffirm one's ancestral heritage, and allow one to emerge with a vision of an existence beyond previous constraints and confines. As the Native American minister Stan McKay describes,

> In humility on the Earth, our mother, in the sweat lodge, which symbolizes the womb of the Earth, our mother, we call on the Creator to bring us new realization. The elder told me when I come out of the lodge, I must remember to say all my relations. And the elder says that includes the wood tick and the ants that are waiting there for us and the fish and the trees and everything that is created and all of you, my sisters and brothers.... And I think if we allow ourselves to share life in natural and creative ways, acknowledging everyone's gifts, the earth will be healed and we too will be healed. (1995, pp. 36–37)

What is being presented here is not the suggestion to dabble in Native American religious ceremonies, nor is it a plea to rush into the marketplace of group dynamics. The sweat lodge ceremony is instructive because it integrates key elements of how individuals can effect a change of attitude and behavior toward others. The willingness, skills, and commitment to engage in culturally sensitive service to minorities derive from more than acquired knowledge, newly found techniques, and good intentions. They stem from something more basic and durable—a profound sense of belonging to the *entire human family*.

REFERENCES

Adachi, F. (1972). *Japanese design motifs.* New York: Dover.

Akeman, T. (1990, June 10). Hopis, who have no word for war, finally wage one. *Sacramento Bee: Forum,* pp. 1–2.

Alexander, E. K. & Lord, J. H. (1994, July 15). *Impact statements.* Washington, D.C.: Office for Victims of Crime, U.S. Department of Justice.

Almeida, R. V. (1993). Unexamined assumptions and service delivery systems: Feminist theory and racial exclusion. *Journal of Feminist Family Therapy, 5*(1), 3–23.

Alter, J. and Starr, M. (1990, January 22). Race and hype in a divided city. *Newsweek,* pp. 21–22.

American Psychological Association (APA). (1995, June). Victims of hate crimes come from all beliefs, races, religions. *APA Monitor* [On-line]. Available: http://www.apa.org/monitor/jun95/hateb.html

Arnold, D. (1990, May 13). Where the relics belong. *San Francisco Examiner,* pp. D-16, D-15.

Askenette, W. (1990, August). *Victim services in Indian country.* Workshop presented at the Sixteenth Annual North American Victim Assistance Conference of the National Organization for Victim Assistance, Lexington, KY.

Associated Press. (1990a, April 16). Ventura County ranch "forced" Mexican workers into slavery. *San Francisco Examiner,* p. A-10.

Associated Press. (1990b, May 9). Columnist punished for racial slurs. *San Francisco Examiner,* p. A-14.

Associated Press. (1990c, May 20). INS agent arraigned. *The Maui News,* p. A6.

Associated Press. (1990d, October 17). Supremacist denies inciting violence. *San Francisco Examiner,* p. D-14.

Associated Press. (1997, June 26). Ex-guard sells alleged abuse story. *San Antonio Express-News: Metro,* pp. 1B.

Attorney General's Asian and Pacific Islander Advisory Committee. (1988, December). *Final report.* Sacramento, CA: Office of the Attorney General.

Attorney General's Commission on Racial, Ethnic, Religious, and Minority Violence. (1987, October). *Implementation Task Force progress report.* Sacramento, CA: Office of the Attorney General.

Attorney General's Commission on Racial, Ethnic, Religious, and Minority Violence. (1990, April). *Final report.* Sacramento, CA: Office of the Attorney General.

Avery, B. (1990). Breathing life into ourselves: The evolution of the National Black Women's Health Project. In E. C. White (Ed.), *The black women's health book* (pp. 4–10). Seattle, WA: Sage Press.

AYUDA. (1997). *AYUDA means help to thousands of refugees, immigrants, children and battered women.* Washington, D.C.: Ayuda.

Bailey, S., Eschbach, K., Hagan, J. & Rodriquez, N. (1996, February). *Migrant deaths at the Texas–Mexico border, 1985–1994: A preliminary report.*

Houston, TX: University of Houston, Center for Immigration Research.

Barr, S. & Fletcher, M. A. (1997, July 9). Changes proposed for racial identification. *Houston Chronicle*, pp. 4A.

Bass, A. (1990, September 9). Fear and loathing. *San Francisco Examiner*, pp. E15, E16.

Bazemore, G. (1992, September). On mission statements and reform in juvenile justice: The case of the balanced approach. *Federal Probation*, pp. 64–70.

Bazemore, G. (1994). Developing a victim orientation for community corrections: A restorative justice paradigm and a balanced mission. [American Probation and Parole Association] *Perspectives, Special Issue: Incorporating Victim Services*, 19–24.

Beane, B. (1997, Winter). Balm for the wounded. [Prison Fellowship Ministries] *Jubilee*, 6–11.

Begay, C. (1990, May 12). *Personal experiences of shamanism*. Paper presented at the Scholar's Conference on California Indian Shamanism, California State University, Hayward, CA.

Belknap, J. (1996). *The invisible woman: Gender, crime, and justice*. Belmont, CA: Wadsworth.

Bennett, C. E. (1995). *The black population in the United States: March 1994 and 1993*. (Current Population Reports, Series P20–480). Washington, D.C.: U.S. Bureau of the Census.

Berrill, K. (1985, October). *Anti-gay violence: Causes, consequences and responses*. Paper submitted to Surgeon General's Workshop on Violence and Public Health, Washington, D.C.

Berrill, K. (1990, June). The second epidemic: Violence against lesbians and gays. National Institute Against Prejudice and Violence. *Forum*, 5(2), 1–2.

Bickham, T. & Rossett, A. (1993, November). Diversity training: Are we doing the right thing right? *The Police Chief*, 43(4).

Billingsley, A. (1990). Foreword: Black families in perspective. In S. Logan, E. Freeman, and R. McRoy (Eds.), *Social work practice with black families* (pp. ix–x). White Plains, NY: Longman.

Blackman, J. (1996, June/July). Race matters: Culture, negative culture and family violence. *Domestic Violence Report*, 1(5), 4, 15.

Blue, A. & Blue, M. (1983). The trail of stress. *White Cloud Journal*, 3(1), 15–22.

Boyd, J. (1990). Ethnic and cultural diversity in feminist therapy: Keys to power. In E. C. White (Ed.), *The black women's health book* (pp. 226–234). Seattle, WA: Sage Press.

Boyer, E. J. (1990, February 13). Grieving father decries violence. *Los Angeles Times*, p. B3.

Branch, T. (1988). *Parting the waters: America in the King years 1954–63*. New York: Simon & Schuster.

Brann, J. (1997, September 27). Through partnerships community policing is taking hold in communities of all sizes across the country. *COPS News*, [On-line], pp. 1–2. Available: http://www.usdoj.gov/cops/

Brazil, E. (1990, March 20). Mexican-American group reactivates census lawsuit. *San Francisco Examiner*, p. A-6.

Brower, M. (1997, September 4). Walter Echo-Hawk fights for his people's right to rest in peace—Not in museums. *People Weekly*, 32, 42–44.

Brown, T. (1990, June 13). Rights abuses called routine in Mexico. *San Francisco Examiner*, p. A-15.

Buckskin, F. (1990, May 12). *Pit River reaction to New Age shamanism*. Paper presented at the Scholar's Conference on California Indian Shamanism, California State University, Hayward, CA.

Buments, P. (1990, September 17). Opening statement, People of State of California C24857, San Mateo, CA.

Burress, C. (1990, March 30). Godzilla takes America. *Maui News*, p. A7.

Butler, J. P. (1995). Of kindred minds: The ties that bind. In M. A. Orlandi (Ed.), *Cultural competence for evaluators* (pp. 23–54). Rockville, MD: Office for Substance Abuse Prevention, U.S. Department of Health and Human Services.

Byrne, J. (1989). Reintegrating the concept of community into community-based corrections. *Crime & Delinquency*, 35(3), 471–499.

Cantrell, C. (1993). *Victim support groups: A model for homicide survivors and the seriously injured*. Irving, CA: Mothers Against Drunk Driving.

Caputi, J. & Russell, D. E. H. (1990, September/October). "Femicide": Speaking the unspeakable. *Ms.*, pp. 34–37.

Caricature in college newspaper sparks protest. (1989, December 20). *Hokubei Mainichi*, p. 1.

Casas, J. & Vasquez, M. (1989). Counseling the Hispanic client: A theoretical and applied perspective. In P. B. Pedersen, J. G. Draguns, W. J. Lonner, & J. E. Trimble (Eds.), *Counseling across cultures* (3rd ed., pp. 153–175). Honolulu: University of Hawaii Press.

Center for Disease Control (CDC). (1997). *HIV/AIDS surveillance report.* [On-line]. Available: http://www.cdc.gov/nchstp/hiv_aids/hivsur82.html

Center for Social Work Research, University of Texas at Austin. (1995). *Cultural competence curriculum for social work educators and health practitioners: Overview module.* Austin, TX: Center for Social Work Research.

Chalfant, H. P., Heller, P. L., Briones, A., Aguirre-Hockbaums, D., & Farr, W. (1990). The clergy as a resource for those encountering psychological distress. *Review of Religious Research, 31*(3), 305–313.

Chin, S. A. (1990a, March 30). Culture-clash defense offered in Shasta Indian's new trial. *San Francisco Examiner,* p. A-10.

Chin, S. A. (1990b, April 8). S. F. launches new attack on hate crimes. *San Francisco Chronicle,* pp. B-1, B-4.

Chin, S. A. (1990c, April 20). Jury hears closing arguments in Croy murder retrial. *San Francisco Examiner,* p. A-11.

Chin, S. A. (1990d, May 2). Indian acquitted in murder of cop after 12 years in jail. *San Francisco Examiner,* p. A-4.

Chua-Eoan, H. G. (1990, April 9). Strangers in paradise. *Time,* pp. 32–35.

The City of Oklahoma City. (1996). *Alfred P. Murrah Federal Building bombing April 19, 1995: Final report.* Stillwater, OK: Fire Protection Publications, Oklahoma State University.

Clinton, W. (1994). *Government-to-government relations with Native America tribal governments: Memorandum for the heads of executive departments and agencies.* Washington, D.C.: Public papers of the President of the United States. Book I at 800–803.

Comas-Diaz, L. & Greene, B. (1994). *Women of color: Integrating ethnic and gender identities in psychotherapy.* New York: Guilford.

Community Oriented Policing (COPS). (1997, September 27). *COPS Stories.* [On-line]. Available: http://www.usdoj.gov/cops/

Coyote, D. (1988 September/October). Ask Dr. Coyote: Dear Stephen. *News from Native California 1*(4), p. 7.

Crim, K. (Ed.). (1981). *Abingdon dictionary of living religions.* Nashville: Abingdon.

Crow Dog, M. & Erdoes, R. (1990). *Lakota woman.* New York: Grove Weidenfeld.

Cursing cop not a crime, court rules. (1990, May 6). *San Francisco Examiner,* p. B-9.

Cushner, K. H. (1996). Culturally specific approaches to knowing, thinking, perceiving, and understanding. In Bayer, A. H., Brisbane, F. B., & Ramirez, A. (Eds.), *Advanced methodological issues in culturally competent evaluation for substance abuse prevention* (pp. 213–240). Rockville, MD: U.S. Department of Health and Human Services, Center for Substance Abuse Prevention.

Davis, A. (1981). *Women, race, and class.* New York: Vintage Press.

Deloria, E. (1944). *Speaking of Indians.* New York: Friendship Press.

Deloria, V., Jr. (1973). *God is red.* New York: Grosset & Dunlap.

DeMallie, R. J. (1994). Kinship and biology in Sioux culture. In R. J. DeMallie & A. Ortiz (Eds.), *North American Indian anthropology: Essays on society and culture* (pp. 125–146). Norman, OK: University of Oklahoma Press.

Department of Finance. (1988, February). *Projected total population for California by race/ethnicity* (Report 88 P-4). Sacramento, CA: Department of Finance, Population Research Unit.

Department of Finance. (1990, January). *Estimates of refugees in California counties and the state: 1988* (Report SR 88–1). Sacramento, CA: Department of Finance, Demographic Research Unit.

Destito, C., Santiago, S. & Darder, T. (1985/1986). Medical protocol for the Latina survivor. In *Protocol for the treatment of rape and other sexual assaults* (pp. 90–93). Los Angeles: Los Angeles County Commission for Women.

de Uriarte, M. L. (1997, September 12). Color fades from academia. *Austin American Statesman,* p. 19A.

Diamond, R. (1990a, April 15). In Brooklyn, bigotry yields to basketball. *San Francisco Examiner,* p. A-8.

Diamond, R. (1990b, May 20). Taciturn mayor struggles to be heard in New York. *San Francisco Examiner*, p. A-7.

Dillon, S. (1997a, August 22). Trial of a drug czar tests Mexico's new democracy. *New York Times*, pp. 4A.

Dillon, S. (1997b, August 31). U.S.–Mexico study sees exaggeration of migration data. *New York Times*, pp. 1, 6.

Draguns, J. G. (1990). Applications of cross-cultural psychology in the field of mental health. In R. Brislin (Ed.), *Applied cross-cultural psychology*. Newbury Park, CA: Sage.

Drummond, T. (1990, April 1). The Barack Obama story. *San Francisco Chronicle: Sunday Punch*, p. 5.

Du Bois, W. E. B. (1969). *The souls of black folk*. New York: New American Library. (Original work published 1903.)

Dunne, J. S. (1972). *The way of all the earth*. New York: Macmillan.

Eddings, J. (1997, July 14). Counting a "new" type of American. *U.S. News & World Report*, pp. 22–23.

Edelman, M. (1990). The black family in America. In E. C. White (Ed.), *The black women's health book* (pp. 128–148). Seattle: Sage Press.

Ehrlich, H. J. (1989). Studying workplace ethnoviolence. *International Journal of Group Tensions*, 19(1), 69–80.

Ellerbee, L. (1990a, June 17). A letter to a leader. *San Francisco Chronicle: This World*, p. 6.

Ellerbee, L. (1990b, July 1). Only when I laugh. *San Francisco Chronicle: This World*, p. 5.

Erlich, R. (1990, March 11). Learning from Fremont. *San Francisco Chronicle: This World*, pp. 15–16.

ESCAPE. (1987, February). *California migrant child abuse prevention plan*. Sacramento, CA: State Department of Education, Migrant Education Office.

Eth, S. (1992). Ethical challenges in the treatment of traumatized refugees. *Journal of Traumatic Stress*, 5(1), 103–110.

Federal Bureau of Investigations (FBI). (1997, January 17). Homicide and nonnegligent manslaughter, 1992. *Uniform Crime Report*.

Federal Bureau of Investigations (FBI). (1997, May). Crime in the United States. *Uniform Crime Report* [On-line]. Available: http://www.fbi.gov/ucr/ucr95prs.html

Feist, P. & Hedgecock, C. (1989, January 25). "Supercharged" is the way Jackson makes them feel. *The Stockton Record*, pp. A-1, A-12.

Ferguson, S. (1990a, May 6). Us against them. *San Francisco Chronicle: This World*, pp. 12–13.

Ferguson, S. (1990b, May 6). A rift in the house of the homeless. *San Francisco Chronicle: This World*, pp. 13–14.

Figueroa, A. (1990a, June 15). Hiding S. F.'s true colors. *San Francisco Examiner*, p. A-25.

Figueroa, A. (1990b, October 17). Gays not satisfied with GM apology. *San Francisco Examiner*, p. A-2.

Fitzgerald, M. (1989, April 27). 100 days of mourning. *The Stockton Record*, pp. A-1, A-10.

Fleming, C. (1995). American Indians and Alaska Natives: Changing societies past and present. In M. A. Orlandi (Ed.), *Cultural competence for evaluators* (pp. 147–171). Rockville, MD: Office for Substance Abuse Prevention, U.S. Department of Health and Human Services.

Forrester, M. (1990, June 13). We need the homeless, just where they are. *San Francisco Bay Guardian*, p. 26.

French, H. W. (1989, September 4). Hatred and social isolation may spur acts of racial violence, experts say. *New York Times*, p. L31.

Gardner, J. (1990, Winter). Senate committee report recommends new Indian policy. *The Tribal Court Reporter*, 3(1), 2–3.

Gay, F. & Quinn, T. J. (1996, September/October). Restorative justice and prosecution in the twenty-first century. [National District Attorneys Association] *The Prosecutor, 16*, 18–19, 20–24.

Giddings, P. (1984). *When and where I enter: The impact of black women on race and sex in America*. Toronto: Bantam Books.

Gilliam, H. (1990, May 13). Immigration—Enough already? *San Francisco Chronicle: This World*, p. 18.

Ginorio, A. & Reno J. (1985, February). Violence in the lives of Latina women. In *Working together to prevent sexual and domestic violence* (pp. 1–3). Seattle, WA: Center for the Prevention of Sexual and Domestic Violence.

Gleick, J. (1990, July 22). The census that doesn't add up. *San Francisco Chronicle: This World*, pp. 7–8.

Goldstein, P. (1990, July 8). Hot dice: Clay on a big roll. *San Francisco Examiner: Datebook*, pp. 35, 36.

Gomez, J. & Smith, B. (1990). Taking the home out of homophobia: Black lesbian health. In E. C. White (Ed.), *The black women's health book* (pp. 198–213). Seattle, WA: Sage.

Goodluck, C. T. & Short, D. (1980, October). Working with American Indian parents: A cultural approach. *Social Casework: The Journal of Contemporary Social Work*, 472–475.

Griffin, N. W. (1990, May 3). Liberal is as liberal does: The faculty fight at Harvard Law. *San Francisco Examiner*, p. A-23.

Gross, J. (1989, May 21). Survivors heal slowly where 5 children died. *The New York Times*, p. 11, 12.

Gudykunst, W. B. & Gumbs, L. I. (1989). Social cognition and intergroup communication. In M. K. Asante & W. B. Gudykunst (Eds.), *Handbook of international and intercultural communication* (pp. 204–224). Newbury Park, CA: Sage.

Gust, K. (1990, February 28). "I want to speak Ah-mur-ican." *Oakland Tribune*, p. D-4.

Gutierrez, C. (1997, Spring). A donor mother's story. [El Paso Regional Transplant Bank] *ReNews*, 3.

Haddock, V. (1990a, March 27). Street people count assailed. *San Francisco Examiner*, p. A-10.

Haddock, V. (1990b, April 1). Census inspires privacy fears. *San Francisco Examiner*, pp. A-1, A-17.

Haddock, V. (1990c, April 16). Census: A bureau of missing persons. *San Francisco Examiner*, pp. A-1, A-26.

Haldane, D. (1990, April 29). Soap-opera therapy for troubled Latinos. *Los Angeles Times: Sunday Punch*, p. 1.

Hall, E. H. & King, G. C., (1982). Working with the strengths of black families. *Child Welfare*, 61(8), 222–230.

Hamann, C. (1996, October 20). Koreans flourish on border. *Dallas Morning News*, pp. 43A, 49A.

Hampton, R. L. (1987, Spring). Race, class and child maltreatment. *Journal of Comparative Family Studies*, 18(1), 113–125.

Hanaver, J. (1990, January 24). Jennings on gun control. *San Francisco Examiner*, p. D-4.

Hardy, K. V. & Laszloffy, T. A. (1994). Deconstructing race in family therapy. *Journal of Feminist Family Therapy*, 5(3/4), 5–33.

Hazama, D. (1974). *The ancient Hawaiians: Who were they? How did they live?* Honolulu, HI: Hogarth Press.

Hecht, M. L., Andersen, P. A., & Ribeau, S. A. (1989). The cultural dimensions of non-verbal communication. In M. K. Asante & W. B. Gudykunst (Eds.), *Handbook of international and intercultural communication* (pp. 163–185). Newbury Park, CA: Sage.

Hecht, P. (1990a, June 10). L. A. County reels as judge throws out voting map. *Sacramento Bee*, pp. A1, A18.

Hecht, P. (1990b, July 1). A gigantic thank-you from Nelson Mandela. *San Francisco Examiner*, p. A-12.

Hecht, P. (1990c, July 8). Fallen politician in San Diego is talk of the town. *San Francisco Examiner*, pp. B-1, B-4.

Hennessey, S. M. (1993, August). Achieving cultural competence. *The Police Chief*, 46(9).

Henry, W. A., III. (1990, April 9). Beyond the melting pot. *Time*, pp. 28–31.

Herek, G. M. & Berrill, K. T. (1992). *Hate crimes: Confronting violence against lesbians and gay men*. Newbury Park, CA: Sage.

Heyck, D. (1990). *Life stories of the Nicaraguan revolution*. New York: Routledge.

Hill, R. B. (1972). *Strengths of black families*. New York: Emerson Hall.

Hilton, B. (1990, July 15). Comedian's joke isn't so funny. *San Francisco Examiner*, p. D-16.

Hinkle, W. (1990, May 20). On the dark edge of hatred. *San Francisco Examiner*, pp. B-1, B-7.

Hinckle, W. (1990b, June 24). Mandela's real thoughts about U.S. *San Francisco Examiner*, pp. B-1, B-7.

Hofstede, G. (1980). *Culture's consequences: International differences in work-related behaviors*. Beverly Hills, CA: Sage.

Holt, D. (1997, September 10). Immigrant smugglers had Dallas link, authorities say. *Dallas Morning News*, pp. 1A, 10A.

Holt, D. (1997, September 18). Border inquiry falls to other investigators. *Dallas Morning News*, pp. 31A, 36A.

Igasaki, P. (1990, June 22). Racial violence and the JACL. *Pacific Citizen*, p. 5.

Ilola, L. (1990). Culture and health. In R. Brislin (Ed.), *Applied cross-cultural psychology*. Newbury Park, CA: Sage.

Indian Assistance Program. (1990). *Field directory of the California Indian community.* Sacramento, CA: Department of Housing and Community Development.

Irwin, J. (1990, January 21). Detroit mom tries to tame violence, heal wounds. *Maui News,* pp. C1, C7.

Japanese students mistaken for Hmong attacked by whites in La Crosse, Wis. (1990, May 25). *Pacific Citizen,* pp. 1, 5.

Jones, C. (1990, February 18). The return of Malcolm X. *San Francisco Chronicle: Sunday Punch,* p. 6.

Jones, W. (1990, January 27). Hit–run victims' parents angry at driver's 4-year sentence. *Oakland Tribune,* pp. A9–A10.

The Judicial Branch of the Navajo Nation. (1997, January 24). *Traditional restorative justice in North America.* Paper presented at the Sixth National Conference of the National Indian Justice Center, San Diego, CA.

Kahn, A. (1990, September 16). Macho—The second wave. *San Francisco Chronicle: Sunday Punch,* p. 2.

Kahn, R. S. (1996). *Other people's blood: U.S. Immigration prisons in the Reagan decade.* Boulder, CO: Westview Press.

Kang, K. C. & Waugh, D. (1990, May 6). Minority students feel like outsiders who were robbed of their past. *San Francisco Examiner,* pp. A-1, A-14.

Kapleau, P. (1989). *Zen: Merging of East and West.* New York: Doubleday.

Kelly, D. (1992, March 24). Rancher to pay $1.5-million fine in slavery case. *Los Angeles Times,* pp. A1, A24.

Kempsky, N. (1989, October). *A report to Attorney General John K. Van de Kamp on Patrick Edward Purdy and the Cleveland School killings.* Sacramento, CA: Office of the Attorney General.

Kim, K. K., Lee, K., Kim, T. (1981). *Korean Americans in Los Angeles: Their concerns and language maintenance.* Los Alamitos, CA: National Center for Bilingual Research.

Kitano, H. (1989). A model for counseling Asian Americans. In P. B. Pedersen, J. G. Draguns, W. J. Lonner, & J. E. Trimble (Eds.), *Counseling across cultures* (3rd ed., pp. 139–151). Honolulu: University of Hawaii Press.

Koltnow, B. (1990, July 11). A busy director tosses the dice. *San Francisco Examiner,* p. C-3.

Korbin, J. (1980). The cross-cultural context of child abuse and neglect. In C. H. Kempe & E. Helfer (Eds.), *The battered child* (pp. 21–35). Chicago: University of Chicago Press.

Kortum-Stermer, J. (1990, February 18). A silence of shame. *San Francisco Chronicle: Sunday Punch,* p. 3.

Lafree, G. D. (1989). *Rape and criminal justice: The social construction of sexual assault.* Belmont, CA: Wadsworth.

Lashley, K. H. (1998, January/February). Secondary Victims; Vicarious Victimization; Compassion Fatigue: The Oklahoma City bombing. *Crime Victims Report, 1*(6), 81–82, 93.

Lashley, K. H. & Ogawa, B. (Forthcoming). The nation's fence: Compassion and hope surrounding the site of the Oklahoma City bombing.

Lee, C. and Armstrong, K. (1995). Indigenous models of mental health intervention. In J. G. Ponterotto, J. M. Casas, L. A. Suzuki, & C. M. Alexander (Eds.), *Handbook of Multicultural Counseling* (pp. 441–456). Thousand Oaks, CA: Sage.

Lee, D. (1986, May 10). *Racism/Sexism: Their combined influence on violence against Asian women.* Panel presentation at the Break the Silence Conference, University of California at Berkeley, CA.

Lefley, H. P. (1989). Counseling refugees: The North American experience. In P. B. Pedersen, J. G. Draguns, W. J. Lonner, & J. E. Trimble (Eds.), *Counseling across cultures* (3rd ed., pp. 243–266). Honolulu: University of Hawaii Press.

Leigh, J. W. & Green, J. W. (1979). The black family and social work. In J. W. Leigh & J. W. Green (Eds.), *Cultural awareness in the human services: A training manual* (pp. 119–168). Seattle: University of Washington, Center for Social Welfare Research, School of Social Work.

Levinson, D. (1989). *Family violence in cross-cultural perspective.* Newbury Park, CA: Sage.

Lewis, G. (1990, March 30). Blacks still suffer from segregation, housing study says. *San Francisco Examiner,* p. A-12.

Logan, S. M. L. (1990). Diversity among black families: Assessing structure and function. In

S. Logan, E. Freeman, and R. McRoy (Eds.), *Social work practice with black families* (pp. 73–96). White Plains, NY: Longman.

Los Angeles County Bar Association and Barristers Domestic Violence Project. (1990). Client information intake sheet.

Los Angeles County Commission on Human Relations (LACCHR). (1990a, February). *Hate crime in the 1980s: A decade of bigotry: A report to the Los Angeles County Board of Supervisors.* Los Angeles, CA: Author.

Los Angeles County Commission on Human Relations (LACCHR). (1990b, February). *Hate crime in Los Angeles County 1989: A report to the Los Angeles County Board of Supervisors.* Los Angeles, CA: Author.

Madriz, E. (1997). *Nothing bad happens to good girls: Fear of crime in women's lives.* Berkeley, CA: Univ. of California Press.

Maloney, D., Romig, D., & Armstrong, T. (1988). *Juvenile probation: The balanced approach.* Reno, NV: National Council of Juvenile and Family Court Judges.

Mann, B. (1990, February 1). Overkill in Boston. *Oakland Tribune,* p. C-4.

Marshall, I. H. (1997). *Minorities, migrants, and crime: Diversity and similarity across Europe and the United States.* Thousand Oaks, CA: Sage.

Martz, L. (1990, January 22). A murderous hoax. *Newsweek,* pp. 16–21.

Maultsby, M. C., Jr. (1982). A historical view of black's distrust of psychiatry. In S. M. Turner & R. T. Jones (Eds.), *Behavior modification in black populations* (pp. 39–56). New York: Plenum Press.

McDonald, W. F. (1997, June). Crime and illegal immigration. *National Institute of Justice Journal,* 2–10.

McEwen, T. J. (1995, May). Victim assistance programs: Whom they service, what they offer. In *National Institute of Justice Update* (pp. 1, 2). Washington, D.C.: U.S. Dept. of Justice.

McKay, S. (1995). A window of opportunity: Native American spirituality as a resource for healing. In T. B. Thelma Burgonio-Watson (Ed.), *Called to make justice* (pp. 32–37). Seattle, WA: The Center for the Prevention of Sexual and Domestic Violence.

McKean, J. (1994). Race, ethnicity, and criminal justice. In Hendricks, J. E. & Byers, B. (Eds.), *Multicultural perspectives in criminal justice and criminology* (pp. 85–134). Springfield, IL: Charles C. Thomas.

McRoy, R. G. (1990). A historical overview of black families. In S. Logan, E. Freeman, and R. McRoy (Eds.), *Social work practice with black families* (pp. 3–17). White Plains, NY: Longman.

Mehren, E. (1990, March 4). Easing heartache. *Oakland Tribune: That's Life,* p. 19.

Melton, A. P. (1995, November/December). Indigenous justice systems and tribal society. *Judicature,* 79(3), 126–133.

Merrill, H. (1990). *The blues route.* New York: William Morrow.

Miller, A. H. (1990, March 27). Founding fathers of racism. *San Francisco Examiner,* p. A-21.

Mitchell, S. R. (1990, March 21). Census bureau seeks out the uncounted. *San Francisco Examiner,* p. A-11.

Moisa, R. (1988, September/October). The Indian Child Welfare Act comes of age. *News from Native California,* 2(4), 10–11.

Mollica, R. (1988). The trauma story: The psychiatric care of refugee survivors of violence and torture. In F. Ochberg (Ed.), *Post-traumatic therapy and victims of violence* (pp. 295–314). New York: Brunner/Mazel.

Montgomery, P. A. (1994). *The Hispanic population in the United States: March 1993.* (Current Population Reports, Series P20-475). Washington, D.C.: U.S. Bureau of the Census.

Mothers Against Drunk Driving. (1997, July 15). *Statistics on Hispanics.* [On-line]. Available: http://www.madd.org/stats/stat_hispanics.shtml

Murdock, S. H., Hogue, M. N., Michael, M., White, S. & Pecotte, B. (1997). *The Texas challenge: Population change and the future of Texas.* College Station, TX: Texas A&M University Press.

Myers, J. (Ed.). (1981). *They are young once but Indian forever.* Oakland, CA: American Indian Lawyer Training Program.

Myers, J. (1996, Spring/Summer). The criminal justice issues of Indian Country. *The Tribal Court Record,* 33–35.

Nakao, A. (1990a, March 23). Mental health system ill-equipped for racial minorities. *San Francisco Examiner,* p. A-12.

Nakao, A. (1990b, September 17). Laotian Americans are targets of vandals. *San Francisco Examiner*, p. A-5.

National Church Arson Task Force (NCATF). (1997, June). *First year report for the President.* [On-line]. Washington, D.C.: U.S. Department of the Treasury & U.S. Department of Justice. Available: http://www.atf.treas.gov/pub/arsonrpt.htm

National Institute Against Prejudice and Violence (NIAPV). (1990, January/February). Group violence in the U.S.A.: The Institute's National Victimization Survey. *Forum, 5*(1), 1, 5.

National Victim Assistance Academy. (1997). *Training manual.* Washington, D.C.: U.S. Department of Justice, Office for Victims of Crime.

Native American Advisory Committee. (1990). *Native Americans.* Conference notes of the 1990 National Association of Crime Victim Compensation Boards Conference, Denver, CO.

Native American Coalition. (1980, Spring). *Working with abusive/neglectful Indian parents.* Tulsa, OK: Author.

NBC sportscaster apologizes for racial slurs in S. F. talk show. (1990, February 16). *Pacific Citizen*, p. 1.

Nesbitt, J. (1990, June 17). Siege mentality in capital of high technology. *San Francisco Examiner*, pp. D-1, D-14.

Ness. C. (1994, April 10). A home of its own lets shelter help more women. *San Francisco Examiner*, pp.B-1, B-8.

Nies, J. (1996). *Native American history.* New York: Ballantine.

Nishio, K. & Bilmas, M. (1987). Psychotherapy with Southeast Asian American clients. *Professional Psychology: Research and Practice, 18*, 342–386.

Njeri, I. (1990, May 2). An L.A. cultural crucible. *Los Angeles Times*, pp. E1–E2.

Norton, I. & Manson, S. M. (1995). A silent minority: Battered American Indian women. *Journal of Family Violence, 10*(3), 307–318.

Norton, J. (1990, May 12). *Ridgewalkers of northwestern California: Paths toward spiritual balance.* Paper presented at the Scholar's Conference on California Indian Shamanism, California State University, Hayward, CA.

O'Brien, E. M. (1989, December 7). Black women additionally victimized by myths, stereotypes. *Black Issues in Higher Education*, pp. 8, 9.

O'Connor, S. D. (1996, Spring/Summer). Lessons from the third sovereign: Indian Tribal Courts. *The Tribal Court Record,* 12–14.

Office for Victims of Crime (OVC). (1997a, February). *OVC Advocate.* Washington, D.C.: U.S. Department of Justice.

Office for Victims of Crime (OVC). (1997b). Children's justice act grant program for Native Americans. In *Fact Sheet* (pp. 1) Washington, D.C.: U.S. Department of Justice.

Oklahoma State Health Department. (1997). *Oklahoma City bombing: Race distribution of fatalities and injuries.* Oklahoma City, OK: Injury and Fatality Prevention Service.

Ogawa, B. (1986, July). Lessons from the Japanese in the recovery from victimization. *National Organization for Victim Assistance Newsletter*, pp. 3, 5.

Ogawa, B. (1988a). Counseling victims of sexual assault. *International Bulletin of Morita Therapy, 1*(1), 19–25.

Ogawa, B. (1988b). Norikoeru: Beyond victimization. Unpublished manuscript.

Ogawa, B. (1989). Practicing Japanese psychotherapy with victims of violent crime. In D. K. Reynolds (Ed.), *Flowing bridges, quiet waters: Japanese psychotherapies, Morita and Naikan* (pp. 71–77). New York: State University of New York.

Ogawa, B. (1994). Culturally diverse victims. In *Focus on the future: A systems approach to prosecution and victim assistance* (pp. C-6–C-13). Washington, D.C.: U.S. Department of Justice, Office for Victims of Crime.

Ogawa, B. (1995). Asian American patriarchies. In Volcano Press (Eds.), *Family violence and religion* (pp. 131–134). Volcano, CA: Volcano Press.

Ogawa, B. (1996). *Walking on eggshells: Practical counsel for women in or leaving a violent relationship.* Volcano, CA: Volcano Press.

Ogawa, B. (1997). *To tell the truth.* Volcano, CA: Volcano Press.

Ogawa, B. (In Press). E hana pono: Issues of responsibility, justice, and culture in the design and practice of prevention programs among Pacific Islanders. In M. O. Orlandi & L. G. Epstein (Eds.), *Cultural competence for professionals working with Asian/Pacific American communities: Theoretical and practical consider-*

ations. Rockville, MD: U.S. Department of Health and Human Services.

Olson, K. (1997, January 23). *Improving federal and tribal response to crimes in Indian Country.* Paper presented at the Sixth National Conference of the National Indian Justice Center, San Diego, CA.

Ortiz, A. (1994). The dynamics of Pueblo cultural survival. In R. J. DeMallie & B. Ortiz (Eds.), *North American Indian anthropology: Essays on society and culture* (pp. 296–306). Norman, OK: University of Oklahoma Press.

Parson, E. (1985). Ethnicity and traumatic stress: The intersecting point in psychotherapy. In C. Figley (Ed.), *Trauma and its wake: The study and treatment of post-traumatic stress disorder* (pp. 314–337). New York: Brunner/Mazel.

Pedersen, P., Fukuyama, F., & Heath, A. (1989). Client, counselor, and contextual variables in multicultural counseling. In P. B. Pedersen, J. G. Draguns, W. J. Lonner, & J. E. Trimble (Eds.), *Counseling across cultures* (3rd ed., pp. 23–52). Honolulu: University of Hawaii Press.

Perea, J. F. (Ed.). (1996). *Immigrants out! The New Nativism and the anti-immigrant impulse in the United States.* New York: New York University Press.

Perry, M. (1990, May 29). Change, challenge and opportunity. Keynote Speech at the Governor's Conference on Victim Services and Public Safety, State of California, Anaheim, CA.

Plank, J. (1989, February 10). Teen stabbed to death while protecting mother. *The Argus,* p. 15.

Poussaint, A. F. (1983). Black-on-black homicide: A psychological-political perspective. *Victimology, 8*(3–4), 161–168.

Pukui, M. K., Handy, E. G., & Craighill, E. S. (1972). *Polynesian family system in Ka-'u, Hawaii.* Rutland, VT: C. E. Tuttle.

Raspberry, W. (1994, November 9). Automatically suspect. *The Washington Post,* p. A19.

Reist, B. A. (1975). *Theology in red, white, and black.* Philadelphia: Westminster Press.

Reynolds, D. (1976). *Morita psychotherapy.* Berkeley, CA: University of California Press.

Reynolds, D. (1989). On being natural: Two Japanese approaches to healing. In A. A. Sheikh & K. S. Sheikh (Eds.), *Eastern and Western Approaches to healing* (pp. 180–194). New York: John Wiley & Sons.

Richie, B. (1990). Aids: In living color. In E. C. White (Ed.), *The black women's health book* (pp. 182–186). Seattle, WA: Sage.

Ridley, C. (1989). Racism in counseling as an adversive behavioral process. In P. B. Pedersen, J. G. Draguns, W. J. Lonner, & J. E. Trimble (Eds.), *Counseling across cultures* (3rd ed., pp. 55–77). Honolulu: University of Hawaii Press.

Ridley-Thomas, M. (1990, September 15). Call racism by its real name. *Los Angeles Times: Commentary,* pp. B7.

Rimonte, N. (1989). Domestic violence among Pacific Asians. In Asian Women United of California (Eds.), *Making waves: An anthology of writings by and about Asian American women* (pp. 327–337). Boston: Beacon Press.

Roark, A. C. (1990, January 13). Mending wounds of a massacre. *Los Angeles Times,* pp. A1, A28–29.

Robinson, W. S. (1950). Ecological correlations and the behavior of individuals. *American Sociological Review, 15,* 351–357.

Rodriquez, A. M. & Casaus, L. (1983). Latino family issues. In *Latino families in the United States* (pp. 41–48). New York, NY: Planned Parenthood Federation of America.

Roll, S., Millen, L., & Martinez, R. (1980). Common errors in psychotherapy with Chicanos: Extrapolations from research and clinical experience. *Psychotherapy: Theory, Research and Practice, 17,* 158–168.

Root, M. P. P. (1985). Guidelines for facilitating therapy with Asian American clients. *Psychotherapy, 22,* 349–356.

Rosales, N. E. (1989). The Latino family: Explorations into cultural values and male roles. In Southern California Child Abuse Prevention Training Center, *Cultural considerations in child abuse/neglect for the primary prevention educator* (pp. 27–40). Los Angeles: California State University, Department of Counselor Education.

Roser, M. A. (1997, September 12). A storm over racial comments. *Austin American Statesman,* pp. A-1.

Ross, J. H. (1990, May 13). Ethnic studies [Letter to the editor]. *San Francisco Examiner,* p. A-16.

Ross, M. E. (1990, July 22). Giving the blues shades and hues. *San Francisco Examiner: Review*, p. 5.

Rural Realignment Project. (1989, December). *New thinking for California agriculture: A discussion paper on farm worker and family farmer relations.* Berkeley, CA: Family Farm Organizing Resource Center.

Samuelson, S. (1990, October 17). Defense witness tells of Salcido's paranoia. *San Francisco Examiner*, p. D-14.

San Francisco Human Rights Commission. (1990, January 17–18). *Proceedings of the community forum,* entitled *"Hate No More: Toward Ending Prejudice-Based Violence,"* San Francisco, CA.

Sanchez, E. (1990). Video illustrates migrant child abuse. *Sacramento Bee*, pp. B1, B3.

Sanders, C. (1997). *Victims of crime: Issues in Indian country.* Washington, D.C.: U.S. Department of Justice, Office for Victims of Crime

Santoli, A. (1988). *New Americans.* New York: Ballantine.

Schiller, D. (1997a, August 16). Drug-related flow of blood continues to shock Juarez. *San Antonio Express-News*, pp. 20A.

Schiller, D. (1997b, August 28). Feds beefing up measures to seal leaks along border. *San Antonio Express-News*, pp. 1A, 4A.

Schiller, D. (1997c, September 16). Officials evaluate border operation. *San Antonio Express-News*, pp. 8A.

Schmich, M. T. (1990, May 27). In the "new Georgia," black man is running for governor. *San Francisco Examiner*, p. A-4.

Schwendinger, J. R. & Schwendinger, H. (1983). *Rape and inequality.* Beverly Hills, CA: Sage.

Seligman, K. (1990, February 18). Telling the truth was her last, brave deed. *San Francisco Examiner*, p. A-1.

Seng, S. M., (1987). One person's story. In B. S. Levy & D.C. Susott (Eds.), *Years of horror, days of hope: Responding to the Cambodian refugee crisis* (pp. 3–13). New York: Associated Faculty Press.

Sharma, S. L. (1989). Transcultural psychotherapy. In A. A. Sheikh & K. S. Sheikh (Eds.), *Eastern and Western approaches to healing* (pp. 516–541). New York: John Wiley & Sons.

Sheikh, A. A., Kunzendorf, R. G., & Sheikh, K. S. (1989). Healing images: From ancient wisdom to modern science. In A. A. Sheikh & K. S. Sheikh (Eds.), *Eastern and Western approaches to healing* (pp. 470–515). New York: John Wiley & Sons.

Shipek, F. (1990, May 12). *Shaman: Priests, doctors, scientists.* Paper presented at the Scholar's Conference on California Indian Shamanism, California State University, Hayward, CA.

Shook, V. E. (1985). *Ho'oponopono.* Honolulu: University of Hawaii Press.

Small, C. (Ed.). (1980). *Justice in Indian country.* Oakland, CA: American Indian Lawyer Training Program.

Smith, G. B. (1990, April 2). Rising U.S. racial bias in spotlight. *San Francisco Examiner*, pp. A-1, A-10.

Sobieraj, S. (1997, January 19). Federal task force spurs arrests in church fires. *Austin-American Statesman*, p. A7,

Southern California Child Abuse Prevention Training Center. (1989). *Cultural considerations in child abuse/neglect for the primary prevention educator.* Los Angeles: California State University, Department of Counselor Education.

Spalding, S. (1990, March 19). Through kupuna program, pupils learn from those who lived lesson. *The Maui News*, p. A-1.

Standing Bear, L. (1933). *Land of the spotted eagle.* New York: Houghton Mifflin.

State Department of Education. (1989). *Language census report for California public schools, 1989.* Sacramento, CA: Author.

Steele, S. (1990). *The content of our character.* New York: St. Martin's Press.

Streshinsky, S. (1990, April 8). The Last Dream of Angela Salcido. *San Francisco Chronicle: This World*, pp. 9–11.

Sue, D. W. & Sue, D. (1990). *Counseling the culturally different* (2nd Ed.). New York: John Wiley & Sons.

Sue, S. & Zane, N. (1987). The role of culture and cultural techniques in psychotherapy. *American Psychologist, 42*, 37–45.

Sundberg, N. D. & Sue, D. (1989). Research and research hypotheses about effectiveness in intercultural counseling. In P. B. Pedersen, J. G. Draguns, W. J. Lonner, & J. E. Trimble (Eds.), *Counseling across cultures* (3rd ed., pp. 335–370). Honolulu: University of Hawaii Press.

Sylva, B. (1990, April 29). At the cultural cross-roads. *Sacramento Bee*, pp. F-1, F-8.

Szapocznik, J. (1995). *A Hispanic/Latino family approach to substance abuse prevention* (CSAP Cultural Competency Series 2). Rockville, MD: U.S. Department of Health and Human Services, Center for Substance Abuse Prevention.

Szapocznik, J., & Kurtines, W. M. (1993, April). Family psychology and cultural diversity. *American Psychologist*, pp. 400–407.

Takaki, R. (Ed.). (1987). *From different shores: Perspectives on race and ethnicity in America.* New York: Oxford University Press.

Takaki, R. (1989). *Strangers from a different shore.* Boston: Little, Brown.

Talbot, D. (1990, July 8). The best defense. *Image*, pp. 6–12.

Tello, J. (n.d.). *Cultural competence in working with Latinos.* Unpublished manuscript. Los Angeles: California Mexican Child Abuse Council (CALMECAC).

Terrell, A. D. (1989, September). Racial violence and the underclass. [National Institute Against Prejudice and Violence] *Forum*, 4(3), 3, 6.

Torres, E. (1990, June 13). The battle for California. *San Francisco Bay Guardian*, p. 20.

Triandis, H. (1972). *The analysis of subjective culture.* New York: Wiley-Interscience.

The Tribal Court Reporter (1990, Winter). 3(1), 13.

Trimble, J., & Fleming, C. (1989). Providing counseling services for Native American Indians: Client, counselor, and community characteristics. In P. B. Pedersen, J. G. Draguns, W. J. Lonner, & J. E. Trimble (Eds.), *Counseling across cultures* (3rd ed., pp. 177–204). Honolulu: University of Hawaii Press.

Umbreit, M. (1997, July/August). Victim–offender dialogue: From the margins to the mainstream throughout the world. *The Crime Victims Report*, 1(3), 35–36, 48.

United Press International. (1990, May 6). Law enforcement learning how words can cuff suspects. *San Francisco Examiner*, p. B-9.

U.S. Bureau of the Census. (1995). *Statistical abstract of the United States: 1995* (115th ed.). Washington, D.C.: U.S. Government Printing Office.

U.S. Bureau of the Census. (1997a). Statistical abstract of the United States: 1996 (116th ed.). *Population.* [On-line]. Available: http://www.census.gov/prod/2/gen/96statab.html

U.S. Bureau of the Census. (1997b, May). U.S. Census Bureau 1996 to 2050 yearly population projections by sex, race, and Hispanic origin, with median age. [On-line]. Available: http://www.fedstats.gov/index20.html

U.S. Bureau of the Census. (1997c, June). U.S. Census Bureau 1997 population estimates by sex, race, and Hispanic origin. [On-line]. Available: http://www.fedstats.gov./index20.html

U.S. Bureau of Justice Statistics. (1997, May). Criminal victimization in the United States, 1994. [On-line]. Available: http://www.ojp.usdoj.gov/bjs/abstract/cvius94.html

U.S. Commission on Civil Rights. (1986). *Recent activities against citizens and residents of Asian descent* (Clearinghouse Publication No. 88). Washington, D.C.: Author.

U.S. Department of Justice. (1994). *Criminal justice in Indian country: A focus on new options.* Washington, D.C.: U.S. Department of Justice, Criminal Division.

U.S. Immigration and Naturalization Service. (1996, November). Immigration to the United States in Fiscal Year 1996. [On-line]. Available: http://www.fedstats.gov/index20.html

U.S. Immigration and Naturalization Service. (1997a, August). Illegal alien resident population. [On-line]. Available: http://www.fedstats.gov/index20.html

U.S. Immigration and Naturalization Service. (1997b). Immigration to the United States in Fiscal Year 1996. [On-line]. Available: http://www.fedstats.gov/index20.html

Vace, N. A., DeVaney, S. B., & Wittmer, J. (1995). *Experiencing and counseling multicultural and diverse populations.* Bristol, PA: Accelerated Development.

Vasquez, G. (1990, May 29). *Welcome to Orange County.* Governor's Conference on Victim Services and Public Safety, State of California, Anaheim, CA.

Vega, W. A. (1992). Theoretical and pragmatic implications of cultural diversity for community research. *American Journal of Community Psychology*, 20(3), 375–391.

Verhoff, J., Kulka, R. A., & Douvan, E. (1981). *Mental health in America.* New York: Basic.

Verhovek, S. H. (1997, August 24). Silent deaths on rise along U.S.–Mexico border. *San Francisco Examiner*, p. A4.

Vobejda, B. (1994, November 9). Smith's kin apologize to Blacks. *The Washington Post*, p. A8.

Walker, A. (1989). *The temple of my familiar.* New York: Pocket Books/Simon & Schuster.

Walters, K. L. (1995). *Urban American Indian identity and psychological wellness.* Dissertation, Unviersity of California, Los Angeles.

Warner Group. (1989, October). *Victim/witness standards and training program.* Woodland Hills, CA: Author.

Warner Group. (1990, February 22). *Victim/witness standards and training technical advisory committee.* Woodland Hills, CA: Author.

Waugh, D. (1990, July 22). Textbooks: An American tragedy. *San Francisco Examiner*, pp. B1–B3.

West, J. O. (1988). *Mexican-American folklore.* Little Rock, AR: August House.

Westermeyer, J. (1988, January). Interviewing the refugee psychiatric patient: Special issues regarding violence and victimization. *Refugee Mental Health Letter* [Minneapolis, MN: University of Minnesota], 5–17.

Wheeler, E. D. & Baron, S. A. (1994). *Violence in our schools, hospitals, and public places: A prevention and management guide.* Ventura, CA: Pathfinder.

Whitaker, C. J. (1990, April). *Black victims* (Bureau of Justice Statistics Special Report NCJ-122562). Washington, D.C.: U.S. Department of Justice.

White, E. C. (1990) Love don't always make it right: Black women and domestic violence. In E. C. White (Ed.), *The black women's health book* (pp. 92–97). Seattle, WA: Seal Press.

Wilson, W. J. & Neckerman, K. M. (1987). Poverty and family structure: The widening gap between evidence and public policy issues. In S. H. Danziger & D. H. Weinberg (Eds.), *Fighting poverty: What works and what doesn't* (pp. 232–259). Cambridge, MA: Harvard University Press.

Wilson, R. & Hosokawa, B. (1980). *East to America: A history of the Japanese in the United States.* New York: William Morrow.

Wilson, J. P. (1989). *Trauma, transformation, and healing.* New York: Brunner/Mazel.

Wyatt, G. E. (1992). The sociocultural context of African American and white American women's rape. *Journal of Social Issues, 48,* 77–91.

Yamamoto, J. K. (1991, June 1). AAs not dealing with violence against women, activist says. *Hokubei Mainichi,* 1.

Yazzie, R. (1994). Life comes from it: Navajo justice concepts. *New Mexico Law Review, 24*(2), 177–180.

Young, M. (1993). *Victim assistance: Frontiers and fundamentals.* Dubuque, IA: Kendall/Hunt.

Young, M. (1994). Responding to communities in crisis. Dubuque, IA: Kendall/Hunt.

Young, V. D. (1986). Gender expectations and their impact on black female offenders and victims. *Justice Quarterly, 3,* 305–327.

INDEX

Abarca, Marco Antonio, 61
Abbey, Edward, 13–14
Affirmative action, 86–87
African Americans
  black churches and, 175–179, 195
  black women, 63–66, 170–171, 175
  blues music of, 22–23
  census and, 13
  diversity within diversity of,
    20–21
  family, 38–40
  gang violence and, 70–71
  Korean merchants and, 95–97
  perceptions of criminal justice
    system, 148–151
  population projections, 10
  response to crime, 73–74
  segregation and, 104–106
  violent crime victimization
    rate, 50
  volunteer services, 194–196
Aguilar, Ignacio, 172
AIDS crisis, 100–101, 102
Alfred P. Murrah Building, bombing
  of (1995), 78–81
American Indian Movement
  (AIM), 32
Anders, Carla, 17
Anti-Defamation League of B'nai
  B'rith, 15
Arguello, Roberto, 140
Arson attacks on black churches,
  178–179
Asante, Molefi, 9
Asian Advisory Committee on
  Crime (AACC), 139
Asian Americans. *See also* Southeast
  Asian immigrants and refugees
  counseling, 168

  diversity within, diversity of, 19
  hostilities toward, 106–113
  mental health and orientation of,
    179–180
  partnerships between criminal
    justice officials and, 139–141
  patriarchies among, 42–44
  population growth of, 10
  response to crime, 76–77
  shame of Asian women, 66–69
  vulnerability of children to crime,
    53–55
Asian Exclusion Act (1924), 107
Asian Women's Shelter program
  (San Francisco),
  191–192
Askenette, Wendell, 188
Automobile industry, 111
Avery, Byllye, 65–66
Avila, Joaquin, 98
AYUDA, 62
Azpeitia, Jorge, 143
Balinton, Mark, 52–53
Banks, Dennis, 32
Banuelos, Clemente, 60
Barfield, Clementine, 175–176
Barrett, Thang Nguyen, 141, 142
Barry, William J., 86
Batiste, Joe, 52–53
Batres, Diane, 117
Battered women, 43–44, 190–193.
  See also Domestic violence
Begay, Carl, 180–181
Bell, Derrick, 91
Belonging, sense of, 190–192, 198
Bender, Thomas, 14
Bennett, William, 114
Bernbaum, Glenn, 110
Berrill, Kevin, 102

Bias-motivated crimes, 83–87
Bilingual/bicultural services,
  126–128
Binational Study on Migration, 60
Binstock, Beth, 36
Black churches, 175–179, 195
Blacks. *See* African Americans
Black Women's Health Book, The
  (White), 65
Bloom, Allan, 14
Blues music, 22–23
Blues Route, The (Merrill), 23
Boarding schools, Native American,
  34–35
Body language, 132–133, 134
Boone, John, 35
Boyd, Julia, 20, 168, 170–171, 175
Branch, Taylor, 66, 83
Brandon, Michael, 153, 154
Brann, Joseph, 135–136
Breslin, Jimmy, 90
Broadcast media, contact through,
  140–141
Bryant-Kambe, Madeleine, 129–130
Buckskin, Floyd, 181
Bumerts, Peter, 46
Bureau of Indian Affairs (BIA), 35
Burress, Charles, 110, 111
Busher, Patricia, 117, 118
Byrd, Charlie, 122
Calderon, Julio, 151, 152
California
  demographic shifts in, 10
  multicultural education in, 17–18
Callahan, John, 91
Cambodian refugees, 27–28, 116–119
Campbell, Ben Nighthorse, 30
Cao, Thien, 26, 138
Caputi, Jane, 103

Carlin, George, 94
Catholicism, 125, 173–175
Census, minorities and the, 11–13
Central American refugees, 183,
    185–186
Chants, 23
Children. *See also* Family patterns,
    minority
    abuse/assault of, 53–56, 75
    Native American, 34–37
Children's Justice and Assistance
    Act (CJA) of 1986, 36–37
Chin, Lily, 110
Chin, Vincent, 110–111
Chinese Americans, 68, 110
Chinese Exclusion Act (1882), 110
Ching, Ed, 57
Chung, Connie, 92
Churches, black, 175–179, 195
Civil rights activism, black churches
    and, 178
Clark, Robert, 91
Clay, Andrew Dice, 90–91
Cleveland School shooting, 115–119
Clifton, Wayland, 136
Clinton, Bill, 157, 178
Club Ped, 54–55
Coalition of Asian Americans for
    Public Safety (CAAPS),
    139–140
College and universities, racial
    hostility in, 86–87
Color blindness, 164–165
Color lines, problem of, 8–11
Communication and outreach
    programs, 126–141
    community-oriented policing,
    135–138
    English only policy and, 126–128
    first contact, 133–135
    partnerships with refugee and
        immigrant communities,
        138–141
    self-translation and, 129–133
Community-oriented policing,
    135–138
Compadrazgo custom, 41–42
Connolly, Brian, 135
Content of Our Character, The
    (Steele), 101
Corporate world, white male
    dominance in, 98–99
Costas, Bob, 92
Counseling, cross-cultural, 165–171
Craig, Vincent, 159
Crear, Joan, 65
Crime, impact on minorities, 48–81.
    See also Hate violence
    bias-motivated crimes, 83–87
    black churches and, 177

cultural misconceptions and,
    63–71
cultural response patterns, 72–81
the homeless as victims, 93–95
minority crime statistics, 49–51
racism and crime, 113–123
underreporting and, 138
vulnerability to crime, 51–63
Criminal justice system, 124–161
    communication and outreach
        programs, 126–141
    minority perceptions of, 147–154
    prerequisites for service, 141–147
    restorative justice, 154–161
Cross-cultural counseling, 165–171
Crow Dog, Mary, 32, 36, 90, 188
Croy, Patrick "Hooty," 119–123
Cultural awareness training, 132
"Cultural defense" argument,
    119–123
Cultural identity, U.S., 13–18
Cultural literacy, 17, 18
Culturally competent approaches
    in mental health system,
    182–196
Cultural pluralism in U.S., 7–47
    cultural keys, 21–25
    "false culture," examples of,
        42–47
    historical perspectives on, 25–33
    minority family patterns, 33–42
    racial and ethnic demographics,
        8–21
Cultural sensitivity, service
    provisions meeting criteria
    of, 171
Culture, deep or subjective, 22–25
Curanderos (folk healers), 173
Cushner, Kenneth, 22, 39, 128
Darnell, Sadie, 137
De Concini, Dennis, 187
de Klerk, Frederik, 99
Deloria, Vine, Jr., 33
Demallie, R. J., 34
Demographics, racial and ethnic,
    8–21
    color lines, problem of, 8–11
    minorities and the census, 11–13
    U.S. cultural identity and, 13–18
    variety within groups, 19–21
Demonstration vs. verbalization
    response to crime, 74–75
Deukmejian, George, 118
de Uriarte, Mercedes, 87
Dichos (sayings), 24–25
DiMaiti, Carl, 115
Dine Alliance, 32
Dinkins, David, 104
Discrimination, 104–106
Diversity within diversity, 19–21

Domestic violence, 43–44, 47, 143,
    159, 190–193
Dominguez, Magali, 153
Donovan, Art, 92
Drug problems, 51–53, 148
Drunk driving victims, 2–4,
    155–157
Du, Tony, 81
Du Bois, W. E. B., 8
Dunne, John S., 163
Ebens, Ronald, 110
EchoHawk, Larry, 30
EchoHawk, Walter, 33
Edelman, Marian Wright, 40
Education, multicultural, 15–18
Eggers, Mitchell, 106
Ehrlich, Howard, 92
Ellerbee, Linda, 91–92, 99
English only policies, 126–128
Estrada, Leobardo, 9, 98
Ethnic humor, 90–93
Ethnic neighborhoods, 104–106
Ethnocentrism, 164, 165, 169
Ethnoviolence. *See* Hate violence
Eurocentric textbooks, 16
European Americans. *See*
    White culture
Executive Order 9066, 108
Fairchild, Flipper, 88–89
Fajardo, Richard, 98
"False culture," examples of, 42–47
Family patterns, minority, 33–42
    African American, 38–40
    Hawaiian *ohana* (family), 37–38
    language ability differences,
        127–128
    Latino (*la familia*), 40–42
    Native American, 34–37
Feminine cultures, 43–44
Feminism, 168
Filipino immigration, 88, 133
First contact with victims, 133–135
Florida Regional Community
    Policing Institute, 137–138
Folktales, 24, 25
Forer, Thomas, 113
Forrester, Mark, 94
Fort Mojave Native American
    Reservation, 186–188
Franco, Roberto, 148
Freedman, David, 12
Fussell, Paul, 15
Gainesville, Florida Police
    Department, 136–137
Gandara, Beatriz, 41
Gang violence, 56–58, 70–71, 77–78
Garcia, Nora, 186, 187
Garden Grove, California Police
    Department, 132, 138
Gays and lesbians, 100, 101–104

Gender roles in masculine vs. feminine cultures, 43–44
Gerrymandering, 98
Ginorio, Angelo, 174
Gleick, James, 13
Gnoss, Ken, 46
Gomez, Jewelle, 101
Good Medicine Society, 80
Graglia, Lino, 87
Gray, Earl, 123
Gray, William H., III, 178
Green, James, 39
Griffith, Michael, 104
Guatemala, refugees from, 183, 185
Gutierrez, Celestina, 155–156
Hacker, Andrew, 18
Hagan, Jacqueline, 58
Haight, Laura, 135
Hall, Edith, 38–39
Hall, Kevin "Sinister," 52–53
Hampton, Robert, 40
Harrold, Steve, 57
Hate Crime Statistics Act of 1990, 84, 85
Hate violence, 83–123
    bias-motivated crimes, 83–87
    ethnic humor and, 90–93
    laws against, 84–85, 86
    police responses to, 145–147
    racial uniforms and, 88–90
    racism and crime, 113–123
    us against them mentality and, 93–113
Hawaiian culture, 6, 7, 17, 23, 37–38, 160–161
Hawkins, Darnell, 64
Hawkins, Diane, 104
Hawkins, Yusuf, 104, 105
Hayden, Iola, 80
Heartland Chapel, 81
Hedgecock, Roger, 59
Hennessey, Stephen, 126
Henry, William, 9
Hernandez, Esequiel, Jr., 60
Hernandez, Lilia, 172
Hewlett, Cloey, 131–132
Hilton, Bruce, 91
Hispanics
    Catholicism and, 125, 173–175
    child victim, case of, 2–4
    cultural traits of, 172
    diversity within diversity of, 20
    family (*la familia*), 40–42
    immigration patterns of, 10–11
    machismo in Latino culture, 44–47
    mental health and Latino cultural values, 172–175
    police responses to domestic violence among, 143

political underrepresentation of, 98
population projections for, 10
response to crime, 74–75, 77–78
violent crime victimization rate of, 50–51
Hispanic victim impact panels, 155–157
Hittson, Jesse Joe "Bo," 119
Hmong refugees/culture, 27, 113, 168, 184
Hmong sudden death syndrome, 166
Home invasions, 56–58, 141
Homeless, the, 93–95
Home visits by advocates, 133–135
Homicide/murder, 50, 51–53, 77–78, 102–103. *See also* Crime, impact on minorities
Homicide survivors group, 73–74, 177–178
Homophobic panic, 101–104
Ho'oponopono, 160–161
Hopi Land Settlement Act (1974), 29
Hopi tribe, 31–32
Hopwood, et al. v. State of Texas, et al., 86
Hosoi, Yuri, 88–89
Housing, segregation in, 106
Howard, Ray, 145–146
Humor, ethnic, 90–93
Huynh, Thong, 112
Identity, U.S. cultural, 13–18
Igasaki, Paul, 83
Ilic, Pedro, 27
Illegal aliens, 58–63
Imamura, Taro, 113
Immigrant smuggling, 61
Immigration and Naturalization Service (INS), 59, 60, 62
Immigration Reform and Control Act of 1986, 63
Indian Child Welfare Act (ICWA), 34–36
Indian Removal Law (1830), 29
Indian Tribal Justice Act (1993), 159–160
Indigenous justice system, 157–160
Institutionalized racism, 87
Internment of Japanese Americans, 108, 109
Interpreters, use of, 130
Interracial marriages, 13, 88–90
Issei generation, 107
Jackson, Michael, 117
Japan, attitudes toward, 109–110
Japanese Americans, 12, 106–111
Jaramillo, Don Pedro, 173
Jefferson, Amber, 146
Jefferson, Jim, 106

Johnson, Charles, 92
Johnson, Norma, 70, 71, 72
Johnson, Steve, 113
Kahn, Alice, 46
Kaufman, Charles, 110
Keating, Kathy, 80
Kenyon, David, 98
Khmer Rouge, 27–28, 116
Kikuchi, Yasushi, 113
Kim, Kenneth, 128
King, Gloria, 38–39
King, Joyce, 17
King, Martin Luther, Jr., 21, 82, 83, 178
Kinship network. *See* Family patterns, minority
Kinzie, D. David, 184
Kitano, Harry, 179
KLANWATCH, 84
Kondracke, Morton, 106
Korean children, sexual abuse of adopted, 55
Korean merchants and black customers, 95–97
Kotobalavu, Fonua, 127
Kuloloio, Alice, 17
Kuloloio, Leslie, 160
Kupuna Program in Hawaiian schools, 17
La Migra, 58–63
Language problems, 126–128
Laotian refugees, 27, 132–133, 145–146
Lashley, Karen Huggins, 78, 80
Latinos. *See* Hispanics
Law enforcement agency. *See* Criminal justice system
Lawson, Katherine (Kitty), 177–178
Lazarus, Sylvain, 88
Lee, Debbie, 44
Lee, K. W., 16
Lee, Marc, 57
Lefley, Harriet, 184–185
Leigh, James, 39
Leon, Modesto, 175
Leong, Tony, 128
Lepine, Marc, 103
Lesbians, violent acts against, 102–103
Levin, Bryan, 84, 86
Levinson, David, 43–44
Liaison work, 132
Lifton, Robert Jay, 9
Literacy, cultural, 17, 18
Literary folklore, 24–25
Loo, Jim, 111–112
Lopes, Elaine, 134
Lopez, Alfonso, 62
Lopez, Diane, 41–42

Los Angeles Commission on
Assaults Against Women
(LACAAW), Survivor series
prepared by, 130–131
Los Angeles County Bar Association
and Barristers Domestic
Violence project, 129–130
Los Angeles Police Department, 140,
142, 143
McClatchy, V. S., 88
Machismo, 44–47
McKay, Stan, 198
Mahathera, Dharmawara, 118
Mandela, Nelson, 99–100
Manning, Arnold, Jr., 112
Manzanar (internment camp), 108
Marianismo, assigned gender role
of, 174
Marriage, interracial, 13, 88–90
Martinez, Jesus, 148
Martinez, Richard, 98
Martinez, Theresa, 47
Masaki, Beckie, 190–191
Masayesva, Vernon, 32
Masculine cultures, 43–44
Massey, Douglas, 106
Means, Russell, 32
Melton, Ada Pecos, 157–158, 159, 160
Menominee Reservation, 188
Mental health system, minority,
172–182
Asian American orientation and,
179–180
black churches and, 175–179
Indian shamans and, 180–182
Latino cultural values and,
172–175
Merrill, Hugh, 23
Metzger, Tom, 97–98
Mexican-American Folklore (West), 25
Mexican Americans, 24–25
Mexico
criminal justice in, 147–148
illegal immigrants from, 58, 59
Mien refugees, 27
Migrant farmworkers, abuse of
children by, 55–56
Miller, Elisabeth, 179
Miller, Marteen, 46
Minorities. *See* Cultural pluralism in
U.S.; *specific minorities*
Mobile crisis units, 134–135
Moisa, Ray, 34, 35
Mollenkopf, John, 104–105
Mollica, Richard, 184
Mondello, Keith, 104
Monkey Wrench Gang, The (Abbey),
13–14
Monterey Park, California Police
Department, 142

Moo, Bertie, 180
Morales, Jessica, 2–4
Morgan, Barbara Goodluck, 187
Mornell, Eugene, 84
Mothers Against Drunk Driving
(MADD), 155–157
Multiculturalism
in education, 15–18
in victim services, 163–171
Multilingual written materials,
130–131
Multiracial choice on census, 13
Murder. *See* Homicide/murder
Music, blues, 22–23
Myers, Joseph, 30, 35
Myung, Seung Sook, 95
Nakagawa, Cressey, 109
National Advisory Council on
Indian Education, 12
National Association for the
Advancement of Colored
People, 13
National Church Arson Task Force,
178
National Congress of American
Indians, 29
National Council of La Raza, 13
National Crime Survey (NCS) data,
49–51
National Gay Task Force, 102
National Institute Against Prejudice
and Violence, 85, 86–87
National Institute of Justice, 60, 126
National Victimization Survey, 85
Native American Heritage
Commission, 33
Native Americans
census records of population, 12
children of, 34–37
counseling, 167
culturally competent victims
services for, 186–188
diversity within diversity of, 19
eagle symbol of, 2
historical perspective on, 29–33
Hooty Croy case, 119–123
justice system of, 157–160
Oklahoma City bombing,
response to, 80–81
shamans, 180–182
sweat lodge ceremony, 197–198
victim impact panels, 155
Native countries, experiences of
justice in, 147–148
Navajo Nation, 19
Navajo Nation Peacemaking, 159
Neeley, Mike, 94
Neighborhood meetings, outreach
through, 141
Neighborhood Watch, 138

New York, race relations in,
104–106
Nguyen, Cal, 141
Nitz, Michael, 110
Norman, Thomas, 52–53
North American Man-Boy Love
Association (NAMBLA),
54–55
Norton, Jack, 181
Noyce, Robert, 109
Nuestros Hijos Project, 55, 56
Oakland, California Police
Department, 138, 139
O'Connor, Sandra Day, 36, 159
Office for Victims of Crime (OVC),
187–188
Ogawa Masanobu, 106–109
Ohana (family), 37–38
Oklahoma City bombing, responses
to, 78–81
Olson, Kristine, 157
"Outing" of homosexuals, 100
Outreach programs.
See Communication and
outreach programs
Paglinawan, Lynette, 161
Pamfiloff, Glenn, 54
Papa, Gerard, 105
Parker, Charles E., 88
Parks, Rosa, 66, 67
Parson, Erwin, 167
Partnerships with refugee and
immigrant communities,
138–141
Patriarchies, Asian American, 42–44
Pedophilia, 53–55
Pena, Raymondo, 58–59
Perceptions of criminal justice
system, minority, 147–154
Perry, Manuel, 9
Persily, Fred, 146
Pham, Luu, 141, 142
Pham, Thuy, 57
Piche, Lloyd, 111, 112
Piche, Robert, 111–112
Pluralism. *See* Cultural pluralism
in U.S.
Police and policing, 135–138,
145–147. *See also* Criminal
justice system
Politics, minorities and, 13, 98
Post-enumeration survey (PES),
11, 12
Post-traumatic stress disorder, 183
Poussaint, Alvin, 51
Powell, Adam Clayton, Jr., 178
Prejudice, 15–16, 84, 144–145, 164.
See also Hate violence
Prosecutors, understanding of
minority victimization, 131–132

Pueblos, 19, 158
Pukui, Mary Kawena, 160
Purdy, Patrick, 115–119
Racial uniforms, 88–90
Racism. *See also* Hate violence
    Asian Americans and, 95–97,
        106–113
    Southeast Asians, 112–113,
        115–119
    behavioral understanding of,
        164–165
    crime and, 113–123
    defining, 8, 164–165
    ethnic neighborhoods and,
        104–106
    institutionalized, 87
    white straight males and, 97–101
Rape, 62, 63–69
    Asian Americans' shame over,
        66–69
    blacks as victims of, 63–66,
        148–151
    of children, 74–77, 148–151
    culturally competent services for
        victims, 185, 189–190, 193–196
    Latina culture and conflict
        over, 174
    of lesbians, 102–103
Rape crisis center, 194–196
Raspberry, William, 115
Rebollo, Jesus Guttierrez, 148
Recruitment of minorities in
        criminal justice system, 141–144
Refugees. *See also* Southeast Asian
        immigrants and refugees
    criminal justice system
        partnerships with
        communities, 138–141
    victims services for, 182–186
Reist, Ben, 8
Relocation of Native Americans, 35
Reno, Jane, 174
Reno, Janet, 160
Reservations, Native American,
        31–32, 35, 186–188
Restorative justice, 154–161
Richards, Angela, 44–45
Richie, Beth, 100–101
Ridley, Charles, 164
Ridley-Thomas, Mark, 146
Rimonte, Nilda, 42–43, 44
Roark, Anne, 118–119
Rosales, Angela, 153
Rosales, Carlos, 153
Rosales, Karla, 153, 154
Rosales, Nydia Eva, 75
Rosa Parks Center, 66
Rossi, Gary, 119, 121
Rothenberg, Charles David, 148
Russell, Diana, 103

Salazar, Chuck, 143
Salcido, Ramon, 44–46, 47
Save Our Sons and Daughters
        (SOSAD), 175–176
Segregation, 104–106
Self-translation, 129–133
Seng, Seang, 28
Seraw, Mulugeta, 97–98
Serra, J. Tony, 119, 120–123
Sexism, 43, 44
Sex roles in masculine vs. feminine
        cultures, 43–44
Sexual abuse/assault, child, 35,
        36–37, 53–55. *See also* Rape
Sexual Assault Crisis Center (YWCA
        Los Angeles Compton Center),
        189–190
Shamans, 166–167, 180–182
Shame, Asian American women's
        sense of, 66–69
Shipek, Florence, 181
Shon, Steve, 169
Shook, E. Virginia, 160–161
Sioux, the, 34, 158, 167
Slave families, 39
Smith, Barbara, 103
Smith, Susan, 114–115
Smuggling, immigrant, 61
Sobieski, Regina, 155
Social cognition, 21–22
South Africa, anti-apartheid
        movement in, 99–100
Southeast Asian immigrants and
        refugees, 25–28, 182–184. *See
        also* Asian Americans
    body language, 132–133, 134
    counseling, 166, 168–169
    home invasions of, 56–58, 141
    mental health service delivery
        to, 180
    racism and attitudes toward,
        115–119
    violence directed against,
        112–113, 115–119
    vulnerability of children to
        pedophilia, 53
Sparks, Keith, 119
Speaking of Indians (Deloria), 158
Stanberry, Felicia, 52–53
Standing Bear, Luther, 31
Stebbins, Maranne, 133
Steele, Shelby, 101
Stereotyping, 164, 169
Stern, Edward, 121
Storefront outreach offices, 140
Storefront victim services center,
        189–190
Stress, 41, 56
Stuart, Carol, 113–115
Stuart, Charles, 113–115

Survivors, feelings of, 3–4
Sweat lodge ceremony, 197–198
Tabarez, Rogelio, 47
Tallchief, Tim, 80
Tanaka, Tsutako Alice, 108
Tang, Lanh, 111
Taylor-Williams, Monica, 189
Tecoatlaxopeuh, 124, 125
Tello, Jerry, 131, 165
Temple of My Familiar, The (Walker),
        22–23
"Termination" policy (federal
        American Indian policy), 29
Termine, Vincent, 105
Terrell, Adele Dutton, 66, 67, 104
Terrorism, 78–81, 103
Texas, demographic shifts in, 10
Thueson, Helen, 68–69, 71
Till, Emmett, 105
Tom, Roger, 18
Trail of Tears, 29
Underreporting of crime, 138
Uniform Crime Reports, 50
Unterriner, Teddy, 53
Us against them mentality, 93–113
Vang, Chong Toua, 27
Vasquez, Gaddi, 141–142
Verbalization vs. demonstration
        response to crime, 74–75
Victim Assistance in Indian Country
        (VAIC) program, 187
Victim impact panels, 155–157
Victim services, 162–196
    culturally competent approaches,
        182–196
    to domestic violence, 190–193
    with Native Americans, 186–188
    with rape victims, 185, 189–190,
        193–196
    with refugees, 182–186
    sense of belonging and, 190–192
    storefront center, 189–190
    minority mental health system,
        172–182
    multiculturalism in, 163–171
Victims of Crime Act (VOCA), 178
Victims to Victory, 177–178
Vietnamese refugees, 169, 182–183
    crime and, 76–77
    diversity within diversity of, 20
    historical perspective on, 25–29
    home invasions of, 56–58, 141
    response to census, 12
Violence. *See* Crime, impact on
        minorities; Domestic violence;
        Hate violence
Violent Crime Control and Law
        Enforcement Act of 1994, 59
Violent crime victimization rate,
        50–51

Voting Rights Act of 1965, 98
Vuong, Vu-Duc, 26–27
Wacinko, 167
Walker, Alice, 22–23, 64
Waukau, Hilary, 31
Way of All the Earth, The (Dunne), 163
Weiss, Joan, 103
West, John, 24, 25
Westermeyer, Joseph, 184
White, Evelyn, 65
White culture
   diversity within diversity of,
      19–20

response to crime, 74–75
   us against them mentality, 97–101
White population, projections for, 10
White supremacist groups, 97–98
Williams, Cecil, 84, 177
Wilson, John, 197
Wilson, Veronica, 177
Wilson, William, 40
Wiltrout, Becky, 135
Women. *See also* Domestic violence;
      Rape
   Asian, sense of shame in, 66–69
   battered, 43–44, 190–193

black, 63–66, 170–171, 175
   Latina, vulnerability to crime of,
      62–63
Woo, Yolanda, 16
Woodard, Michael, 106
World of Difference program, A,
   15–16
Xenophobia, 14
Yellow peril, 106–109
Young, Andrew, 114, 178
Yuh, Ji-Yeon Mary, 90